HOCKEY TOWN

CANADA

HAROLD GARTON

Published by
Creative Bound Inc.
P.O. Box424, Carp, Ontario
Canada K0A 1L0

ISBN 0-921165-25-0
Printed and bound in Canada

Cover design by Wendelina O'Keefe
Photo of author by Jo-Anne Marion Photography, Beachburg, Ontario
Printing and camera-work by DFR Printing, Pembroke, Ontario

Canadian Cataloguing in Publication Data

Garton, Harold
    Hockey town, Canada

Includes index.
ISBN 0-921165-25-0

   1. Hockey--Ontario--Pembroke--History.   2.
Hockey -- Ontario, Eastern --History.   I. Title.

GV848.4.06G37 1992   796.962'097138 C92-090643-5

Creative Bound Inc. gratefully acknowledges the support of the Government of Ontario
through the Ministry of Culture and Communications.

This book is dedicated to
Don "Brownie" Andrews
who, in addition to several big assists and
many small ones, understands.

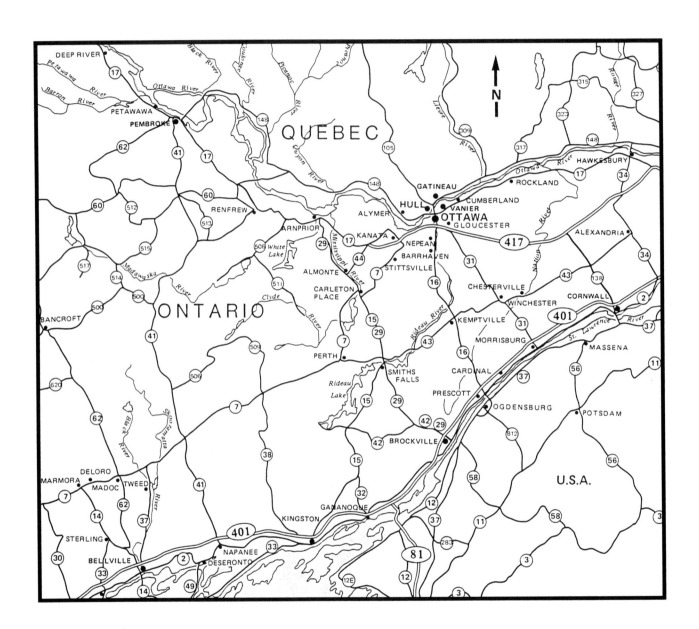

Contents

Foreword

In a fine late-1920s' analysis of how sport reporters conduct their business, the *Renfrew Mercury* suggested that they rely a bit too heavily on their memories "with memory often making for imagination tinctured with local prejudice."

Harold Garton has not had the luxury of memory in writing *Hockey Town Canada* but if a slight bit of local prejudice has "tinctured" his story, he can be excused. As Harold writes early in his book, hockey and Pembroke are inseparable, then he proves it beyond any doubt with his unusual but very effective games-participants-adjuncts approach to telling the story of a town and its game.

Instead of memory, Harold has relied on exhaustive research to create his story and he has important evidence to show that some form of hockey was played as early as 1837. He did miss something, didn't he? Wasn't Gordie Howe a rookie that season?

The game, the characters who played hockey and those who helped shape Pembroke are here in abundance in what is far more than a sports book. It's a history book but one told with that strong thread of a sport and the great love that Canadians have for hockey as the pivotal factor.

Long ago in Ottawa, a trophy "for the most useful player on his club" was awarded, the precursor of most valuable player awards. That laurel should be resurrected and presented to Harold Garton. He's the most valuable writer hockey has had in recent memory.

Frank Orr
Toronto Star

ABBREVIATIONS

MAAA:	Montreal Amateur Athletic Association	IPU:	Interprovincial Union
OAAC:	Ottawa Amateur Athletic Club	CCHA:	Central Canada Hockey Association
O&DAHA:	Ottawa & District Amateur Hockey Association	NOHA:	Northern Ontario Hockey Association
ODHA:	Ottawa District Hockey Association	OHA:	Ontario Hockey Association
OVHA:	Ottawa Valley Hockey Association	OAHA:	Ontario Amateur Hockey Association
OVHL:	Ottawa Valley Hockey League	IPHL:	International Professional Hockey League
UOVHL:	Upper Ottawa Valley Hockey League	IHL:	International Hockey League
UOVSHL:	Upper Ottawa Valley Sr Hockey League	FAHL:	Federal Amateur Hockey League
UOVIHL:	Upper Ottawa Valley Intermediate Hockey League	PCHL(PCL):	Pacific Coast Hockey League
UOVJHL:	Upper Ottawa Valley Jr Hockey League	WCHL:	Western Canada Hockey League
LOVHL:	Lower Ottawa Valley Hockey League	WHL:	Western Hockey League
LHL:	Laurentian Hockey League	NHA:	National Hockey Association
BHL:	Bonnechere Hockey League	NHL:	National Hockey League
NRHL:	North Renfrew Hockey League	ECHA:	Eastern Canada Hockey Association
		PCI:	Pembroke Collegiate Institute
		PHS:	Pembroke High School
		RHS:	Renfrew High School
		AHS:	Arnprior High School

The County Town	Pembroke
The Creamery Town	Renfrew
The Woollen Town	Arnprior
The Factory Town	Almonte
The Junction Town	Carleton Place

CREDITS

Research Funding assistance: *Canada Council Explorations Program*
    Ontario Arts Council
    Ontario Heritage Foundation
Publishing Funding assistance: *Ottawa Valley Historical Society*
    City of Pembroke
    G.K. (Gerry) Gordon

Pembroke Observer
Pembroke Standard
Pembroke Standard-Observer
Pembroke Bulletin
Pembroke Times
Renfrew Mercury
Carleton Place Herald
Arnprior Chronicle
Ottawa Citizen
Ottawa Journal

Pembroke Public Library
Renfrew Public Library
Champlain Trail Museum

Diane Seager, University of Waterloo
Jim Swartz, Waterloo County Hall of Fame
Diane A. Imrie, North-Western Ontario Sports Hall of Fame
Garry Lovegrove, NHL Central Registry
M.H. "Lefty" Reid, Hockey Hall of Fame and Museum

Special thanks to:

My wife, Yvonne, for shoves and pats as required.
My friend Mickey Hammond, who let me attack his fine memory with reckless abandon.
Dr. & Mrs. Carl Tripp, for their help and support.

Introduction

The Pembroke men were a fine looking sinewy set of fellows, and played throughout with the utmost pluck and good humour, but neither in skating or stick-handling were they up to the mark.

So said the *Ottawa Journal* following an initial attempt by Pembroke men to play hockey. Rarely would the negative part of that observation accurately describe a County Town team again.

It was in 1986 at the fiftieth anniversary of Pembroke's great 1936 Jr club that MPP Sean Conway suggested to me someone should write the hockey history of this town because "it has to be one of the most fascinating tales ever." I took him up on it. Actually, my preference was to write Pembroke's story, with hockey central to it. Long before my research was completed the question proved academic: Pembroke and hockey were inseparable.

A town created by teamwork tends toward team sports and this Ottawa Valley community met the criteria. Lacrosse, curling and baseball were established pastimes when hockey crept up the river. However, Valley hierarchy found the new and vigorous winter game to be a fine vehicle for settling old scores . . .

Arnprior, Renfrew and Pembroke began competing for the county seat in 1862. Arnprior was given little chance, being too close to Ottawa and therefore not central enough. Renfrew had a decided advantage: well located, established and wealthy. Pembroke, relatively insignificant and difficult to reach, ran a poor second.

Knowing it would take more than simple lobbying, a group headed by John Supple caught their Creamery Town counterparts a tad complacent by inviting the Governor General to visit. Pembroke town fathers gave him a grand time, culminating the day with a river cruise to Des Joachims, as far upstream as one could navigate both then and now. Returning at sunset, the all-powerful gentleman took one look at old sol gleaming off "the bright cornwall tin roofs" and declared Pembroke the County Town then and there. The ceremony officially took place October 10, 1866.

Renfrew powers-that-be were furious. Winning normal everyday scrimmages, which they usually did, would no longer suffice: they must humiliate their rival. There is nothing like sports to accomplish that goal; however, none of the currently popular activities were all-encompassing enough to achieve that satisfactorily.

Then hockey came along . . .

But there is much more to this story.

National heros: Frank Nighbor was the most skilled player in his day and worthy of a book alone. Hugh Lehman was the epitome of goaltenders for twenty-two years. Harry Cameron was a gifted free spirit before his time. Pembroke born and raised, all three are members of the Hockey Hall of Fame. Then there's Dave Trottier, a brilliant NHLer who should have been honoured with the three above. And Leo Reise, Bob Trapp . . .

Local heros: Dave Behan devoted decades of playing and teaching. J. Deacon Taylor gave decades of sponsorship. Jack Sarsfield had decades of service.

Characters: Orin Frood was a brilliant rebel. Sarsfield Brennan loved the limelight and always seemed to find it. Charlie Delahey could do anything, anytime he felt like it.

Mystery men: Solomon "Hum" Lance played, and played, and disappeared. Melville "Fats" Larwell played, and departed, but left a trail.

Imports: Sam "Shinny" Shaughnessy, Skene Ronan, Hamby Shore, plus unexpected others were all from that incredible first decade of the century.

Pembroke has exported hockey players to every corner of Canada and beyond. That's why, when you ask anyone between Vancouver Island and Newfoundland their first thought when you say "Pembroke," the inevitable answer is "Lumber Kings." However, as you will see, the County Town has contributed to many sports, including "flagpole sitting"—if that doesn't stretch the definition too much.

Also, you will read about Herb Mackie. He didn't have much to do with hockey but was involved in just about everything else; his story will never be fully told. On the other hand there was Lennox Irving, a man just as socially enmeshed but who documented every single moment. You will find bits and pieces on most Pembroke pioneers then follow their descendants through an exciting adventure that became a horrible war. Read of montrous fires, robberies, chases, intrigue and murder.

But most of all you will find humour, even when you don't expect it. Perhaps especially when you don't expect it. Certainly when you need it.

Setting the Scene

This is a story about Pembroke. And hockey. And their marriage; tranquility, storms and all.

Technically, the town is older than the game. Peter White meandered up the Ottawa River in 1828 and put down roots a few hundred yards east of the Muskrat River outlet. By 1840 he had been joined by such pioneering names as Dunlop, O'Meara, Moffat, Biggs, Edwards and Sweeney. They incorporated as a village in 1858 and created a town of fifteen hundred souls January 1, 1877.

The Canadian Central Railway pushed through town in 1876 and it wasn't long before local entrepreneurs began building the Pembroke Southern to Toronto. That industrious group got as far as Booth's Ottawa, Arnprior & Parry Sound line at Golden Lake then decided it wasn't necessary anymore. Phones and hydro arrived in 1885, Pembroke becoming the first community in Canada to have street lights when J.A. Cone installed one on the corner of MacKay[1] and Pembroke Sts. This is still one of those things we brag about. A waterworks was installed in 1892 and sewage system in 1904.

Pembroke wasn't called Pembroke right away. First it was Campbelltown, after hotel owner Campbell Dunlop. Next, Mirimichi, in honour of refugees who settled here after being burned out of their New Brunswick community of the same name. Then Alexander Moffat, who built a Muskrat River grist mill, saw his surname mark the spot before someone gave it the short-lived tag of Sydenham. Then came Pembroke.

You'll find this town about a hundred miles upstream from the city of brotherly love. Between Pembroke and the Quebec mainland is a bulge in the Ottawa River called Allumette Lake in the middle of which

---

1. Now don't you locals blast me for saying MacKay instead of McKay. The spelling comes officially from city hall.

sits Allumette Island, a large piece of real estate that is part of Quebec. Just downstream from Pembroke are much smaller Morrison's Island (Quebec) and Cotnam's Island (Ontario). The part of the river running between the big isle and Quebec is narrow and has been bridged since away back when. However, transport to Pembroke with its hospitals and shopping was confined to ferry—a service highly susceptible to weather and politics. Naturally, during freeze-up and break-up, island residents could only gaze across.

However, when our tale begins politicians were saying they were thinking about building a bridge. Islanders didn't quarrel with that . . .

Originally considered a German settlement though sporting quite an ethnic mix, Pembroke began as a railroad and logging community. The people of Pembroke were a rough and ready lot, and being tough and talkative, stories of such exploits as these were often handed down.

Davidson & Hay employee James McCaghery was on a horse buying trip to the Markstay area. While inspecting a team, one of the animals kicked him over two sets of log sleighs. As his peers arrived to pick up the pieces, Jim rose on his own, completed the deal and caught the next train home.

Then there was Constable Barrand, who journeyed just south of town to arrest James "Gypsy" Williams for thumping on his wife. Gypsy politely invited the lawman to sit and chat, during which time he surrounded himself with a pick, shears and manure fork while pouring four bottles of porter in a bowl. After downing the contents, Gypsy told the policeman what he could do with his warrant. Barrand was thus required to obtain assistance before completing the task at hand.

Every Canadian community big enough to contain both Tories and Grits boasted two newspapers. In Pembroke we had the Liberal *Observer* which began in 1855 and the Conservative *Standard* that sprang into action twelve years later. Such rigid political bias softened after WWI and many newspapers merged, as this pair did. Meantime, sports reporting was very slow to materialize, being considered far too trivial a matter to include in the paper. The type of news reported was often trivial enough, however.

Catch this lovely sample of writing from 1888: *A strange woman with a young lad was seen wandering the roads in the Renfrew area. A son, who lives in Washington, arrived in Pembroke while searching for his mother and young brother. She was supposed to visit him and never showed up so he came here thinking she may be somewhere between Renfrew and Eganville because people she knew lived in the area.* This preamble concluded with *Catherine Cox—about 50 years old, grey hair, short and stout, about 5' in height and supposed to be insane. Son—about 14 years old, about 5'2" in height, complexion fair, delicate health and of strange disposition.*

Setting Another Scene

I would have loved to find some form of hockey played in 1828, giving us a uniform start so to speak. But it was not to be. Mind you, there are those that claim a reasonable facsimile thereof transpired even before 1800. Some say, when white men stepped ashore, they found natives carrying bent gads running up and down river ice pursuing a chunk of you-know-what. Apparently these "Indians" even had a name for it: "Hogee," which means "it hurts." If you've ever been hit by a frozen horse ball at thirty-five below you'd say they were right on.

The closest year I could find any reference to hockey was 1837. On the last Saturday in February, Dorchester and Uptown battled it out for the championship of something or other in Montreal. It seems the first team to score three times was the winner. However, when Dorchester notched one the fans became so exuberant events ground to a halt. Remember, rinks were built for skating only and had no boards; as late as 1892, Ottawa and Quebec City players were obliged to join hands during a match and push back two thousand spectators. There were many cracked shins and misdirected bodychecks before a one inch wall became three and a half feet of protection.

The game was called "Hoguet" then, a French word meaning "shepherd's crook" or "bent stick." Played with eight players per side, the "home" position soon went the way of the dodo bird but "rovers" remained until 1912 in the east and survived ten years longer out west.

We know some version of the sport was played in Ottawa before Ontario's first official "hockey" game took place at Kingston in 1886. Queen's University and Royal Military College (RMC) engaged in conflict on a rink owned by Captain Joseph Dix that had a bandshell smack in the middle!

There was one goal scored in that game, by Pembroke's Lennox Irving.

Lieutenant Irving wasn't with RMC either, but a law student at Queen's. I give you his own description of this historic event, as described in *Hockey's Captains, Colonels and Kings*. "I feigned a skate around the left side of the bandstand, but suddenly swerved up the right side and let fly a drive at the goal. The cadet goal-keeper cleverly stopped the hexagon which bounded back and the great 'I', though skating for all I was worth, struck the puck on its return and through the RMC goal." Lennox exuded a certain confidence, don't you think? As for that "hexagon," it was squared from a lacrosse ball by Ottawa's Fred Booth, in order to "slide more and bounce less."

Pembroke's First Game

When Lennox Irving came home to set up a law practice, he and friends created a hockey team. Pembroke had had a covered skating rink for several years already but manager George Selwood, a Guelph native, wasn't keen on people shooting pucks through windows and banging up the framework. The building was located on Isabella St, east of what is now the police station, and sported just enough space between the ice and outer wall for two walking abreast. Skating and carnivals reigned supreme, for which the H&L Band (Hook & Ladder Co.) played, if "sufficiently encouraged."

So, this rough new sport began on rivers; in Pembroke's case either the Ottawa, Muskrat or Indian.

On December 28, 1893, Pembroke Srs (meaning anyone familiar with the rudiments of hockey) journeyed to Ottawa's Rideau Rink where they took on the Ottawa Amateur Athletic Club (OAAC), number one capital team and frequent national champion before Lord Stanley had presented his cup the previous spring. OAAC enjoyed the services of such stars as goaltender Albert Morel, Weldy Young, Chauncey Kirby, Fred Chittick and Charlie Spittal. It was seven man hockey played in thirty minute halves without substitutes and, in tradition that would continue well into the next century, goal scorers were not recorded, as it was considered poor form to encourage individualism in a team sport.

An element of mystery created great interest in the capital, advance tickets selling out within hours. The welcoming crowd was taken aback when a 6' 6" fur-coated youngster named Herb Mackie, who was probably given the honour of being team manager, led his entourage from the train, possibly fortifying what one County Town supporter wrote his friend: "If your Ottawa men expect a gentle walk-over they will be severely disappointed. Our boys are not only good hockeyists, but they are rapid skaters and in the pink of condition."

So much for propaganda. OAAC won 13-1. However, the post game bash—a ritual sustained until discouraged by war—eased the pain.

Many moons later, Lennox Irving claimed Pembroke Srs were obliged to defeat an Arnprior team in a home and home (H&H) series to earn the privilege of meeting OAAC. If so, the match must have taken place the previous winter and gone totally unrecorded as much was made of the fact Pembroke faced OAAC without benefit of a single practice.

Pembroke's First Team

The goaltender was Albert Mackie, Herb's brother of similar size. Edward Irving, brother to Lennox, played point and Peter White, Pembroke's third by that name though not a direct descendant of the founder, was at cover point. As opposed to present-day defencemen, these two lined up in front of one another. Lennox Irving, Billy Williams and J. Robert Moffat were the forward line while Fred Supple roamed free as rover.

White, Williams, Supple and Lennox Irving all became lawyers; White built a huge practice in Toronto, Williams and Supple stayed in the County Town while Lennox Irving combined a military career with practices first in Pembroke then Renfrew. Albert Mackie, after marrying Edna Dickson, Billy Williams's aunt, also moved to Toronto. Robert Moffat joined the Bank of Nova Scotia and Edward Irving got into lumbering.

The club played two more games that first season, defeating a Pembroke High School (PHS) team 3-0 then hosting the capital's second best club, Ottawa Electrics, losing 7-0 on the Ottawa River. A very young Wallace Pink played goal during those matches and Robert Gibson saw some action.

Chapter 1

PRECURSOR TO LEAGUE PLAY

1894/95 to 1897/98

Games

1894/95

Though a large number of aspiring players participated, the Sr team apparently never left town, playing younger fellows in what best could be described as training sessions. A group of boys from PHS visited their counterparts in Renfrew and won 5-4 in overtime. Big Herb Mackie, proving he could play like his older brother, scored four of the five goals, including the winner. The team also played in Arnprior's (the Woollen Town) curling rink; roaring game devotees didn't really appreciate pebble being removed by skates but facility-short youngsters were often accommodated thus during the early years.

1895/96

Hockey rinks began appearing on school grounds, and even a few private individuals, such as W.B. McAllister, flooded their yards for this new purpose. "Evidently mere skating around without any particular object in view is losing its charm around here," said one town official.

A Jr team (read beginners) was organized by Gus St.

James and a group of girls prepared to play. But the weather turned so mild at Christmas that pansies sprouted, farmers worked the fields and loggers called it quits. In fact, except for a few days at New Years, the only cold weather that winter was a couple of weeks in March.

But New Year's Day was memorable. Pembroke Srs invited Ottawa Varsity to town and, "the rink ablaze with electric lights," played a night game on the river! Joe Bourke invited everyone to his dancing facility after Pembroke's 5-1 victory and the students enjoyed themselves so much they stayed for a bachelor's ball the following evening.

During March, the Srs managed a win and tie with Renfrew then a loss and tie with Eganville. During that last game, a referee named Cavanaugh learned fans were already more expert than he—judging by the snide remarks. A Montreal team was supposed to stop for a game while passing through town but it failed to do so, generating more mumblings.

The Jrs, called Crescents, lost 4-0 and 1-0 to Arnprior but it seems the girls had found better things to do as their team never got underway.

1896/97

The season was a complete lost cause. It should have been a success as organizers were fired up early on, but perhaps the poor previous season left residents uninterested. A meeting called for Labour Day was ignored and another in November fared no better. Between Christmas and New Year though, representatives from Pembroke, Renfrew, Arnprior and Ottawa Victorias met to discuss forming a league. No one had much in the way of hockey facilities and, when Woollen Town curlers declined to allow use of their building on a regular basis, the project died. Pembroke Srs and Ottawa Victorias (Vics) played H&H exhibitions but that was about it.

Hockey enthusiasts should have taken a page from the curlers book; they bought property next to Chambers Bakery on December 1, 1896 and "commenced to erect a commodious curling rink thereon." The finished product, 150' x 34' with an adjoining 26' x 12', was awaiting ice-making weather December 18, 1896.

1897/98

This season it was the end of January before ice could be made—and we wonder what's happening to today's weather.

Then Arnprior Srs visited, allowing five goals in each half while scoring only one. Fans were noticing—and being confused by—an inherent difference between hockey and other team sports. Speed and rapidly changing possession, without benefit of the forward pass, encouraged individualism, yet all the experts clamoured for "combination play." The design flaw survived thirty years and more.

Though newspapers still considered any sport as beneath Fourth Estate responsibilities, an *Observer* observer made this observation after the above contest: "While the visitors stuck to the different tactics of individual rushes it was amusing to watch the embarrassment on their faces, when after a brilliant dash by one of their forwards with the almost certain expectation of scoring, to see the puck picked up by C. McPhee and carried up the other side . . ." Naturally, he declined to mention if Cliff scored or not . . . nor was it proper practice to use first names. It was noted, however, that fellows like Billy Wallace, Frank McDonnell and Bert McPhee, Cliff's brother, moved up from "Jr."

Then the club brought shame to itself. Following a 5-4 defeat in Renfrew, certain players not only blamed referee N. Mitchell for the loss but ripped Renfrew's club banner off their building. That was Jack Poff's first game too; he and Tom Dunbar were destined to become goaltenders but at that time Wallace Pink had the position sewed up so they played forward. Prominent on the Renfrew team were goaltender Joe Martelle, James Ferguson, Alex Box and Robert Scott plus Alex and Sam McDougall.

Pembroke Srs, coached by a playing captain, as were most clubs, earned five straight wins after that, the last being a 3-2 defeat of Carleton Place with Cliff McPhee in goal and Dunbar still playing forward.

Participants

Considering most players were either lumbermen, railroaders, teachers or college students, few were available regularly. For instance, Bert McPhee taught all over the county and brother Cliff went from coast to coast building railroads, while David P. Kennedy, enrolled at Osgoode Hall, got home when the opportunity presented itself. Following a couple of games in 1901, David moved to Wolseley, Saskatchewan, eventually becoming mayor. He passed away February 2, 1931. Of course, others moved away too, such as Robert Gibson who departed for Vancouver in 1898.

Wallace Pink, of the logging tool manufacturing Thomas Pink family, took TB after the winter of 1898 and spent many months in a sanitorium at Seneca Lake, New York. Home only a few weeks, Wallace headed west, settling in Calgary. Doing well in the cattle business, he suddenly suffered a relapse and died in 1900.

Adjuncts

At this time the hottest news was the Georgian Bay canal. It was to go up the Ottawa to Mattawa to North Bay then down the French, bringing ocean liners to our door. Folks couldn't see that thing down Welland way at all . . .

MP Tom Mackie, in keeping with the custom of the day, took full advantage of his position to establish timber holdings nation wide. Son Herb, though a lieutenant with B Company by 1898, actually kept books in one of his father's bush shanties. On the provincial front that year, Tory

Andrew Thompson White—the Honourable Peter White's brother—defeated Grit Henry Barr, though Liberals gained control of the legislature. Municipal politics was dangerous; two hundred people were rallying in a London, Ontario hall when the floor collapsed, killing thirty and injuring the rest.

Prominent lumberman Tom Murray, a true Grit but retired, contented himself with driving around town behind his team of moose. "They were sleek and handsome and well mated as to size and appearance," said the *Observer*, which went on to suggest the beasts were obedient as well-trained horses, willing to trot but preferring to walk.

Some of the mainstays of pioneer life advertised at this time were South American Nervine Tonic, Kendall's Spavine Cure for man or beast, Dr Thomas Eclectric Oil for almost anything wrong with a horse, Dr Low's Pleasant Worm Syrup, and Cook's Cotton Root Compound for ladies monthly discomfort.

Two carloads of reindeer, enroute to the Yukon, were parked in a Smith's Falls siding, waiting for a load of dogs to catch up. A large crowd gathered. The Laplander attendant opened a door and one reindeer escaped. For two hours, half the town residents gave chase while the other half cheered. This entourage later frustrated Pembrokeites, chugging through town unannounced, and therefore unseen.

A Welland Vale bicycle cost $100, so Jim Anderson built a two-wheeler himself, "making every part of it except the tires, which were Dunlop." Meantime, John Lorne Hale and Edward A. Dunlop rode factory-made jobs to Ottawa in nine hours, earning Gold Century Bars from the Canadian Wheelman Association.

Tidbits: From 1886 to today, Petawawa's name evolved through Petawawe—Pettewawa—Petewawa—Petawawa . . . 45 percent of students actually attended classes—and that didn't include those who never registered at all . . . Multi-businessman Ed Behan cut ice from the Ottawa River and sold it door to door by wagon . . . the Mary St. bridge collapsed in 1898, its first such plunge . . . and the CPR built such a beautiful station it was praised from all quarters; the firm ignored pleas eighty years later and tore the building down in minutes, replacing it with a tin shack.

Lastly, many newspapers published hotel registrations weekly, complete with full names and addresses—take that you philandering . . . !

Chapter 2

GREAT FUN—LEAGUE PLAY

1898/99 to 1901/02

At this time Goal nets began replacing posts with no cross-bar; some leagues even allowed goals that ricocheted through from behind! Hockey gloves made an appearance.

Games were conducted by one referee and two goal judges, called umpires. These umpires, often prejudiced locals and just as often overruled by the on-ice official, regularly paid for their indiscretions through rough treatment by fans.

Teams invariably travelled by train, often "specials" carrying only players and fans. Seasons opened with carnivals and visiting teams brought a band, which alternated shifts with the local contingent. Half time featured races plus whatever goofy endeavour could be conceived. Incorporating these traditional events with the new game of hockey softened the attitude of arena managers, bringing more games inside the privately owned buildings, most now equipped with rink boards.[1]

Games

1898/99

At a meeting in Renfrew, Friday, December, 16 1898, the Ottawa Valley Hockey League (OVHL) was born. Charter officers were Renfrew's J.E.H. Barnet (President), C.G. Pennock also of the Creamery Town, R.J. Slattery of Arnprior, J.S. Oliver from Carleton Place and Pembroke's Frank McDonnell. Those four communities where scheduled to play each other twice between January 6 and February 17, 1899, with the top team taking the championship. First-place ties were to be broken in a sudden-death game.

Pembroke Srs president was Mr and Mrs Arunah Dunlop's twenty-two-year-old son Edward. Ed's bicycling buddy, Lorne Hale, was a prominent member of the team. Local businessman Fred Cockburn became vice-president and the other executives were Peter White Jr and Robert W. Ranson. Team colours were red, white and black, barberpole style.

The league adopted Ontario rules as opposed to the more popular Quebec version. The main difference was that the OHA allowed a skater to pass the puck then continue ahead, taking out his man, and a team mate could pick the puck up so long as he was not further advanced down ice than the passer at time of reception. We might call it an early variation of the pick play. Quebec rules forbade any forward pass unless touched by an opponent in the process.

---

1. Tom Dey's new arena took over from the Rideau Rink as Ottawa's premier hockey facility in 1896/97, maintaining that status until the Auditorium was built in 1924.

Substitutions were not allowed; in the event of injury, a player was dropped from the opposing team to "even up." Later, mutually agreed to replacements were permitted, though infrequently.

The County Town team began with a flourish, winning 7-2 in Renfrew. That same evening, Carleton Place shut out the Woollen Town 6-0. Right away there was rivalry. Held up by a storm, Pembroke arrived late, the game getting underway at 9pm. Since no contest began before 8:30 you'd expect suffering to be minimal but Renfrew fans, anticipating a big crowd, arrived early making it seem longer; long enough for the local *Mercury* to take a strip off Pembroke, railroads, hockey in general and apple pie.

Pembroke players included a goaltender named Buchanan, who played three more games then disappeared. Ed Jones was point man, with Cliff McPhee at cover point, while the forwards were Jim Stewart, John Lorne Hale, Bert Summers and Ed Irving. Fred Cains of Montreal refereed. Two Renfrew notables were Robert Carruth and Larry Gilmour; Robert continued many fine seasons with Renfrew while Larry became one of the earliest professionals.

Our heroes went on to beat Carleton Place 7-5, lost 6-5 in Arnprior and defeated Renfrew 8-5 in Pembroke. Then G. Peden took over in goal, finishing the season there. The club concluded events with a 4-4 tie in Carleton Place, then hammered Arnprior 13-1, giving the team a 4-1-1 record and first place tie with the Junction Town.

A one-game title match was ordered to be played in Renfrew, on Monday February 27, 1899. Pembroke Srs bombarded Carleton Place goal tender Peter Murphy, winning 11-3 and taking the first OVHL championship. C.G. Pennock officiated and a league-purchased trophy was presented. From a $120 gate, Renfrew firemen got $60 and the clubs split $60.

Only one 1898/99 OVHL game was free of protest, prompting Valley weeklies to suggest a possible oversight. Here are two examples.

Carleton Place defeated Renfrew 4-3. Carleton Place fans arrived on the 5pm local, sporting all manner of noise makers. Pandemonium reigned in Eureka Rink, prompting referee Fred Cains to order a house cleaning at half time. Police Chief McDermott flung a few out, lowering the octaves a level or two, but Cains paid dearly, suffering fans on the ice after every whistle. Then, when a Carleton Place goal was allowed that even Junction Town supporters agreed didn't go in, intimidation reached such levels that the umpire considered changing his mind—until a burly visitor changed it back again.

At a 4-4 tie in Carleton Place, referee Fred Chittick ordered overtime, as stipulated in the rules. Carleton Place captain McLaren pulled his team, claiming the referee "favoured Pembroke" and "Mr Chittick's rank decisions disgusted the spectators." Fred awarded the game to Pembroke, sparking a vicious letter writing exchange between him and OVHL secretary J. Stewart Oliver of Carleton Place. The OVHL eventually overturned Chittick's ruling, leaving the game tied, but the *Ottawa Citizen* stopped printing a seemingly endless string of insults only after Fred wrote, "His language was of the vilest and filthiest and I would suggest that your executive (OVHL) would grant a small sum to Mr J. Stewart Oliver, secretary of the league, that he might procure at the nearest drug store a brush and some soap, so that the next time he meets a gentleman his mouth will have been thoroughly cleaned and disinfected."

1899/1900

Pembroke Srs line-up for this season remained constant throughout, the one and only time it happened. Paddy Howe, the spare, never played.

Same team—same format. Pembroke Srs dropped their first two games before hammering Renfrew 10-2 (team names had yet to become popular in the Valley). Again, Carleton Place and the County Town finished tied, this time at 4-2. Also again, they met in Eureka Rink, March 21, 1900. What was an exception, after OVHL president C.G. Pennock dropped the puck, fans were treated to a fast, clean, protest-free game. Billy Wallace and Sam Shaughnessy scored for Pembroke in the first half then Tom Dunbar held off a furious Carleton Place rally to win 2-1, taking the second league title in a row.

Naturally, the above conclusion came via a rocky route. We take you back to game four; opening night for Arnprior's new arena. A CPR special left Pembroke with the team and two hundred fans, picking up twenty-five in Cobden and eighty in Renfrew before arriving at 8.30pm. With opening ceremonies, play didn't begin till 9:15. Each team scored twice in the first half. During the break, world figure skating champion George Meagher put on a demonstration (he later performed in Pembroke). Neither club scored during the second half nor did they through two ten minute overtime periods. Since there was no return special layed on, it was necessary to catch the 11pm local—and everyone did!

You might wonder, since Pembroke finished with a 4-2 record, what happened to the above tie. Simple—Renfrew's Larry Gilmour turned up in an Arnprior sweater; Pembroke protested and won.

You might also wonder why that final game was so late in the season. For whatever reason, probably weather, there was a month delay between games five and six of the schedule. During that time Pembroke Srs entrained to North Bay for a game, the outcome of which is a mystery. We do know Billy Wallace and Tom Dunbar were obliged to wage war on some bedbugs with their hockey sticks before getting any sleep that night. On the way home, they stopped in Mattawa for a game on ice separated from the curling rink by a "fragile fence." Mattawa's Don Hogarth, who later became a Major General in Toronto, came barrelling down on Wallace, who stepped into him, obliging the speedy forward to complete the rush on another rink!

1900/01

Suddenly, everyone was playing. Muskrat and Indian River ice became home to teams like Daisies, Young Hills, Back Streets and Tin Cans. So many girls turned up at an organizational meeting in Belle Campbell's home they put together two clubs but we don't know if they actually played.

Finally, there was an early freeze-up; rink manager Max Runge got his opening carnival over well before Christmas. Pembroke Srs captain Jim Stewart led his team, which sported new sweaters, to a 6-1 win over Carleton Place in the poorest played OVHL game to date.

It was an omen. A much improved Renfrew team visited and won 3-1, the first home-ice defeat for Pembroke since league play began. Still, our heroes arrived at a 4-1 record with one game to go, but it never came off. Carleton Place, after two fine campaigns, had lost every game badly; neither players nor fans were showing up, so they quit. You guessed it; that left Pembroke and Renfrew in a dead heat.

Led by Larry Gilmour, the Creamery Town won 8-2, securing it's first OVHL title. David Kennedy got home for the game and Tom Dunbar relieved Jack Douglas in goal, all to no avail.

There was not a single protest all season!

This was in sharp contrast to the town league, I can tell you. One match featured "slashing, smashing and dashing . . . several players were chucked through the window."

When Cans visited Westmeath, goatender Dunbar claimed he was obliged to "send a few headlong into the boards" in order to protect himself. Maybe it's how you look at it; Daisies and Mintos played what one described as "fast and furious, but not extra rough, although some of the players were the recipients of smashed mouths and black eyes, etc . . ."

Lorne Ranson's "Jr" team got in a few games before his highly touted star, Herb Jamieson, took sick in February, dying almost instantly. Typhoid was rampant, and even Dr Fred Delahey came within an ace of succumbing. In fact, sufferers were given a badge to discourage vigorous handshakes.

*****

Woodstock lost to Paris in OHA playdowns. Next day, this appeared in a Paris newspaper:

DIED
At Paris, Feb.11 1901
WOODSTOCK HOCKEY CLUB
From a dose of Paris Green

1901/02

As expected, Carleton Place dropped out of OVHL play, leaving Pembroke, Renfrew and Arnprior to go it alone. Action commenced January 10, 1902 with the Woollen Town visiting. A full house was royally entertained, the home club prevailing 7-6.

Then Renfrew visited, winning 5-3. Young Paddy Howe did not perform up to the expectations of impatient fans and suffered long-distance references to his heritage as a result. Insults of that nature came with the territory then and he survived three more solid seasons.

Pembroke Srs took a 5-3 decision in the Woollen Town, setting up an interesting conclusion to the four game schedule in Eureka Rink.

Referee Sam Rosenthal faced arguments throughout—and newspaper flack afterwards—but he maintained control. It was Jack Poff's first game in goal, following Tom Dunbar's last. Bert McPhee returned to action, helping his team secure a 2-1 victory, the town's third OVHL title in four tries—this time without a play-off.

Post-season competition nearly developed; a lower valley division of the league (LOVHL) had been formed—won by Hawkesbury—but talk of a winner-take-all game never bore fruit. So Pembroke Srs, with plenty of winter left, entrained to the Soo and lost 3-1, Lorne Kennedy registering their only goal.

Participants

Edward Irving was twenty-six years of age when he took part in Pembroke's first hockey game. He and Lennox were two of six children born to Andrew and Mary (Cannon) Irving, their father being the first registrar of Renfrew County. An exceptional lacrosse player, McGill-educated Edward captained the 1898/99 Srs then departed for Yukon gold with buddies Roy Moffat and John Ritchie—an eleven month trek fraught with grief. Roy froze to death. Jack returned safely but was killed in France during WWI. Ed got back as far as Kenora—then called Rat Portage—where he took up lumbering until the war broke out. Claiming to be much younger than his actual forty-nine years got Edward into the army, only to be wounded in France. After recuperating in Burlington, Ontario, Ed moved to Brockville where he remained until 1942. Ailing, Edward Irving then took up residence with Pembroke relatives, Mr and Mrs George Fenton, passing away a year later.

John Lorne Hale stopped playing hockey after that first OVHL championship. Son of lumberman Tom Hale, he enrolled in engineering at McGill in 1895 but when his father died in Bermuda of typhoid three years later, Lorne came home. Lorne never married and died in 1932 after a lengthy illness. This is a good spot to note that Tom's widow, shortly after he died, bought a Pembroke St home, tore it down and built a new one—that is now the Legion Hall.

Of the 1899/1900 players, bookkeeper Tom Dunbar, moved to Boston; "Tough Guy" Shaughnessy also went state-side; Albert Summers became a doctor in Ottawa and moustached Frank MacDonnell ended up in Australia. The rest stayed in town.

Captain Adjutant Herbert J. Mackie departed for the Boer War from Kingston in charge of "C" Battery. After a successful campaign with Charles Warren's famous Scouts, he hustled home for Christmas 1900, arriving several days late—but his horse came in on time.

*****

At Rat Portage, Wabigoon Division Court was scheduled during an important play-off game. All parties agreed to a 2am session, allowing everyone, including the judge, to entrain at 4am. A good time was had by all, including one legal beagle who was heard to exclaim "court proceedings should not at any time interfere with attendance at a hockey match."

Finally, let's tune to a game in Perth, when Smith's Falls was the visiting club. Overtures between bands from both towns led to such a crescendo the melodious masters began arranging each other's physical composition—how's that for brass?

Adjuncts

The *Pembroke Observer* was owned by one Martin Ringrose, a devoted Liberal whose scathing political prose was unmatched until he lost interest a couple of years before selling the newspaper in 1911. But Martin was not a sports fan, as this initial attempt at game coverage exemplifies. "After ten minutes waiting for wind, the puck again commenced to sail up and down the ice and the home team started in to do or die . . . Tim got the puck, drew the goal keeper and umpire's attention, shot it past Dunn between the umpire's legs—but he didn't see it." We wonder, of course—who didn't see it, and, was it a goal?

Speaking of Ringrose, which we will do on occasion, he sent Dan Jones to northern Ontario on assignment but the young man kept right on going, west. Eventually, Martin decided Dan was no longer an employee. But we haven't heard the last of Dan either . . .

Pembroke's first electric clock, installed on the Canada Atlantic Railway station, prompted one *Observer* to declare it "a marvellous affair—requiring no winding at all."

Andrew T. White, third son of Pembroke's founder, was elected MPP in 1898 but dropped dead at the dinner table two years later. James Munro took over the political position and it was James, in 1901, who brought a record square timber raft down the Ottawa River. A floating city, it contained 4057 pieces in 168 cribs. Turn that sucker crossways and it would have bridged the bulge!

Albert Cockburn quit his job with Pembroke Navigation Co. in 1900 to take over John Cockburn and Sons Boat Building, keeping alive the most famous pointer boats in history for another sixty plus years.

Ever hear of quinzy? Neither had I, but here's an example of where curiosity can lead. Noting that twenty-three-year-old George McDonnell, who worked at Gray's Drug

Store, died from the tonsil infection, I enquired of a doctor friend and learned something about Mr Gray in the process. A wealthy but frugal man who tied his shoes with string, Mr Gray had a daughter, Annie, who married, then lived for many years in the big house at Margaret and Moffat Sts (later owned by the Sisters of the Precious Blood and now a private home again). Annie created a private park on the property, which extended down to, and across, the Muskrat River. Many years after leaving Pembroke, she gave that land to the city and now Pansy Patch Park is the prettiest spot in town.

In 1901, Lieutenant Colonel Lennox Irving wrote to a Pennsylvania millionaire and received the following reply.

Lennox Irving
Pembroke, Ont.

Dear Sir:

Mr Carnegie does not think that $1000 a year would maintain a library suitably, but if Pembroke will give a suitable site and pledge itself to maintain the library, Mr Carnegie will give, say ten times the amount of annual maintenance guaranteed for the erection of the building. This is his usual rule of procedure.

Respectfully yours,

James Bertram—P. Secy.

Pembroke opened that library thirteen years later, and it is still one of the finest and most functional buildings in town.

Did you hear about the well-dressed gent who, having consumed his share of the glorious twelfth, eased to a table in the Pembroke House dining room? Seems he tried to shoo flies from a plate of bread before him. The insects persisted so he did too, employing some ill-chosen words while shaking both the dish and food in unison. Only then did fellow diners advise him it was currant loaf.

1896. Percy Doran and a bike to be proud of. Courtesy Carol Doran, his granddaughter.

1893/94 Fort William lacrosse team. Third from left, standing, R.J. Bob Manion: Pembroke-born lad who earned a Military Cross at Vimy and became National PC leader in the 1930s. Courtesy N–W Ontario Sports Hall of Fame.

Pembroke lacrosse club, 1897. Bill St. James is the father of Earl St. James, well-known former night clerk of the Pembroke Hotel. This is our only picture of David P. Kennedy. Others from the hockey world are Frank McDonnell, Jim Stewart—who previously played in Renfrew, Eugene "Paddy" Howe, Bert and Cliff McPhee and Jack Poff. Hiram Griffith is an uncle to local singer and community supporter Joyce Moore. Also note the Hon. Peter White and Peter White Jr. Courtesy Don Stewart, Jim's son.

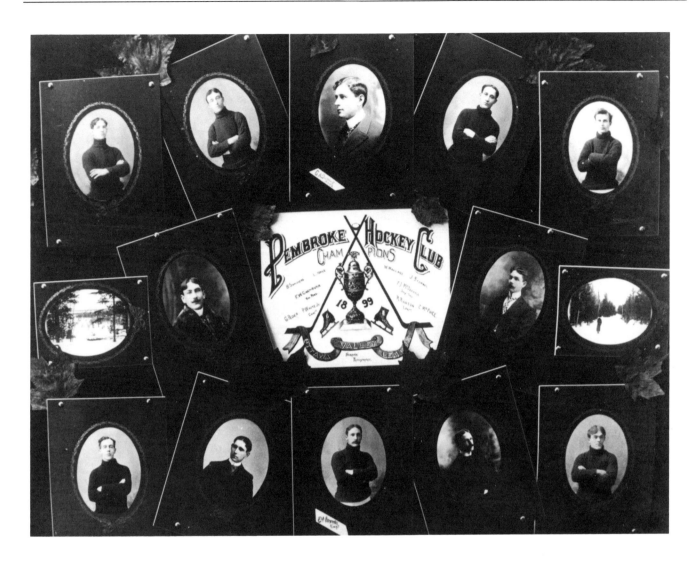

Pembroke Srs 1899. Top, left to right: Bert Summers, Lorne Hale, Edward A. Dunlop (president), Billy Wallace and Jim Stewart. Middle row: Fred Cockburn (vice-president) and Frank McDonnell (player/secretary-treasurer) Bottom row: G. Peden, Peter White Jr (exec.), Ed. Irving (captain), R. Ranson (exec.) and Cliff McPhee. Courtesy Don Stewart.

The P.S.R. Station. When the railroad became the Grand Trunk in 1914, Gordon's store was incorporated into a new station; opposite of the old one. Pembroke St E. runs between the stop-block and post office, now city hall, seen behind. Courtesy Jean Cringan.

R.W. Gordon's (Grant's father) store. Courtesy Jean Cringan.

1900 Srs. Great old picture. Note inserts of the 1897, 1898 and 1899 teams, small as they are. Courtesy Gerry Gordon, Grant's son.

Above: Pembroke, pre-1908. Looking west over the Muskrat River from atop Middleton's house, 329 MacKay St. Right, beyond the Mary St bridge, is Pembroke's first covered skating rink. (It's roof collapsed in 1908) Extreme right, the P.S.R. station—over that rectangular chimney and the post office beyond. Note spur tracks at the bridge, from a main line south of town. Courtesy Allan Levoy.

Right: 1901/02 Pembroke Srs: From top, left to right: Billy Wallace (left wing), D. Burns (vice-president), Shinny Shaughnessy (centre), Tom Jones (rover), W.D. McLaren (secretary-treasurer), Lorne Kennedy (right wing). Centre, left to right: A. Thomson (commissioner), Bert McPhee (point), J.E. Wallace (commissioner), J.R. Grieve (commissioner), Eugene "Paddy" Howe (cover point), W. St. James (commissioner). Bottom, left to right: Herb Mackie (commissioner), Jack Poff (goal), Lorne Ranson (spare), W. Cockburn (president). Courtesy Pembroke Jr Lumber Kings.

Chapter 3

EXTENDED LEAGUE, NEW TROPHY — GREATER FUN?

1902/03 to 1904/05

In the beginning, most games belong to the players. If it remains essentially a participation sport, attracting few spectators, rules will be developed only for the players. But let it develop excitement on the street and manipulation begins. Hockey was getting people's attention.

In 1903/04 the International Professional Hockey League was born; until then every player had been an amateur. You're familiar with the difference: a professional gets paid for his services and an amateur services those who pay him. Not unexpectedly, Sault Ste Marie Algonquins and Toronto University were quickly black-listed by the OHA for playing exhibition games with "tainted" pros, establishing a conflict that lasted for years.

Meantime, the OHA ruled referees could no longer overturn an umpire's decision, a flawed though well-intendedidea. Also, beginning with 1903/04, substitutions, as opposed to "evening up," were allowed in the event of injury, and it was surprising how suddenly vulnerable some players became.

Games

1902/03

With the OVHL now sporting the prefix "Upper," the *Ottawa Citizen* ensured a UOVHL–LOVHL play-off would take place by creating an incentive. The *Citizen* Shield, eventually provided for all levels down to bantam and still available at intermediate level today, quickly became the Ottawa Valley trophy.

The addition of Almonte brought UOVHL strength to four again so a six-game schedule was organized. Headed by captain Robert Scott and goalie W. Egan, Renfrew swept to a 6-0 record, rarely allowing a goal.

Anchored by Jack Poff and Paddy Howe, Pembroke Srs rebuilt with several budding stars. As an example, in the H&H matches with Renfrew, Poff was in goal when Pembroke lost the first encounter 2-1, but for game two, a 1-0 loss, Jack had given way to a kid off the local creeks and rivers named Frederick Hugh Lehman, a goal tender destined for the NHL Hall of Fame.

Vankleek Hill overcame Hawkesbury, Lachute, Rockland and Buckingham for LOVHL honours and thus met Renfrew for the first Shield. That game took place in Dey's Arena, March 2, 1903, and we'll never know what happened to the firepower of Larry Gilmour, Roy Anderson and Co.; suffice to say Vankleek Hill won the game that quickly deteriorated to water polo, 5-2.

The LOVHL played by Quebec rules so the contest was split 50-50, first half one way, second half the other.

Morgan's Nationals won the first duly organized town league in Pembroke thanks to outstanding goaltending by J. Douglas Campbell, a chap who would have doubtless seen action in the Sr nets had he not moved to Smith's Falls, where he lived until passing away in 1947. Nationals played Eganville several times, a team blessed with the talents of Basil and Greg George, who were eventually to star with Queen's University, first Allan Cup winners in 1909.[1]

1903/04

Renfrew began the season by defeating Pembroke 6-3, January 8, 1904. Harry Airth played goal for the Creamery Town, though he soon gave way to one W. Campbell. Harry was a driving force in Renfrew baseball until dying quite young of a heart attack, May 7, 1928. R.D. Scott was in the midst of his best years with that club; he died in 1949 at the age of seventy. A newcomer to Renfrew was Nellum Kimpton, a marvellous talent who had been playing with his brother Jim for Ottawa Capitals. Many wondered what mysterious force had propelled him Renfrew way.

Suddenly Arnprior upset Almonte 17-4. Thus Pembroke arrived in the Woollen Town tentatively, despite having former Arnprior star Frank Sargeant in the line-up. Pembroke also boasted rapidly improving goal tender Hugh Lehman, but the feeling of apprehension proved legitimate. Our heroes lost 7-1.

What brought about Arnprior's sudden resurgence? Firstly, Harry Smith, was coaching and playing centre, and on the sideline, brother Alf was offering verbal encouragement. Of Ottawa's seven Smith brothers, Harry, Tom and Alf had significant careers in hockey. To be fair, Harry was just beginning, while Alf probably made more money for yelling instructions. We know how much the veteran Sargeant cost Pembroke: 2 1/2 months board, a pair of socks and unspecified clothes, totalling $32.25.

Pembroke's only two wins came at the expense of Almonte, the Factory Town being shut out altogether. Fine play by Lehman had forced both Jack Poff and Tom Dunbar to forward positions. When Tom was injured midway through the game in Almonte, his brother Jim, also normally a goaltender but on this occasion just along for the

ride, was pressed into service under the new substitution rule. Technically then, Pembroke had more goalies on the ice than forwards.

Really, the team was improving. Second-year players Roy McVean and Tom Jones held great promise, newcomer Hugh Fraser demonstrated all kinds of talent and veteran Billy Wallace steadied the ship.

Most interesting was the final league game between Renfrew (5-0) and Arnprior (4-1). The clubs had built quite a head of steam, what with their competition for "unpaid" imports and constant debate over acceptable officials. They were tied 1-1 late in the first half when Harry Smith took a fifteen minute slashing penalty. Renfrew scored three times. When Harry returned he engineered five in a row, giving his club a 6-4 victory, and forcing a play-off.

That took place in Almonte on February 26, 1904. Arnprior went all out; not only were Harry and his brother still involved, but Alf was flanked on the sidelines by Bouse Hutton and Harry Westwick, his Stanley Cup winning Silver Seven teammates. Harry scored three goals and his club won 6-2. To reduce prolonged pre-game arguments over officials, Toronto Marlborough referee F.C. Waghorne was recruited. He ruled with an iron hand.

Arnprior met LOVHL champion Lachute in Ottawa's Aberdeen Pavilion, March 15, 1904 for the *Citizen* Shield. It was a super game. Led by goaltender Willie Hayes and Willie Pearson, a methodist minister's son who played point and flattened people, Arnprior won 2-1. Also on that talented club were Melford Milne, John Fraser, John Campbell and one of the finest players that town ever produced, Prosper Dontigny.

1904/05

Renfrew opened a so-so season with a new arena, and Ottawa Jr champion Victorias were in town for the christening, January 6, 1905. Improved lighting over the 75' x 175' surface eliminated a favourite trick of the time; high backhanders into the gloom that bounced before startled goaltenders. Incidentally, two hundred and forty thousand board feet of lumber went into that building.

After the previous disastrous season, Almonte was coaxed to try again, then suffered through another frustrating campaign.

As for Pembroke Srs, captain Tom Benson was lost for the season right off; Willie Pearson stepped into him mid-

---

1. Record books show Ottawa Cliffsides to be the initial Allan Cup winners, in 1908. Actually, Allan Cup trustees awarded the new trophy to Cliffsides, in 1909, based on their 1908 record. Cliffsides lost it within weeks to Queen's.

way through the first game in Arnprior. Harry Bowden, irascible clothing merchant and team official, immediately swore out an assault and battery charge against Willie. Arnprior countered in kind, naming Tom. The case actually went to court in Arnprior, January 20, 1905, before Magistrate McGonigal. The Woollen Town team produced dozens of witnesses, including the inimitable Mr Chittick, a bunch of Smiths, Harry Westwick and even Frank McGee. Alas, Pembroke sent only Harry and fellow club executive D.W. Campbell. They didn't have a chance.

But County Town players did; they hammered Arnprior 11-2 in the return match. The UOVHL secretary received this letter immediately thereafter:

Dear Sir:

Take note that the Arnprior Hockey Club protest the league match between Pembroke and Arnprior on the evening of the 3rd of February 1905, on the following grounds:

> *That one Ranson, who played for the Pembroke team, has played on other teams, is not a resident of Pembroke for thirty days preceeding the game and is not otherwise qualified.*
> *That the referee ruled according to Ontario Hockey Association rules, whereas the game should have been played under Quebec rules.*
> *That the rink is not properly lighted; that it is not regulation width and length, that the rafters interfere with the proper playing of the game and that spectators at one end of the rink were on the ice and interfered with the players and puck during the game.*
> *That spectators were allowed on shelves erected on the sides and struck at Arnprior players with sticks and other missiles.*

Dated at Arnprior this fourth day of February 1905.
(signed) R.J. Slattery, sec–treas Arnprior Hockey Club.

M.G. Milne, Captain Arnprior Hockey Club.

Needless to say, nothing came of that protest.

By defeating Renfrew 5-3 in the final game, Pembroke Srs created a tie with Arnprior for league honours, forcing another sudden death match up, this one taking place in the Creamery Town, March 7, 1905.

Despite a productive forward unit of Lorne Ranson, Tom Dunbar and rookie Curley Campbell (who would also become a member of that 1909 Allan Cup winner at Queen's), several hundred fans and a lucky rabbit decked out in team colours, Pembroke lost 4-2.

Led by the scoring of Earl McMillan, Arnprior won its second Shield in a row by upsetting Hawkesbury 5-3 in Dey's Arena, March 15.

Participants

Two sad items to report:

During February of 1905, Pembroke's Robert Fraser, sixteen, was playing with friends on an outdoor rink. In pursuit of the puck, he fell backwards, striking his head. Carried to the clubhouse, he seemed to recover then suddenly died. Robert's brother Gordon and nephew Ivan are covered extensively later in this book.

One week later, during a game in Maxville with Alexandria the visiting team, Alexandria's Alcide Laurin was killed by a blow from the stick of Maxville's Allan Loney. A coroner's jury found Loney guilty of "a swift, heavy blow . . . and judging from the evidence not in self-defense." Loney pled not guilty at the murder trial. Twenty witnesses appeared before Justice Teetzel of Cornwall, including former Pembroke player John Robert Moffat, then manager of Maxville's Bank of Ottawa and in attendance at the game. It looked bad for Loney, a condition not eased by Teezel's charge to the jury. Nonetheless, they took only four hours to find him not guilty. While announcing their decision, the jury foreman launched into a lengthy dissertation on roughhouse tactics in not only hockey but lacrosse and football, concluding it was reporters, "in giving space and prominence to those contests, are largely responsible morally for these results, as they unquestionably fire the imaginations of some less level-headed spectators, who by voice and manner encourage and excite heated players to deeds of violence towards an opponent."

Judge Teetzel told Loney the jury had been merciful.

Adjuncts

The most bitter provincial election in local history took place January 1905. Tory Edward A. Dunlop and Grit Dr McKay, who had been friends previously, and were again after a decent interval, lambasted each other mercilessly.

Both McKay and his party lost.

That same winter, Pembroke's Thibideau block went up in flames, taking out Grieve Shoes, Goody Paints, Harrison Jewellers, Martin's Grocery and Pembroke Electric Light Co. offices.

Tom Mackie died in May, at seventy. The father of Albert, Herb, Leonard, Bill and Gordon was a high profile businessman, and his wife, Jessie, is of the well-known Shaw family, a current example being Herb Shaw and Sons Ltd; one of the area's largest lumber companies.

Getting back to that bridge. Allumette islanders hired engineers to investigate the possibility of a railway-road-way structure stretching 3000 feet from White's Dock to Sand Point. August Demers and Tom Dunbar supervised the project, and politicians, while collectively admitting it might take some time, got right on it . . .

Chapter 4

WHO REALLY "PLAYS" THIS GAME?

1905/06 to 1908/09

This story is full of items ranging from routine to amazing but nowhere will you find four seasons in a row that equal this period.

An important advance was the arrival of tube skates, gradually replacing "two-enders." Fred Weghorne, who refereed for fifty years, introduced dropping the puck instead of placing it gently between the sticks; he'd had his knuckles rapped enough. Fred also reintroduced the whistle; hockey officials began with whistles, but as they froze to lips, switched to bells. Now, with covered buildings on the increase, Fred was the first to switch back. Also, a "judge of play" began appearing. This referee's assistant, was not on the ice but he did have a whistle. This position remained with the game until two referees were introduced. Meantime, blurred authority led to some hilarious scenes.

It was Pembroke's turn to build a new rink. The MacKay St Arena, destined to serve the County Town for forty-five years, opened Christmas Day, 1905. Mayor W. H. Bradley cut the ribbon and everyone they could cram on 179' x 80' of ice skated to the 42nd Battalion Band. The 206' x 100' building sported a balcony all around and four dressing rooms over the reception area, obliging players to negotiate stairs on skates. It was also a signif-

icant drop to ice level, prompting players to jump through the opening in full flight. Many were unlucky enough to pull a groin muscle if not careful to check their skate blades for foreign material first.

Billy Bogart, a painter, was president of the privately owned facility for decades; his yet-to-be-born son, Arthur, grew up to become manager.

Games

1905/06

W.D. McLaren served both Pembroke Srs and UOVHL as president. This season Almonte did pull out, leaving Pembroke, Renfrew and Arnprior to visit each other twice.

The County Town cast varied little. J.A. Merkley, a late arrival the previous season, played one game at point then disappeared, Roy McVean taking his place. Eugene "Paddy" Howe would have been part of the club were it not for typhoid fever; the five-year veteran recovered but never played again. Robert Coxford served as spare but wasn't used. That left Hugh Lehman to play goal—his only full season in Pembroke, McVean, captain Tom Benson—cover point, while Tom Jones centred Billy Wallace and almost-rookie Hugh Fraser. That left the rover position for Orin Frood, a Renfrew lad that Creamery Town officials let get away because he was too small and couldn't skate.

Prosper Dontigny and his Arnprior teammates were first to visit MacKay St Arena, January 5, 1906. Only he, goalie Willie Hayes and Melford Milne weren't rookies and things didn't go well for them. Jones, Fraser and Frood built a 3-0 lead for the home team before Arnprior scored; at that point referee J. McLaren of Carleton Place called roughing penalties on Hugh Fraser and a fellow named Banks that Arnprior had brought in from Buckingham to provide muscle. Dontigny was so incensed that Banks went off with Fraser, he pulled his team, refusing to return. McLaren had no alternative but to award Pembroke the game. It turned out that Banks didn't meet the ninety-day residency rule so league officials ordered him out. Arnprior threatened to quit the league. They didn't, but did manage to sneak Banks into one more game before being forced to conform.

Pembroke then won 5-2 in Renfrew and 2-1 in Arnprior before hosting them in that order, taking 4-0 and 4-3 decisions. Former Arnprior player Peter Murphy refereed that 4-0 game in which Lehman was brilliant while Fraser and Frood shared the goals. The team won 3-2 in Renfrew then scored a last minute goal in Arnprior to prevail 5-4.

That game cinched the title, making the last game at home against Renfrew anti-climatic, though Hugh Lehman couldn't see losing if at all avoidable. With Pembroke leading 3-1, which was how the game finished, Larry Gilmour came steaming in on Hugh and shot, piling into the young goaltender for good measure. Not sure if the puck crossed the line, Hugh stuffed it into his paraphernalia before they untangled. The puck couldn't be found—until Hugh disrobed in the dressing room.

The Shield game was played in Dey's Arena, March 9, 1906. Four thousand fans watched Pembroke defeat Hawkesbury 5-0, a contest so lopsided that one Ottawa scribe said, "Lehman enjoyed the game from his box seat." Referee Bob Meldrum added the last few minutes of the first half to the second after a Hawkesbury shot broke the light over Lehman's head. Harvey Pulford and Fred Cockburn umpired Pembroke's first Shield victory, suffering nary a challenge. Frood scored two while Jones, Benson and Fraser tallied one each.

Pembroke Srs played two post-season games, both at

MacKay St Arena. Ottawa Vics, considered legitimate Stanley Cup contenders, lost 7-2, mainly on the strength of four goals by Orin Frood. Lastly, Pembroke defeated an LOVHL all-star club 5-1. Not counting the all-star game, for which no summary could be found, Orin Frood scored twenty goals during Pembroke's biggest year to date, surpassing second place Nellum Kimpton by nine markers. Kimpton, who operated a restaurant in the Creamery Town, was mistakenly called Nelson most of the time.

Standard publisher, Mr Bone, and his *Observer* counterpart, Martin Ringrose, organized a banquet at Mr Bourke's Copeland House for Pembroke Srs and everyone enjoyed themselves, especially after learning the new champions finished $200 in the black, even after everyone received gold watches that cost the club $565.

No player was paid a cent. Referees earned $10—including expenses. Pucks cost 20¢ to 35¢ and a stick 40¢ to $1.50; the team bought those, did the laundry and provided oranges and gum each game.

It was a great season, talked about to this day. I must, however, refute a claim made frequently that Pembroke Srs' undefeated season went 14-0. Despite exhaustive efforts on my part and the famed perseverance of community statistician Donald "Brownie" Andrews, we find only eleven games. Unless yellowed documentation surfaces to the contrary, we say 11-0.

1906/07

The 1905/06 season infuriated Renfrew. It was bad enough letting Arnprior stretch the rules with all those Smiths but seeing the hated County Town with the Shield, especially using a Renfrew man their team had rejected, left Renfrew furious. But not for long; the O'Briens, Barnets and Lows, already dreaming of a Stanley Cup, decided OVHL domination would not only generate necessary credibility but exact some up-river retribution as a secondary benefit.

First, the residency rule must be eased. This proved to be no problem; the moment Pembroke and Arnprior objected, Renfrew pulled out, returning only under "compromise" conditions.

Meantime, thanks to a winning season, Pembroke Srs boasted a huge executive and over thirty patrons. On the ice, Jack Poff became goal tender again because Lehman turned pro with the Soo. Initially, the only other addition was Roy Anderson, a Buckingham native who saw action with the 1904/05 team.

Pembroke opened the eight game schedule in Arnprior, arriving an hour late after the train suffered a hot box. Only Milne and Hayes were still with the Woollen Town, and Milne was about to turn pro. The main addition was Antoine Rattez, there briefly between stints in the Soo. Former Renfrew player R.D. Scott refereed the 3-2 Pembroke win, having been forced from the Creamery Town line-up by the numbers game.

When Renfrew, now called Riversides, invaded MacKay St Arena, only Larry Gilmour and Jim Carruth were from the previous team. At least forward Louis Imbleau and netminder Bert Parsons were Creamery Town natives, but the rest of the team were "instant locals" such as Bobby Rowe, Steve Vair, Ernie Williams and a guy named Black. They were all from Barrie and among the best in the business. Renfrew won 6-3.

Before Arnprior arrived for the next game, Pembroke officials made an effort to compete, at a cost of $25 to $45 weekly, per player. Tom Benson lost his cover point position to Charles Douglas "Baldy" Spittal, a thirty-one-year-old veteran of six seasons with Ottawa's best, one a Stanley Cup club in 1903. Billy Wallace was replaced by Eddie Roberts, fresh from Pittsburgh of the IPHL (Roberts broke his collarbone the next season while with Ottawa Vics). And Roy Anderson gave way to a fellow called Johnston, who turned out to be Erskine "Skene" Ronan.

Apparently, Spittal and Roberts were re-instated amateurs while Rowan had already turned professional. Why Renfrew wasn't tagged for similar aquisitions is anyone's guess. Skene, recognized during the next game, earned a national one-year suspension. Then he embarked on a nine-season pro career, mostly with Ottawa but including the 1918 Stanley Cup winning Canadiens. However, it was Skene's two-game stint in Pembroke that got the County Town labelled "initiator of local professional corruption," by press across the land, and the stigma stuck for years.

The contest ended 3-3 but overtime was prevented by train schedules.

A suddenly poetic Ringrose described the game: "At 7:30 in the evening the air was frosty. Indeed, the cold was intense. But, in spite of it all, a hurrying procession wended its way down each thoroughfare that led to the icey arena.

Like the Romans of old, in a sense, they thronged to see the gladiators fight. Here and there a scurrying of some dainty-footed maiden betokened that Jack Frost was playing the part of Jack the Hugger. Now and then a slip on the icey pavement was followed by a peal of girlish laughter giving an inkle of the happiness that anticipation sometimes stirs in the hearts of us all. Anticipation of victory and its realization were not too far apart Tuesday night."

When Pembroke Srs visited Renfrew, Riversides boasted Williams, Black, Kimpton, Gilmour, Vair, Rowe and a new goaltender named Bert Lindsay (bumping Parsons to forward) who had been playing in Ottawa but was originally from West Garafraxa County, near Guelph. The visiting club included a still masquerading Ronan, Hugh Lehman—home for a visit and his only 1906/07 appearance, plus Sam Hamilton "Hamby" Shore, a twenty-year-old emerging Ottawa Senators (formerly Silver Seven) star. Hamby played the one game, returned to Ottawa and except for a season in Winnipeg stayed with the Senators till he died of influenza in 1918. This game ended 5-5 and though it was imports Rowe and Vair who did the scoring, the *Renfrew Mercury* printed the outcome "Renfrew 5, Pembroke 3, Ottawa 2." Riversides protested of course; not Hamby and the "mystery man" though, but Lehman and Roy McVean! Nothing came of it.

Dan McLaughlin, who was president of the league as well as Arnprior Srs, wanted Peter Murphy to referee a Pembroke-Arnprior contest. Pembroke objected to the veteran Arnprior player, saying anyone but Murphy. McLaughlin said Murphy or nobody. Pembroke sent a telegram quoting the league constitution, which provided for disputes over officials to be settled by a neutral team. They would accept anyone Renfrew chose, except Murphy. McLaughlin wired back; to heck with Renfrew—the game's off. And so it was.

Then the UOVHL decided to have a meeting. Though it was almost February, they tore up the old schedule and wrote a new one, which apparently fixed everything.

When Riversides next came to MacKay St Arena, the host club "delayed a long time" but the imported players never showed up. Pembroke reverted to rejects, getting thumped 10-2. Billy Wallace broke his shoulder in this game; he played very little over the next couple of years then switched to officiating.

Pembroke Srs won and lost against Arnprior then finished in Renfrew with several youngsters from the newly formed Debaters team, such as Tony Kutchaw, George Valin and H. Scott. The game was never completed; Riversides pounded on Tom Jones till he quit, so the entire club packed up and came home.

The team played one more game, an exhibition in New Liskeard, taking along the athletic but wild Ernie Taylor, younger brother of J.Deacon Taylor, a local jeweller soon to be Pembroke's most prominent hockey executive. Baldy Spittal refereed the tied game, Pembroke's first introduction to a "judge of play."

Two new teams appeared on the local scene, Jr Mintos and the aforementioned Debaters. The Mintos didn't survive but Debaters—debating clubs were quite popular at the time—became famous in the Valley, frequently starting the careers of some outstanding talent. The team toured Northern Ontario during this charter season.

April 8, 1907, Westmeath defeated Beachburg 8-4 on a surface described as "ideal," the latest game I know of played on natural ice to date.

As for Renfrew, the team lost one league game, 9-6 to Arnprior, frustrating a pre-season determination to match Pembroke's record of a year earlier. While waiting for a LOVHL winner, Riversides defeated Ottawa Senators 9-5, qualifying them to challenge for the Stanley Cup, a privilege granted the following year. They then took the Shield, defeating Vankleek Hill 9-3.

1907/08

This could be called a threatening season. Arnprior threatened to pull out and Renfrew threatened to produce two teams—one to go after the big trophy and another "secondary outfit" to meet UOVHL standards. Pembroke threatened to threaten anyone found susceptible to threats.

In the end Arnprior stayed in the league, having obtained Jack Fraser of Brandon, Manitoba, who was said to be a franchise saver.

The Renfrew team was now called Creamery Kings. President Tom Low got word they were to play Ottawa Victorias in a two-game, total-goals Stanley Cup qualifying round between Christmas and New Year. They were allowed four "outside" additions, present team members obviously considered "inside." Anyway, Low immediately signed Ottawa's Horace Gaul, Fred Lake, who had been playing in the IHL, and Harold Armstrong of Smith's Falls.

Steve Vair had gone to Guelph but responded in a hurry to Low's call. A grab at Fred "Cyclone" Taylor was quickly rebuffed by his club, the Senators. These new players, added to Lindsay, Rowe, Kimpton and Gilmour, met Vics December 27. Vics, sporting the likes of Eddie Roberts, Charlie Ross, Jack Ryan of football fame and, oddly enough, Jack Fraser, won 4-1.

Renfrew tried buying more good players. Brandon star Con Corbeau was rushed in. Baldy Spittal was enlisted and Arnprior even lent Prosper Dontigny. A second attempt to recruit Cyclone failed, though he accepted $800, played an exhibition game, then was forced to return to the Senators—giving back the $800 to boot.

Creamery Kings defeated Vics 3-1 in Renfrew, thus losing on the round by a goal. The Montreal Wanderers later hammered Vics 9-3 and 13-1 in the Cup series so Renfrew had a ways to go anyway. Meantime, Creamery Kings entered the UOVHL for a season in which every game began with protests, most goals were disputed and few umpires avoided banishment; the rule about not being overruled having been ruled out.

Pembroke Srs, still with Fraser, Frood, Jones and McVean, were pleased to see Lehman return, bringing fellow home-towner and Soo teammate, Bob Scott, with him. Bob, by this time a doctor, left Pembroke after the 1903 season and played for Calumet, Michigan until breaking his leg in 1905. Hugh also brought veteran point man Eddie "Dutch" Schaeffer, also known as "Germany" Schaeffer. Eddie, who had served several teams and was always known as "a swift, manly and clean player," was Pembroke's only true import.

Renfrew made a move on Schaeffer after he signed with Pembroke, but team officials screamed so long and loud that Low and Co. had a rare failure. Oddly enough, the only Pembroke player over whom Renfrew maintained a constant protest was Lehman.

Shortly thereafter, Pembroke attempted to sign Eddie Roberts but Arnprior objected vehemently, winning the case.

The County Town team opened with exhibition wins over Ottawa Emmetts and Cornwall of the Federal Amateur Hockey League (FAHL). After four seasons of Stanley Cup level standings, the FAHL lost its best players to the new Ontario Professional Hockey League (OPHL) and was one campaign from extinction. The OPHL, known as the Trolley League because member towns were in close proximity to one another, survived four tumultuous years, with only Berlin and Brantford in for the duration.

Following those successful warm-ups, Pembroke Srs played only four more hockey games, but what a quartet they were.

Game one: Arnprior visited. Arnprior added Bob Harrison, former Vics star, to the likes of Dontigny and Fraser. Pembroke protested. Arnprior countered, naming Scott. Eventually they played. Referee Tom Ellis was obliged to replace both umpires within three minutes. There were lots of penalties, but finally Pembroke won 7-2. Frood scored four while Harrison got both his team's goals. Arnprior pressed their protest but it was thrown out.

Game Two: In Renfrew. Pembroke had Jack Ryan available but decided not to play him. Renfrew, on top of all that power, hired Montreal's Ernie Liffiton, who was equal to any on hand. The County Town didn't bother to protest, no doubt pleasing referee Chauncy Kirby who had all he could handle anyway. The visitors belted Rowe so often he finally withdrew; Jones going off to even up. Though a special train had taken hundreds of fans, they didn't help their team. Creamery Kings won 8-1, Vair getting four. Descriptions of the game varied widely, right down to the *Citizen* saying conditions were ideal and the rival *Journal* claiming ice was soft.

Game Three: In Arnprior. Started late. Jones, too badly banged up from game two, was replaced by Roy Anderson. Ottawa's Ted Groulx played goal for Arnprior. Percy LeSueur, famous Silver Seven netminder and eventual Hall of Famer, was referee and had a nightmarish evening. The umpire disallowed Pembroke's first goal. Roy McVean argued with the official, who gave Roy a punch in the mouth. Percy restored order. When Arnprior suffered a similar fate, a fan clobbered the umpire. Percy restored order again. Frood and Scott registered three goal evenings and Pembroke won 6-4. Dontigny was the big man for Arnprior.

Game Four: Renfrew Creamery Kings visited Pembroke Srs on Friday, January 17, 1908. This game, which was included in every banquet speech for decades and suffered gross distortion as a result, fired imaginations throughout the Ottawa Valley like no other single contest before or since. In fact, rumours of something unusual brought representatives from not only Ottawa press, but Toronto and Montreal as well.

Creamery Kings' president Tom Low, as did most of his peers, enjoyed the odd wager. Tom had sufficient confidence in his expensive athletes to indulge that pleasure regularly.

Mr Low arrived by train, with his team and supporters, one being Billy O'Brien, who eventually became trainer of the Montreal Maroons. As you know, railroad employees were quite familiar with the O'Briens', particularly Michael J. O'Brien, the family patriarch who layed much of the track in this country. Therefore, we should not be surprised that a note was delivered to this family member enroute. An unnamed conductor wondered, on paper, what three members of the Montreal Wanderers were doing aboard, and where they might get off.

Mr Low was advised. No one would blame him, should the mystery trio appear on MacKay St Arena ice in Pembroke uniforms, for declaring all bets off. On the other hand, it was not an era kind to welchers . . .

Meanwhile, two thousand faithful flocked to the rink, spurred onward by rumours of a talent display unlike any seen before. Then, just before game time, word circulated that Baldy Spittal was going to put Orin Frood out of commission—permanently. How much could the fans stand?

Tom Low stood by the Renfrew dressing room door, assuring one and all he was a man of his word.

Finally, through the end zone opening popped Lehman, Schaeffer, Scott and Frood plus the three Montrealers: Jack Chipchase, Tom Hooper and, captain for the night, Art Ross.

The crowd went bananas. Lindsay, Gilmour, Spittal, Rowe, Vair, Gaul and Liffiton watched.

They began with the required protests and finally started to play at 9:25pm. Referee Eddie Phillips, rated anywhere from superb to inept depending on the source, called only life threatening infractions—thirteen in all. Creamery Kings, displaying some familiarity with one another, built a 4-1 lead by half-time. Chipchase and Hooper showed little but the talent of Ross was obvious if he ever got going.

The fifteen-minute half-time break became a half hour due to light failure. When the teams returned, Ross was wearing his Wanderers sweater and about to perform thirty minutes of hockey to a level even he would never surpass.

Switching defensive positions with Schaeffer, the twenty-two-year-old Naughton, Ontario native began from the opening face-off by stripping Rowe of the puck then successfully challenging Vair, Gaul, Spittal and Gilmour—in that order—before scoring on a fake that left Lindsay out on MacKay St. A safe place, given that the rink seemed about to cave in.

Unfortunately, Ross mesmerized his teammates, who stood around watching while he played one against seven for most of the second half.

At last, with only a few minutes left and Renfrew leading 7-4, Baldy checked Frood, knocking him cold. Orin was barely through the exit, feet first, when constable Tom Dickson arrested Spittal.

It's a wonder there were no fatalities. Captains Ross and Gilmour spent half an hour with authorities, both league and legal, trying to get the game finished. Finally, Rowe went off to even up for Frood, Baldy was incarcerated so Scott retired, and Gaul took a five-minute penalty with less time than that remaining. Thus, with nine players on the ice and the band playing "Home Sweet Home," the contest ended at 12:20 am .

Renfrew prevailed 8-6. Steve Vair scored five goals for the winners and we'll never know, with absolute certainty, who fired the other three. Despite various claims during succeeding decades as to the recipients of Pembroke's markers, let it be recorded once and for all that Art Ross scored five and Orin Frood one.

Tom Low and George Barnet put up $500 each in order to take Spittal home, but he was ordered to appear before Magistrate Mitchell a week later. Fortunately for Baldy, though already on probation for hitting a player named Blatchford the previous season in Montreal, Pembroke police dropped the charge within two days. Actually, Spittal was not a dirty player and a fan likely started the rumour. Furthermore, Frood was far less damaged than some of his teammates—or dozens of warring fans.

The referee immediately blamed gambling, getting considerable flack for that opinion from local papers but gaining support from the *Toronto Globe* writer in attendance, who said "The Pembroke crowd had the satisfaction of telling referee, Ed Philips, of Ottawa, that they thought he was a robber, but these are the regular accompaniments of Ottawa Valley league games, which seem to be run for the cheap gambles that follow them."

The "ringers" returned to Montreal, having been paid $200 collectively for their services. Chipchase was immediately released by the Wanderers, for whom he had seen spot duty over four seasons. Hooper, elected to the Hall of Fame for many great seasons in Rat Portage which included a Stanley Cup, came to Montreal when that team folded and

retired after this campaign. Art Ross completed fourteen years of top flight competition until 1918, including that Cup win with Hooper in Kenora. He then retired to coaching and managing. A great innovator, the Hall of Famer after whom the NHL scoring champion award is named, invented both the modern net and modern puck. He died in 1964.

Two games were merely postponed before Pembroke Srs officially folded for the season. Though given permission by the league to pick up three replacements for the walking wounded, none could be found and there was little heart to continue anyway. Later, a group that included the Beamish boys, Alex Thrasher and young Allan Wilson got together for a visit from Ottawa Seconds, then played a game in the Soo. Schaeffer went to Brantford for three contests before that club's campaign ended.

Renfrew romped over Arnprior then played exhibitions until Buckingham and Hawkesbury resolved the LOVHL title. In fact, that series took so long Renfrew was given permission to play Ottawa Seconds for the Shield; the Creamery Kings won easily. Then, when Buckingham finally came out on top, the club refused to meet Renfrew. Later, at the capital banquet in Ottawa, Horace Gaul was asked to get up and tell how Renfrew won the *Citizen* Shield. He got up and left.

On January 13, 1908, four days before that fateful fourth game, Brockville and Cornwall played an FAHL match. Brockville won 12-0. In the winners line-up were Bert Lindsay, Larry Gilmour, Steve Vair, Horace Gaul and Ernie Liffiton. Vair scored five, Gaul four, Liffiton two and a regular Brockville player, Simpson, got one. OVHL officials said not a word.

*****

In local action, the Debaters joined what was called a Jr circuit with Renfrew Rivers and Eganville. The *Eganville Star* publisher Dan A. Jones was first league president. Rivers won the league.

The North Renfrew Hockey League, soon to be Laurentian Hockey League, began in 1908. Original members were Pembroke YMCA, Westmeath, Beachburg and Cobden; only the latter did not have an indoor facility. Westmeath merchant and political aspirant Norman Reid put up a trophy and W.M. Fraser of that community held the chair. YMCA had won the trophy, until questions arose whether all players were club members.

1908/09

UOVHL fans could be forgiven for expecting the return of common sense, especially after learning Renfrew had enrolled Lindsay and Co. in the faltering FAHL, where they ran roughshod over Cornwall, Smith's Falls and Alf Smith's Senators. But Renfrew also entered a second team, called Rivers, in the UOVHL. Further hope arose when Almonte and Carleton Place re-entered the league, saving it from oblivion because Arnprior had called it a day. At the first league meeting, under new president G.H. Dunbar of Pembroke, the key word was "amateur." Anyone who had played more than one professional game was ineligible to play in the UOVHL.

To begin 1908/09, brothers Fred and Alex Thrasher, Rowan Stewart and Milt Horn joined veterans Poff, Fraser, Wallace and McVean for a match with Ottawa College, losing 13-7. Hugh Fraser and Billy Wallace scored all the Pembroke goals. There was one other little guy who joined the fray, a boisterous, unpredicable teenage husband and father named Harold Hugh "Harry" Cameron. Pembroke's second contribution to the NHL Hall of Fame. That season was the closest Cameron ever came to playing with fellow Hall of Famer, Hugh Lehman, who had turned pro with Berlin and was on his way.

Led by goalie Allan Lowry and superb new forward Stan McGregor, Almonte arrived to open the season fresh off a 19-2 thumping of Carleton Place. Horn, Cameron and McGregor scored two each, which translated into a 4-2 Pembroke victory.

Cameron got two more when the Srs played in Renfrew, but Rivers scored twelve. The Creamery Town, population four thousand, crammed the rink for both FAHL and UOVHL games. In what other community could you see Steve Vair score ten times and Lindsay take a shot on net, as they had twenty-four hours before this game, then next evening observe the contingent of goaltender Norman Budd, Jim Carruth, Louis Imbleau, Bert Parsons, Charlie Logan plus Bill and Tom Fishenden clobber somebody? Vair, by the way, recorded fourteen goals in one game that season, during a 23-2 thrashing of Smith's Falls, a record unsurpassed.

The County Town team kept plugging along, adding youngsters Jim McAlindon, Allan Wilson and Emmett Duff. They defeated Carleton Place twice and Almonte again on their way to a title showdown with Rivers.

The game was played at MacKay St Arena and Pembroke won 5-2, halting Renfrew's drive for a third straight Shield and permanent possession. It looked like the end of a rational and entertaining UOVHL season.

But that was not to be. Rivers protested Billy Wallace and Roy McVean, claiming they were "professional." The "no professionals" rule had to mean everyone who played in the UOVHL during 1908; no other scenario makes sense. Yet, with both Almonte and Carleton Place new to the league and the entire 1908 Renfrew team transferred to the FAHL, such a ruling could only affect Pembroke! Would the new teams have favoured such a decision? Would Pembroke have used Roy McVean, the only 1908 player, if the rule was clear? It was a bum rap on Wallace for he had played in only one 1908 game, and an exhibition one at that. We can understand Renfrew waiting for the right moment, but why didn't the other two teams protest Roy immediately?

UOVHL vice-president Dean, who was also Rivers league representative, ordered league secretary-treasurer Rosamond to call a meeting, which he did, for Wednesday, February 17, 1909 in Almonte. Upon learning of this affront, UOVHL president George Dunbar declared that date inconvenient, rescheduling the event for February 22, in Pembroke. Almonte and Carleton Place representatives refused to attend any meeting in Pembroke, unless expenses were paid. They then went ahead with the February 17 meeting (without the president), upheld Renfrew's protest and awarded the championship to Rivers.

President Dunbar waited one hour past the specified time for his meeting and, when no one showed up, officially awarded the title to Pembroke.

Meanwhile, Pembroke Srs played an exhibition with the FAHL Senators, contaminating the entire team (Horn scored four and Pembroke won 8-7). So, when Hawkesbury took LOVHL honours, the club advised all and sundry they would have nothing to do with that "team of Pembroke professionals" then played Rivers for the Shield in Hull's Parc Royal Rink, March 12, 1909, before two thousand fans, few of whom were from Renfrew. Rivers persevered 14-12, taking the first *Citizen* Shield permanently. It's still in the possession of Renfrew's Fishenden family.

The *Citizen* Shield was specifically donated for competition between Upper and Lower OVHL champions, and therefore was not a challenge trophy like the Stanley Cup. However, since the award was now theirs, Rivers accepted a challenge from the Gatineau Hills community of Kazubazua, Que. Only a handful turned out to see the visitors lose 7-1. The match was pointless in any event because, had Kazubazua won, they would have lost through protest for including in their line-up Roy Anderson—another "Pembroke professional."

*****

Pembroke had a four-team town league in 1909, under president Anthony Kutchaw. Star of the PHS team was P. Cornell, a one-armed athlete, who brings to mind two more valley performers so handicapped. One appears later in this book, and the other, an outstanding example of such determination today, is Pembroke's Graham Mathieu, who has capably participated in various sports for many years.

The Debaters won the town title in 1909, defeating Strathconas 3-1, the last Debaters goal being credited to a skinny youngster named Francis "Frank" Nighbor, Hall of Famer #3.

Participants

Steve Vair, of Barrie, played for Renfrew on three separate occasions as well as for the Wanderers, Edmonton, Cobalt, Toronto Tecumsehs and Ontarios. He left the pro circuit in 1914, and then coached for many years, winning an Allan Cup with Port Arthur Bearcats 1928/29. Vair was an average skater and poor shot, but with a heavily taped stick he manoeuvred his way to dozens of multi-goal games.

Bobby Rowe, another Barrie product, stayed with Renfrew through 1911 then joined Victoria of the new Pacific Coast Hockey Association (PCHA) where he played for four seasons. Nine campaigns with Seattle of the same league followed, including a Stanley Cup win in 1917. He finished one of the longest professional careers on record with a couple of 1925 games in Boston and as many with Portland in 1926. Rowe is one of the few players who remained in the Patrick's PCHA from its 1912 inception untill it merged with the Western Canada Hockey League (WCHL) in 1925. That he's not in the Hall of Fame is an immense miscarriage of justice, for many less qualified are.

Ottawa native Nellum Kimpton, a six-year veteran of hockey and lacrosse in Renfrew, began the 1907/08 season but came down with Bright's disease mid-campaign. He died May 17, 1908.

Horace Gaul played one 1906 game for Brooklyn Athletics then was suspended for not signing first. This caused the Amateur Hockey Association of America to temporarily ban all Canadians.

There was another hockey fatality in 1907. Cornwall's Owen McCourt died during an FAHL game with Ottawa after being accidently struck with a stick.

Tom Benson arrived in Pembroke with the Quebec Bank in 1904, being transferred again in 1907. Tom quickly left the bank and returned to Pembroke, entering first the furniture then the milling business. His marriage to Enid Burritt in 1911 produced sons John and Allan. In April 1929 he caught the train to Ottawa on business but a bad cold developed into pneumonia and he was rushed to the Civic Hospital, almost upon arrival. He died shortly thereafter, at the age of forty-eight.

Tom Jones, who had played more games for Pembroke than anyone, called it quits after the 1908 fiasco. Tom then moved to Calgary where he remained, passing away after a long illness in 1934. Some Pembrokeites confuse this Tom Jones with his cousin, who played in the town league for several years after WWI. This second Tom Jones, a third cousin to Louis Riel, was a crack rifleman and fine baseball pitcher who often threw two games in one day—using either arm. At this writing, his widow and four daughters are in Pembroke, and both his sons on the West Coast.

Orin Frood was born February 10, 1889; one of four children produced by Mr and Mrs Peter Frood, who operated a restaurant and grocery store in Renfrew. Two weeks after being carried off MacKay St Arena ice he surfaced with the Fredericton Capitals. To escape the "Pembroke Pro" stigma he became Claude Orin, and a favourite among Capitals fans. Alas, he was recognized by a railway conductor from Moncton, home of the reigning league champions, and reported. Declared ineligible just before a game, Frood's absence sparked a riot during which troops were called in, but fans wrecked the arena anyway. They didn't let up either. Later, during play-offs, Bob Meldrum, referee of the 1906 Shield game and considered a top drawer official, was hired to maintain order. Fredericton went on to win the Starr Trophy but was ordered to return it for using ineligible players. The Capitals refused, and were suspended for one year as a result.

After the 1910 season with Haileybury, where it was said $35,000 changed hands during every battle royal, Orin switched to Berlin of the OPHL for two campaigns, winning the scoring title both years. One of Frank Selke's favourite stories was of a game in which Berlin trailed 3-0, despite the best efforts of goal keeper Hugh Lehman. Orin had been suspended by his own team for a previous escapade and was warming the bench. He constantly begged to play. With only a few minutes remaining, Orin blew up, telling the coach he might as well get involved because all was lost anyway. Exasperated, the boss sent him on; Orin scored four in a row and Berlin won.

Frood averaged two goals a game with Berlin, assists still not being recorded.

At home during the summer of 1911, Orin saw an ad for a bookkeeper in Medicine Hat. He visited the prairie town and was hired by Birnie Bros Hardware, becoming a shareholder of that firm in 1913. About all we know from then until he arrived in Toronto to join the 67th Battalion June 16, 1916 is that he played hockey every year, either in Medicine Hat or Saskatoon. Gassed and blinded August 21, 1917 in France, he returned to Canada and recovered enough to take a job with George Taylor Hardware in Haileybury, only to lose everything in the great fire.

Orin Frood married Hulda Keats of North Bay, in New Liskeard, April 18, 1923. His children Orin Jr and Lois were born there. Orin even served on the New Liskeard Srs executive a while but the man was irrepressible, moving lock, stock and barrel to Dundas, Ontario in 1925 and going from one job to another in the Hamilton-Galt area until taken by a heart attack January 14, 1943.

Lois married US Colonel George Blackwell; they retired in Fairfax County, Virginia. Dr Orin Frood Jr retired in Ottawa.

Hugh Lehman was born October 17, 1885, and kept goal professionally for twenty-two seasons, if you count the 1908 "Pembroke pros." One in the Soo, three OPHL campaigns, three with New Westminster, then twelve in Vancouver where he too went from beginning to end with the PCHA, then a pair in Chicago before retiring. That final season, 1927–28, Hugh played four games, being co-coach with Barney Stanley under Major F. McLaughlin, Black Hawks owner. The man was still good enough though, at age forty-three, to inspire a Boston play-by-play announcer, who exclaimed "They ought to send that fellow Lehman to Mexico to stop the revolution, he's stopped everything around here."

A regular season average of 3.60 and 2.86 during playoffs brought Lehman but one Stanley Cup, in 1914/15 with Vancouver. He does, though, share a unique distinction from the days of Stanley Cup challenges with just one other player, Percy LeSueur. He contended for the trophy with two different clubs in the same season. Galt challenged Ottawa Senators January 5 and 7, 1910 and lost, with Lehman in goal. Then Senators went west to face an unsuccessful bid by Edmonton and when they returned, Berlin was waiting for a shot, having acquired Lehman from Galt in the meantime. Lehman lost again, March 12, 1910. However, the Wanderers relieved Ottawa of the prized mug before season's end.

Hugh Lehman was a superb puck-handler and often stick-handled to centre ice before passing it off. It is said he scored a goal one time but that cannot be confirmed.

After leaving his home town, Lehman seldom returned, spending his summers in Windsor, then Toronto where he obtained an off-season job with Warren Bituminous Paving Co. Soon after retiring from hockey he was named president of Warren, the firm that reconstructed Pembroke's main street during WWII Hugh Lehman was inducted into the Hall of Fame in 1958, the same year he paid his last visit to Pembroke, for the village centennial celebrations. He died April 8, 1961.

Adjuncts

In 1907 Pembroke Electric Light Co. opened a new power plant at Waltham, Que. A worker was electrocuted within the first two months . . . Eganville's Albert George bought the area's first motorcycle that year, driving it home from New York; so Allan Hale bought a new car in Detroit, driving it home . . . and, on the question of whether or not a Mr Hyman of the provincial government had resigned his seat, the headline read "Is Hyman in or out?"

Petawawa was a six-week summer home for four thousand troops and one thousand horses, and had been since long before the Boer War. By 1907 the federal government had spent $40,000 on buildings and was about to make it a permanent militia base when a squabble erupted over the price of land relinquished by Pembroke Lumber Co. Arrangements were completed to locate the camp elsewhere when an eleventh hour agreement was reached. So the camp stayed, but it didn't become year-round till after WWII.

Summer 1907 found County Towners ready to revolt. Horse-powered buggies and delivery wagons were rounding corners much too fast, endangering life and limb. Worse, town council was satisfying political expediency by putting sidewalks around trees rather than removing them, making already narrow streets narrower. Talk must have intimidated one nag because, on a busy afternoon, it chose to lay down smack in the middle of Pembroke St W and wouldn't move for anyone. Finally, Police Chief J.H. Butler arrived and laid down the law, which went right over the animal's head. Disgusted, Butler deputized a number of bystanders and they pried the creature to its feet; it immediately trotted away like a colt.

On a cold January morning in 1908, fire destroyed Singer Sewing Centre, Sparling's Machine Shop, Kitt's Real Estate plus the better part of Barrand's Butcher Shop and Cadden's Harness Works. However, if you'll excuse the expression, that was just a warm up to the following November 4.

At 4 am, fire broke out in National Manufacturing Co., downtown. It would easily have been contained but for gale force winds blowing off the river; by 6am much of the business community was ablaze. A CPR road crew, working nearby, joined the fray. Renfrew firemen loaded their equipment on a flatcar and were in action at 10am, helping to bring the fire under control by noon.

What a disaster! Fifty buildings were totally destroyed. Everything from the Ottawa River to Victoria Hall between the Muskrat river and Victoria St was levelled. Correction: Barr's Carriage Shop and the market building were inexplicably spared. The Copeland House was saved, with considerable effort, but the conflagration got around it and consumed more buildings to the west. After National, the largest structures to go were the grist and woollen mills. Also reduced to ashes were Taylor's P&W, the Library, Manitoba House plus some factories, restaurants and other businesses. Tom Delahey and Harry Irwin lost their Renfrew St homes before the horror was halted.

The *Pembroke Standard* went up in smoke, with every printed word to date. Mr Bone was in Ottawa and his daughter escaped with only the ledgers. He immediately sold the property and new owners were in business by February.

It looked like the brand new Leland Hotel would be saved but the wind changed and the place burnt. Mayor J.S. Fraser, concerned about drunks getting in the way, ordered all bars closed. This being a 4 am to noon blaze, one wonders how many bars were open.

After everything settled down, one fire engine suffered a burnt tire and Officer Campbell, the night policeman, jammed his leg. Total loss, a half million dollars.

46

Chapter 5

METAMORPHOSIS

1909/10 to 1910/11

Two new terms began appearing during this season: "coach" and "defenceman." The latter replaced point positions within a couple of seasons but coaches, whether playing or behind the bench, did not completely dismiss "best player authority" for twenty or more years. Substitution was still not allowed except in the case of injury, but rumours of "three periods" replacing "halves" were heard.

The average professional, such as Galt's Louis Berlinquette, earned $60 per week plus his board. This was several times what a labourer pulled down.

Games

1909/10

When they were rejected by the ECHA (Eastern Canada Hockey Association), J. Ambrose O'Brien and friends formed the National Hockey Association of Canada (NHA) and swallowed the old league by mid-season. Michael J. O'Brien's energetic son also donated the O'Brien Cup, an NHA championship trophy presently in the NHL Hall of Fame, and played a major role in creating another league member, Les Canadiens de Montréal.

Thus Renfrew Creamery Kings began an unsuccessful two year Stanley Cup pursuit. With wealthy owners pur-

chasing players at any cost, such as $3000 each per season for Frank and Lester Patrick, fans nicknamed the club "Millionaires," though it was never an official handle.

Renfrew came up with a UOVHL entry too. When S.E. McLeod of Almonte was named league president at the annual meeting, Rivers officials successfully spearheaded a motion to bar every former 1900-1908 player. Then, opening in Arnprior January 7, 1910, Renfrew Rivers attempted to ice several players from those very years. Naturally, Arnprior took exception, and when the protest was upheld—Rivers withdrew from competition!

Arnprior had replaced player-shy Carleton Place, and Almonte decided to give it another try. Under President Joe Murray, Pembroke Srs also hung in there. A rewritten schedule began mid-January.

On the Pembroke team, Tom Dunbar's brother Jim took over in goal while Rowan Stewart and Ralph Lett made debuts at point and counter point. Lett played only that one season, as did Quebec Bank employee Ernest Cunneyworth. Gordon "Brick" Fraser began the first of two local campaigns and J. Parnell Duff was launching a lifetime of community activity. Jack Teevens managed MacKay St Arena, a job few survived beyond one term.

On opening night, Arnprior was in town. Tied 6-6 with ninety seconds left, Arnprior withdrew over a disputed penalty, refusing to return. Team captain Emmett Duff performed the ritual of scoring in an empty net.

Pembroke finished a high scoring eight-game season at 6-1-1, Cameron and Duff providing most of the goals. The loss was a 13-2 hammering in Arnprior and they tied in Almonte. That should have given Pembroke the title but Arnprior officially protested game one, and, believe it or not, a replay was ordered.

Due to mild weather, weeks went by without the game being played. Meantime, Hawkesbury took LOVHL honours and, claiming to tire of waiting, challenged Renfrew Rivers to an "Ottawa Valley Championship" contest. Mercifully, that potential pot boiler never occurred. A mid-March cold snap allowed the County and Woollen towns to meet, Arnprior winning 3-2. That created a first place tie, forcing another battle, which brought the same result.

Eight days later, March 24, 1910, Arnprior met Hawkesbury in Ottawa. Officials Russell Bowie and Duncan Campbell of Montreal Victorias, noting a poor crowd and ice covered with an inch of water, refused to perform unless paid $35 each in advance. The money was gathered in small quantities and Hawkesbury won 5-1. As the *Citizen* had not yet come up with a new Shield, no trophy was awarded.

******

Led by Frank Nighbor, Debaters took town honours over Bankers and PHS, going undefeated. A Jr team played the odd game while the girls teams, Cyclones and Whirlwinds, met occasionally on behalf of charity.

Speaking of cyclones, this was the year Cyclone Taylor was supposed to have scored for Renfrew while skating backwards. Much has been made of the feat but very little of the story; it was a late season nothing game that ended 17-2, with ample evidence of pre-game celebrations.

1910/11

Carleton Place returned to the UOVHL fold but an application by Renfrew was rejected—could Creamery Town influence have been reduced by its involvement with the NHA?

This was the only year Harry Cameron and Frank Nighbor played together in Pembroke uniforms. Close your eyes and take yourself back to January 1911. You're leaning over the upper railing in a cold MacKay St Arena.

Brockville's in town for a season opening exhibition. Fans are trickling in, anxious to watch Harry Cameron warm up by elbowing his way through teammates for a shot at Jim Dunbar. Word is that eighteen-year-old Frank Nighbor will get his first taste of Sr action, could he handle the heavy going? This should be a good team with Stewart, Duff and Fraser who had proven their worth and young Morand's no slouch either. There's Captain Tache, who manages the place, and Harry Jenks, who provides the music, in a far corner discussing half-time entertainment. You wonder, while stomping your feet to keep warm, if any of these high-spirited observers have the slightest inkling what hockey will become, and to what degree two of the men they'll be watching will contribute.

Billy Wallace is referee tonight and he'll be working with a "judge of play" for the first time in Pembroke. That ought to be something: two guys blowing whistles!

Pembroke wins 6-4. Sure enough, Cameron scores most of his team's goals, despite fans yelling at him about being all speed and little else. Nighbor can handle the puck; wait till he learns what to do with it . . .

Pembroke opened in Carleton Place, winning 6-4 and discovering a new problem. Renfrew players, without a team, were attempting to catch on with not only Carleton Place but Almonte and Arnprior as well. Rivers players were ineligible but every game brought protests on that very subject. For instance: Arnprior, having chosen the name Shamrocks, used Norman Budd in goal against Almonte, which had Luke Imbleau and Charlie Logan in the line-up. Both clubs protested.

Pembroke's second game featured a visit by Shamrocks, who now had goaltender Julius C. Kittner, a jeweller who soon moved to Pembroke and donated a trophy over which many a town league season was fought. Cameron, Duff and Percy Wilson tallied two goals each in the 6-2 victory. But when Almonte arrived, Imbleau and Logan were still in harness. Pembroke protested a while then dropped it; Almonte was weak and lost 10-1 anyway. Only Dunbar didn't score, Nighbor getting his first Sr marker.

Sporting new uniforms, Pembroke visited Arnprior and won 10-4. Rookie J. Reginald "Bedu" Morand Jr put on a dazzling display. Before the game, fans were asked if they'd like to see three periods; everyone agreed and found the configuration quite acceptable.

Then in Almonte, Pembroke lost the game 7-5, and Rowan Stewart to boot. The burly defenceman went down with a broken collarbone and, except for a brief post-war effort, never played again. Lindsay Fluker took his place, making a good job of it too.

Carleton Place visited to close out the schedule. Percy Wilson booked off sick so Graham Fenton was promoted from the town league Red Sox. Only three hundred fans saw the 12-1 laugher; Nighbor getting four and Morand three. A 5-1 record gave Pembroke Srs UOVHL honours.

The new *Citizen* Shield was administered by a board of trustees, a move toward better control that enjoyed brief success. Vankleek Hill and Pembroke Srs played for it in Dey's Arena Wednesday March 1, 1911.

Led by Art and Albert Blanchard, coach Bill Chambers' Hill squad was favoured, so Joe Murray brought in Fred Lake for a week of intensive counter-coaching; unfortunately Morand was injured during the rigorous practices and couldn't dress for the big game.

Fans saw an exciting see-saw battle, officiated by Percy Lesueur and Ernie Butterworth. Midway through the second period, Brick Fraser took a penalty; Vankleek Hill scored three goals while he was off. So the big hitter came back breathing fire, scoring twice and scattering bodies. Meanwhile, influenza sufferer Percy Wilson was forced to retire after two periods, allowing Lindsay Fluker twenty minutes of service. Lindsay scored three straight goals and Pembroke won 10-8, taking the new Shield.

Something else new that season was the A Rosenthal & Sons Trophy. Russell, champions of Russell County, came up with the trophy and challenged Pembroke for first possession. So, back to Dey's Arena, March 9, 1911. Pembroke fired seven in the third period to win 10-3, Morand recoved to score a pair and Nighbor got four. MP Gerald White, who paid Fred Lake out of pocket, treated the team to lunch on Parliament Hill.

Strangely, this unique and talented hockey club, as opposed to the 1906 team, is virtually forgotten in local folklore.

*****

Debaters, using every Sr except Fraser and Wilson, swept through Red Sox and Bankers undefeated, taking the Munro Cup. Red Sox was actually Jim Bresnahan and Anthony Stoqua's baseball team; they also created a Jr squad that leagued with Business College, operated by Sarsfield Brennan, and PHS, where Edward "Ted" Behan

and Harold Duff starred. The league soon restricted use of graduating players, bringing Debaters more in line with the rest of the competition.

Westmeath embarrassed every team it played, regardless of calibre. Even their fans were embarassed; they went home after two periods of their first three-period hockey game.

Participants

We should devote a capsule comment to Michael J. O'Brien, about whom much has been written. The native of Antigonish, N.S., who left school at fourteen to seek his fortune, was sixty when son Ambrose and friends created the NHA. M.J.'s holdings at that time included timber limits the breadth of Canada; mica, gold, copper, silver and nickel mines; prairie farms, several factories and the odd quarry, in addition to his railroad operations.

Bert and Cliff McPhee moved West. Bert settled in Cranbrook, B.C. with the telephone company, later starting an electrical contracting business. Semi-retired and keeping books for a sash and door factory, he died suddenly at the age of sixty-four, in 1942, leaving his wife and four children. Cliff, who farmed not far away, died six months later.

Mr and Mrs George Thrasher had three sons: Alex, Fred and Harry. Alex opened a pharmacy at Fernie, B.C. in 1909; his brothers came out a year later and were immediately hired by Fernie Lumber Co. Alex, who married but never had children, died in Phoenix, B.C. during the early 1940s. Fred played and managed hockey teams while operating sawmills around the province, meeting his second wife, Marjorie Duncan, in Snowshoe, now one of B.C.'s famous ghost towns. Fred retired to Vancouver in 1957, passing away ten years later. One of the lumberman's four children, Ann, was back east tracing her father's footsteps when her mother passed away in 1988. Harry worked for Fred for several years then settled in Kelowna, where he died July 1962.

On Friday, October 10, 1910, three Pembroke men went out in rickety canoes hunting ducks on Mud Lake, an aptly named pond if ever there was one. Searchers found their bodies Saturday night, mired in muck; they probably died as much from exposure as drowning.

Lost were businessman Herman Christman, druggist Harry Temple and Pembroke Srs captain Emmett George

Duff. Emmett, brother to J. Parnell Duff, was only twenty but already a husband and father of two. His wife, Ida May Kutchaw, Tony's sister and first cousin to Frank Nighbor, married twice more and lived a long life.

As for Tony Kutchaw, he joined his ailing father in Sudbury, soon opening his own business. Tony wasn't there long before getting lost while hunting partridge, spending two nights in the bush. Quite a search party was formed to look for him.

George Dunbar married Ida May Coxford before becoming a Smith's Falls businessman.

Gordon "Brick" Fraser, nicknamed because of his red hair but also because of his style of play, moved to Cobalt and became a top scorer in the Silver City League before enlisting. He was wounded and never fully recovered. Fraser eventually the joined the Engineers at Camp Petawawa, dying after a long illness in 1949.

Joe Murray moved to Renfrew toward the end of WWI, where he became mayor and later donated the Murray Cup, an unusual hockey trophy detailed later in these pages.

Jim Dunbar was only eighteen when he back-stopped Pembroke's second Shield win. Jim worked for Lee Manufacturing, a large firm that made incubators and provided employment for hockey players; Cameron and Nighbor worked there too.

Speaking of that pair, let's track them. Harry, with Frank in tow, headed for the Lakehead, having turned down lucrative offers from Schrieber and Montreal Wanderers. Playing for Port Arthur, he picked up a $400 signing bonus on top of $25 a week and expenses. Warming the bench, Frank made little, but he studied teammate and poke-checking expert Jack Walker; a piece of homework that served his future very well indeed.

Adjuncts

Fire: Dunlop Hardware burned Easter Sunday, 1909: a mower could be had for $41.50 at the fire sale. In 1911, the big Thomas Pink plant went up in smoke, as did People's Theatre and Pembroke Library, again. Meanwhile, the town fire alarm went off so often it created a "cry wolf" syndrome. Actually, Carleton Place suffered most: a 1911 blaze took forty downtown businesses.

Water: A new idea, run that Georgian Bay canal through Cobden and Muskrat Lakes, to avoid river rapids. And where's that blamed bridge?

Planes: McCurdy and Baldwin spent considerable time at Petawawa trying to get their "Silver Dart" airborne before military brass arrived to pass judgement. Though success was measured in feet, most were impressed, except General Otter, who "did not care to express an opinion."

Cars: A two-cylinder, 20hp Reo, winner of the 1700 mile endurance run in 1908, sold for $650.

Lorne Hale hired Montreal's T. Twohey and C.K. Batchelder of Vermont to race his 60hp Stearns at Blue Bonnets; they crashed and were both killed, causing Hale to give up the sport. In Ottawa though, he was accused of doing 30 mph in a 7 mph zone, until he proved his car had been stolen.

Police Chief J.H. Butler asked council for a car, having commandeered one once on the spot to catch a thief. He was still turned down. Too much racing about, it seems. One editor wrote "If a horse were driven on main street the speed automobiles are, the driver would be up before the cadi (judge) in short order. But this world is full of privileges."

Horses: Anthony Merrifield rode his bike into one, which kicked him within inches of death; he survived and became quite a hockey player.

Newspaper notice: "We advertised last week for a horse and got several offers by letter. We don't need a roadster. We want a cheap plug of a horse to send to Cobalt to use as an express horse for a store."

Newspapers: Martin Ringrose's interest in newspapers began to waver, as indicated by starting articles on page five and finishing them on page one. His editorials became more boastful and rambling, and in mid-1911 he sold the *Observer* to none other than Daniel A. Jones, his former employee and past publisher of the *Eganville Star-Leader* which had burned in 1908. Martin had already purchased a general store in Chapeau, Quebec and his last few editorials were little more than advertisements for that establishment. Within the next three years Martin sold that business, bought the *Cobalt Star* and adjacent hotel, both of which burned, purchased a fruit farm near St. Catherines and sold it, acquired the St. Lawrence Hotel in Port Hope and sold that, then returned to Pembroke. Stay tuned . . .

Dan Jones promised "to temper the dogma." He did. Meantime, F.B. Elliott sold the *Standard* to former *Alliston Herald* owner A. Wigelsworth and a new era in County Town publishing began.

Trains: While walking along the Grand Trunk Railroad track one night, Nelson Montgomery discovered a washout.

Knowing a train was due shortly, the lad ran for help, bringing Bill Noack and a lantern with moments to spare. Incidentally, the GTR station was at Pembroke St, connected by a spur to the main line. Now and then a car would get shunted through the stop-block onto main street. It happened again in 1909, this time smack into the post office opposite, tying up traffic all day.

Friday, January 10, 1910 saw one of Canada's worst train wrecks. Two CPR passenger cars plunged into the Spanish River between Sudbury and Sault Ste. Marie, killing forty-two and injuring scores more. Rev. Stephen Childerhose of Cobden and Beachburg veterinarian Dr. McLennan were two of the victims.

Somebody tipped off a Pembroke game warden and he examined two trunks in a CPR freight car, finding eight hundred neatly packed partridge, headed for Montreal. He diverted them to Belleville's Institute for the Blind. One could legally sell game birds in 1911, but not in those quantities.

Fort William, Ontario: a railway employee refused to stop whistling in the bunkhouse so a fellow worker shot him four times, dead, and got away!

Populations in 1911: Pembroke 5624, Arnprior 4395, Smith's Falls 6361, Brockville 9372, Hawkesbury 4391, North Bay 7718, Sudbury 4140. Canada was nine million. AND, the post office showed a profit of one million dollars on an income of nine million!

Lastly: Pembroke's Jim Munro, president of Massey Lumber Co, director of almost every other company, and unsuccessful Grit candidate when Borden swept to unexpected power in the famous reciprocity election of 1911, was taking a bath in his Soo hotel room when he noticed a stream of water going up past his window. Rising enough to see out yet maintain propriety, James determined the gravity defying liquid was being hosed to the roof. He sought pants and hastened streetward. Damage was confined to the top floor.

51

Pembroke lacrosse team, 1903. Earliest portraits of Harry Cameron and Hugh Lehman(n) as well as Hugh Fraser and Milt Horn. Others who played hockey are Jack Poff, Charlie Hout, Paddy Howe and H. Scott. Also note Augustus St. James (Bill's half brother), Hiram Griffith, Andrew White and Walter Chambers. Courtesy Moodie Doering.

Morgans of Pembroke 1903/04. No written records of 1903/04 exist so this beautiful picture is all we know about town hockey. Considering the players it is not difficult to understand how they accumulated so much silverware. Left to right: Harry Cameron, Hugh Lehman, Emile Hout Tom Dunbar, Jack Poff, George Beamish, Leo Alphonse "Babe" Chaput, D. Dunbar, H. Brown, C. Anderson (or Roy), Charlie Hout, Milt Horn, Colin Bogart and Hugh Fraser. Courtesy Ted White.

The great 1906 Pembroke Srs. Standing: Billy Wallace, Jim Coxford and Roy McVean. Seated: Hugh Lehman, Tom Jones, Tom Benson, Orin Frood and Hugh Fraser. Courtesy Margaret Willison, a niece of Roy McVean.

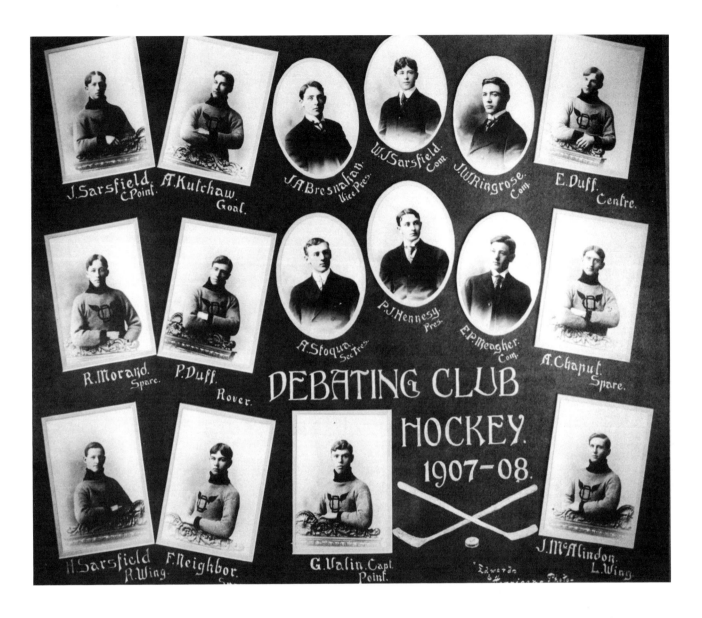

Pembroke Debaters 1907/08. This is probably the Debating Club's first hockey team. Left to right: Jack Sarsfield, Anthony Kutchaw, Jim Bresnahan, Bill Sarsfield, Bill Ringrose (Martin's son), Emmett Duff, Reginald "Bedu" Morand, J Parnell Duff, Anthony Stoqua, P.J. Hennesy, E.P. Meagher, Leo Alphonse Chaput, Harry Sarsfield, Frank Nighbor, George Valin and Jim McAlindon. Courtesy Champlain Trail Museum.

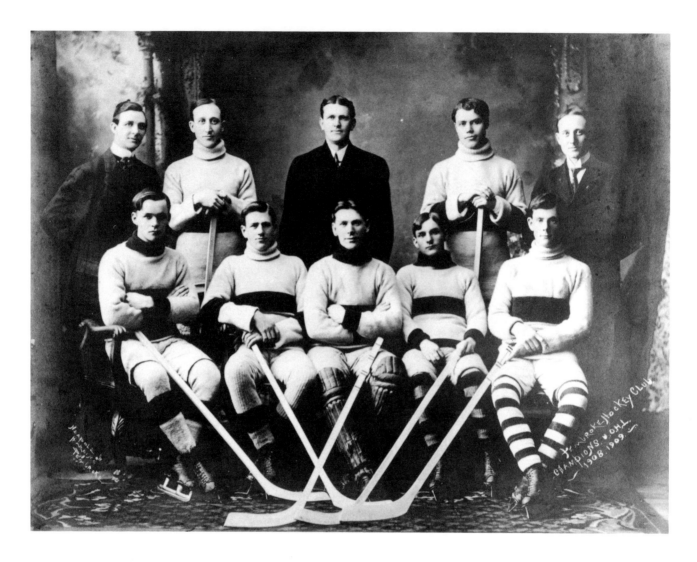

Pembroke Srs 1908/09. This may be the only time two teams, playing in the same league, in the same year, were both marked Champions (see photo on facing page). Back row, left to right: Walter Chambers, Billy Wallace, George Dunbar (probably), Roy McVean and Jack Wallace. Front row, left to right: Harry Cameron, Milt Horn, Jack Poff, Emmett Duff and Hugh Fraser. Courtesy Champlain Trail Museum.

Renfrew Rivers 1908/09. Left to right: Norman Budd, Charlie Logan, Jim Carruth, Tom Fishenden, Bill Dean, Gilbert "Bert" Parsons, Bill Fishenden, Howard Box and Louis Imbleau. Courtesy George Fishenden, Tom's son.

Pembroke Red Sox base-
ball team, 1910. Harvey
Blakely, J.N. Gray,
W. Depine, L. Farlinger,
G. Irving, Charlie Ramsay,
D. Gurtin, E.S. Webb,
Alex Millar, Sarsfield
Brennan, J.M. Moran,
William Sharpin, Gordon
"Brick" Fraser, George
Campbell, Joe
Beauchamp, Harry
Cameron.

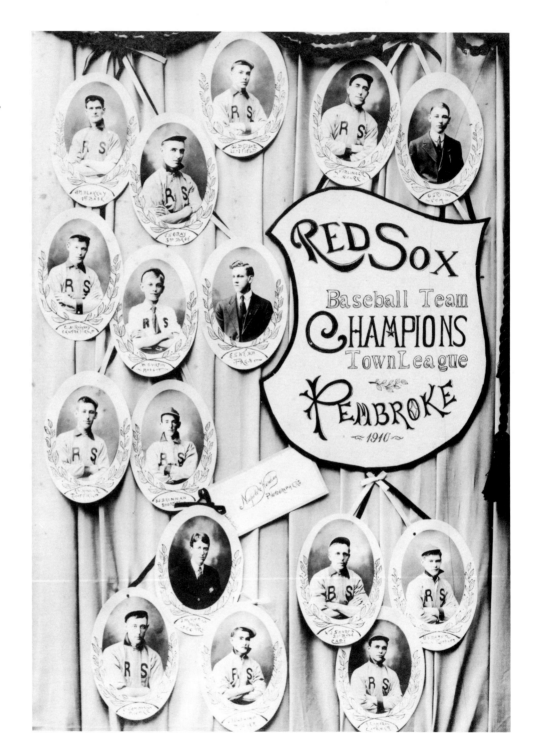

Comets baseball team 1910. Anthony Stoqua, Emmett Duff, Andrew Thomson, Wib Behan, Ab Strutt, Dave Behan, William Sarsfield, J.J. O'Brien, Parnell Duff, Fred Lance, Bedu Moran, Philip Martin, Cecil Giroux, Ted Behan. Courtesy Vic Gauthier.

Chapter 6

BOOM TIMES—WHO COULD ASK FOR MORE?
1911/12 to 1913/14

The NHA adopted six-man hockey in 1912 but the West retained rovers another decade. Red goal lines came into use. More colourful uniforms appeared, with numbers yet. Programs appeared in some arenas, inaccurate as they sometimes were. Assists were still rarely given. Goalkeepers, at the professional level, were fined $2 every time they left their feet.

Games

1911/12

Having given up the Stanley Cup quest, Renfrew underwent a complete overhaul. However, an executive consisting of Jimmie Jackes, George Martel and Billie Dean chose the Interprovincial League over UOVHL wars.

The UOVHL began as usual. At first, there were no problems, then Almonte dropped out. Smith's Falls entered. A schedule was written. Then Carleton Place departed, despite having just opened a new rink. League president Joe Murray suggested they fold. So Almonte returned. Then Joe quit. Arnprior's Emmett Hogan took over. A thirty-day residency rule was struck, players lists submitted, schedule re-written, and play began January 19.

Lorne Hale began as president of Pembroke Srs, then went south for the winter, leaving Frank Garrow to take over. Ben Hollinger gave them a hundred bucks to get started and Billy "Sunshine" O'Brien, affable Copeland House day clerk, coached the club to a 3-2 win over a collection of local guys attending Queen's University. Visiting Fred Thrasher played that one game while all the other players except Morand were rookies. In Renfrew for a second pre-season encounter, the club lost 7-5 to a hot though reluctant goalie named Roy McVean—Roy was working in the Creamery Town.

Pembroke opened by defeating Maurice Lynch's Almonte club 14-8 at MacKay St Arena. Morand and Wilson, plus youngsters Ted Behan and Sarsfield Brennan, shared the fourteen goals.

But they lost 11-5 in Arnprior, then protested the Shamrocks use of Len Smith, team leader but not an Arnprior resident. We'll see . . .

A 4-3 loss in Smith's Falls was Vessie Cadden's last local game. Renfrew's IPHL club had already used Vessie once without Pembroke's knowledge and was about to do so again when Frank Garrow got wind of it. Joe Murray, acting on Pembroke's behalf, marched into the Creamery Town rink and began reciting rules, delaying a contest considerably. In the end, Vessie backed off himself and within ten days "packed his turkey and entrained to Nelson, B.C." Fernie, B.C. is where he actually played.

That left the door open for Solomon "Hum" Lance, the talented goaltender who became Pembroke's main backstopper for six straight years.

Then, at a meeting called to hear several protests over Shamrocks players, Arnprior took it on the chin. Ernie Stavenow of Mansfield (practically Arnprior) and Len Smith of Fitzroy Harbour (visible on a clear day) were both on the submitted player list but no team protested until suffering a loss to them. Asked to drop both men, Arnprior chose to quit, washing out all results involving the club and leaving Smith Falls 2-1, Pembroke 1-1 and Almonte 1-2.

Lance debuted spectacularly. Pembroke built a home-ice lead of 4-0 over Smith's Falls before Billy Wallace penalized Allan Wilson a total of twelve minutes; Hum was sensational preserving a 4-3 win.

Pembroke, however, lost 9-7 in Almonte, leaving all three teams at 2-2. The UOVHL decided Almonte and Pembroke would meet in Renfrew, the winner to play Smith's Falls in Carleton Place a week later.

Cyclone Taylor and Herb Jordan officiated the exciting first contest before fifteen hundred fans. Led by star Wilbert Monterville, Almonte built a 4-1 lead but couldn't hold on, Pembroke prevailing 9-7. But how about this for a measure of changing times; the special was halfway home before someone realized two Pembroke players weren't aboard. No problem, the engineer simply threw the engine in reverse and recovered the delinquent duo.

Something else happened that night. Bill Roland packed his Casino Theatre with fans then verbally relayed game information taken by electronic means. A pre-Foster Hewitt's play-by-play?

Next, Pembroke Srs built a 5-0 lead in the new Carleton Place arena but Smith's Falls kept chipping away, actually tying it before defenceman Jim Coxford made a rink length dash then rebounded a shot off the backboards, which Morand poked home—creating one of the most hilarious situations in this book.

Smith's Falls protested, claiming the goal was offside. President Hogan, still seething over the Smith–Stavenow incident, called a meeting in Arnprior, which everyone ignored except him and someone from Smith's Falls. They decided the game must be replayed. Meantime, Pembroke was scheduled to meet Rockland for the Shield in Ottawa,

March 15, 1912 and when plans for that event continued, Hogan threatened an injunction. Fliers began circulating throughout the Valley, promoting the replay which would take place in Arnprior. So it came to pass that the Smith's Falls team, band, and fans entrained to Arnprior, there guided to the rink by a torchlight procession. The club lined up, referee Charlie Logan dropped the puck and a goal was scored. Thus UOVHL president Hogan proclaimed Smith's Falls champion and Rockland's next opponent.

Referee Ernie Butterworth, who allowed the disputed goal but had never been consulted by anyone, decided to make a statement. He said, "Coxford carried the puck down and shot it. The puck struck behind the Smith's Falls goal and bounded out in front, striking one of the Smith's Falls men as it did so. One of the Pembroke forwards, who had been fifteen feet behind the man who shot it, seized the rubber and drove it into the net. It was the fairest earned goal that I ever saw scored."

Referee Jack Ryan called only two penalties during a supurb Shield game that ran two extra periods before Rockland prevailed 3-2, the first of such matches to enter overtime. Ted Behan tallied both Pembroke markers while Lance and M. Dion were outstanding in their respective goals. To no one's amazement, Emmett Hogan walked into the Rockland dressing room and advised Mr Marion his team would still have to play Smith's Falls if they wanted the Shield. A reporter sifted this translation from Marion's reply "he gave him to understand there was something wrong with his headpiece . . ."

Still, a Smith's Falls official wrote Citizen *Shield* Board of Trustees Chairman L.N. Bates, belabouring the point further. Bates spent an hour with Butterworth then declared the matter closed, once and for all.

NRHL champion Westmeath challenged Rockland to a Biesenthal Cup match, which the LOVHL club had won by defeating Vars. Officials told Westmeath a qualifying H&H with Pembroke would be required; the village managed a 5-5 first game before losing the second contest 8-2. They put up a $200 bond for a third try but Pembroke declined to continue.

*****

Debaters chose an exhibition schedule over playing in the town league, which was won by Business College. The chuckle of the season came in a game when Bankers played their counterparts in Renfrew. Larry Gilmour, refereeing yet coaching the home club, kept a steady string of visitors in the penalty box. When that didn't prevent Pembroke from taking a two goal lead, he withdrew his team, and the nets, drawing a full round of boos from his own fans.

1912/13

This season MacKay St Arena was professionally managed by E.D. Otter, fresh from operating Broadview Outdoor in Toronto, which was said to accommodate eighteen hundred skaters. He installed lockers, sold season tickets and employed a band twice weekly. Otter also organized a pre-hockey-season six-team indoor baseball league, won of course by Debaters. He too survived but one campaign.

There was a new league, the winner of which would enter the Allan Cup playdowns. Pembroke, Renfrew, Arnprior, Almonte and Carleton Place formed the Ottawa Valley Hockey Association (OVHA) and affiliated with the Interprovincial Union (IPU), becoming one of three sections. The other two were City with Stewartons, New Edinburghs and Ottawa U, and the Western with Perth, Smith's Falls and Brockville. Members posted $100 bonds with $25 to accompany every protest. Arnprior dropped out before play began.

Frank Garrow remained president of Pembroke Srs and Billy O'Brien continued as coach, manager, water boy, etc. They opened by hosting Renfrew for the first time in three years. Rivers, sporting goaltender Norman Budd, Louis Imbleau, Charlie Logan, the Fishenden brothers, Ian McKinnon and Alf Anderson, pounded the home team 9-2. Gordon Fluker took five penalties—then a job in Ottawa. It was also Charlie Thorpe's single attempt at goaltending. Midway through the lopsided contest, coach O'Brien lifted Morand and Dan Durick in favour of railway employee Milt Horn, who was home after a three-year absence, and nineteen-year-old David Edward Behan. No name appears more often in this story than that of Dave Behan; he was beginning over six decades of involvement in Pembroke hockey, golf and horse racing. He died November 25, 1989, two weeks short of his ninety-seventh birthday.

With Lance back in goal, Pembroke won 5-2 in Carleton Place. This was Oliver "Dooney" Landriault's first game, and it would be 1925 before Pembroke Srs played without him or a brother.

Though Dave's cousin Ted Behan and Milt Horn were splendid talents, Pembroke Srs could do nothing with powerful Rivers, who finished the schedule undefeated. However, Rivers suffered decisive losses during an exhibition swing through the Cobalt area, indicating the new league may not have been up to Valley standards.

While deciding the Western champion, Smith's Falls and Perth got in such an argument over player eligibility that a game never got started. Finding the box office locked when they returned for refunds, fans proceeded to wreck the Smith's Falls arena. Both clubs were suspended—finally Renfrew and New Edinburgh met for IPU honours. Renfrew lost 2-1 and won 3-2, forcing a third game which Burghs took 4-0. Bert Parsons was the Renfrew leader while Dave Gill's powerful club featured Bud Slack, Angus Duford and Gordon Dunlop plus Basil and Greg George of Eganville.

*****

No town league that season, but boys clubs were beginning three decades of prominence. The first was El Shadi, a Wesley Methodist Church group organized by Mrs Robert (Isabel) Booth. She headed that club until ill health forced daughter Gertrude to take over in the mid 20s. Immediately behind El Shadi came St. Columbus Boys Club (SCBC) and Holy Trinity Boys Club (HTC); they, along with Debaters, often formed the town league.

As for Cameron and Nighbor, they were both with Toronto St. Pats of the NHA. Frank made the Art Ross all-star team while Harry drove manager Jack Marshall to distraction. He was too valuable to trade, ignore or sit out, so Marshall simply fined him.

1913/14

Sheriff Alex Morris managed the rink, Bill Harvey, after returning from Renfrew, took over the team presidency, with a large committee, and smilin' Billy coached again. M.J. had enticed the younger O'Brien to leave Pembroke and take over his Dominion House but Billy didn't stay. The league structure remained the same.

When the team opened with a 3-2 defeat of Carleton Place, Omer Landriault, Dooney's brother, scored in his first Sr game. Arnprior native Archie Dimmell, who had gotten a job in Pembroke, also saw his first action.

Then everyone entrained to Renfrew, $1.15 return. Fans had a ball in the "Bonnie Heilan Toon," were a person could "get a drink anywhere except a hotel, and you can get one there if you know how." It was not a good score though: Ian McKinnon tallied four and his team won 7-4. Dan Durack and Dave Behan shared the Pembroke markers.

Though Jim McAlindon had returned from three years in the Soo and Hugh Fraser came home briefly, plus the fact that Harold Duff and Jim Cully showed promise, Renfrew still prevailed. Mind you, Pembroke beat them once, 5-3; fans were so excited they damaged MacKay St Arena quite severely.

So Rivers entered IPU playdowns once again, in their old, inimitable fashion. Disqualified at the last minute for not paying a $25 registration fee, Renfrew countered claiming no OVHA clubs had done so, in protest of "ringers" used by City and Western teams. But IPU officials didn't agree so they re-aligned matches; City to play West, winner plays Intercollegiate champs, that victor plays Renfrew.

Did you follow that? Renfrew gets disqualified for not paying dues then is given a bye to the final round!

That's how it went. City beat West, Queen's beat City, and Renfrew. Ironically, Ian KcKinnon was by then with Queen's, spearheading the defeat of his home team.

*****

There was no town league again. But Westmeath, virtually owning ex-MLA Norman Reid's Cup, put it up to challenge. Debaters tried, and got hammered. Arnprior Kits suffered likewise. Pembroke Srs, such as they were, took on the village and were humbled 7-2. Then Renfrew got in line, but wisely backed off at the last minute.

Pembroke players who had turned pro were doing well, on the whole. Cameron won a Stanley Cup with Toronto. Nighbor played for Vancouver. Lehman missed all but eight games with New Westminster due to a broken hand but still made the PCHA all-star team. For the off-season: Frank had a forestry job in Port Arthur, Harry split his time between Pembroke and Toronto, while Hugh was already into paving.

Participants

Bill and Nellie Bogart's son Arthur came into this world September 14, 1912. His mother died of pulmonary trouble a year later and it wasn't until Billy married Greenwood Methodist Church organist Lillian Whitmore on October 9, 1916 that Arthur and his brother had a mother again. Art, like Dave Behan, spent more time in or around the sport of

hockey than any dozen Pembrokeites put together.

Milt Horn worked for the CNR, generally in Sudbury. Jim Coxford went wherever Herb Mackie's bush operations took him, mostly B.C. P.J. O'Brien married Beatrice Bresnahan and moved to Smith's Falls, then Sudbury.

Allan Wilson spent the 1912–13 season in Glascow, N.B., earning all-star status. Next year found him with the Ottawa Senators, where he was good enough to draw special attention from hardrock Odie Cleghorn of the Wanderers. Allan later enlisted.

After 1911/12, Sarsfield Brennan received offers from as far away as Trail, B.C. He played for Port Arthur the next year, taking Dooney Landriault with him. Brick Fraser, Steve Vair and Bob Scott were all in that league. Then the boys joined St. Paul, Minnesota, where the *Pioneer Press* and *Daily News* of that city praised their performances on numerous occasions.

Adjuncts

Captain W.L. Murphy joined Captain Jim Higgins and employed Joe Trottier to build them a new ferry, replacing the old 78-foot *D.B. Mulligan* with a $10,000, 98-foot vessel. A huge crowd gathered to watch the April 30, 1912 launch. This was a fine time to discover the slipways were too level. It was nearly morning when an exhausted and totally unobserved crew finally cast the monster adrift. Murphy then bought out Higgins and decided *Pontiac of the Ottawa* would nicely identify his new craft only to have it rejected by the Department of Marine. How about *Pontiac 1*, Murphy asked. Sorry. *Allumette?* Nope. *W.L. Murphy* then! Sure.

The *W.L. Murphy* was christened right and proper by Tom Murray, who fetched a load of cattle across. The trouble was, slippery footing made unloading adventuresome and one got away, bolting down the CPR tracks. Urged on by an approaching train, Tom took after it, but he got his foot caught between the ties. Friends pulled him free with seconds to spare but the beast wasn't as lucky.

Remember the *Mayflower*? No, not that one, the old relic that sank in Lake Kaminiskeg below Barry's Bay in the fall of 1912. Nine people drowned that day, and three floated ashore with a loaded casket. You might call it Eastern Ontario's Titanic, six months late. Speaking of that ocean disaster, one victim was GTR President C.M. Hays; his successor being E.J. Chamberlain, President of Colonial Lumber Co. in Pembroke.

The County Town was without much power through half

of 1912. Ice smashed the Waltham plant, forcing PELC to resurrect the old and inadequate steam facility, and residents to renew relations with coal oil.

The weather went goofy in 1913; river ice carried log sleighs in April yet summer brought a combination of dust and caterpillars. It affected some people. A nervous thief committed Pembroke's first robbery by pulling a gun on Joe Burke one evening, then, given Joe's loose change, nearly shot himself in the foot while running away. The incident so unnerved everyone, a chap was later knocked to the sidewalk for simply reaching in his pocket while walking by a chatting threesome. That trio finished up in front of Magistrate Stewart.

It really was boom times. Sub-divisions went up everywhere. Lots sold for $100 or more. Workers were imported from Montreal. Most of them complained only of the constant "local option" debate (wet or dry); hotels opened and closed accordingly. The first ambulance service arrived and Wm. Markus Co. built an Opera House, which Bill Roland managed for a time along with his Casino and Crystal theatres. Hundreds canoed the Ottawa and the Steamer *Oiseau* was loaded to the gunnels every trip upriver; in fact she sank once under the strain but was later recovered. And the *Montreal Daily Mail* arrived every day, by mail, on time, for $3 a year.

And cars: Why you couldn't buy a Willys-Overland for under $1250 and a McLaughlin cost all of $2750. Henry Ford doubled salaries overnight! With 20,000 horseless carriages on Ontario roads, driver's licences and livery vehicle permits were born. "These autos!" once said Farmer Jones, in caustic, acrimonious tones. "When folks tear by me with a whiz, I wonder what the pleasure is in sailing through a dusty shower at ninety-seven miles an hour, if this is what is now called sport, the government should cut it short. It gets me mad to have these chumps go sailing over ruts and bumps, cavorting down the country road where I am driving with my load, and as they pass my prancing team to hear them cough or bark or scream or bellow like a frantic cow, the horns they have on those things now which jar all ears for miles around with hideous, discordant sound have scared my cattle all to bits and put my horses on the fritz, they've got my hens and pigs and sheep so that they're scared to go to sleep. 'Twas quiet round here once, by gum, but now these wretched autos come and fill the atmosphere with howls and grunts and snorts and yelps and yowls and fiendish forty-horsepower shrieks which linger in the air for weeks. The noisy chaps who swiftly slide through miles of quiet countryside with glaring lights and loud alarms have chased more people off the farms than any other single cause," and savagely he snapped his jaws.

Now that we're in the mood . . .

The difference between slop and swill. Slop: "A hogs relish of fine ingredients." Swill: "Dish water and soap suds polluted with unhealthy refuse."

Upon being asked why he failed to print obituaries of non-subscribers, a Texas editor replied "People who do not take their home paper are dead anyway and their passing away has no news value."

Soo *Star* ad: "Pious party wants board with family where his good example will be considered sufficient recompense."

Lastly, a local merchant received this order: "Please will you send me the oder skirt this same his that one if she is shorter than one she to long. Send it down went the team be down and if she the same lent don't mine. I be up me selft some time."

*****

February 1912. Since becoming a widower seventeen years previously, Francis Henry Switzenburg had lived in an Alice township cave, with Mary Summerfeldt, for the past ten years. The man was never seen and, except for an occasional begging trip, neither was the woman.

Finally, Reeve George Biggs and a councillor were asked to investigate. They found a rank crawl space without heat, light, furniture or food. The pair spoke only German.

Under warrant, they were brought to town, handcuffed, on the floor of a sleigh as both refused to use the seat. They were housed in the jail until officials were able to accommodate them in Perth's House of Refuge. The *Perth Expositor* reported a week later: "One day at the home appeared to work wonders as the woman was hardly in the home until she had her apron on and was in the kitchen hard at work. She is one of the cleanest, tidiest and best workers in the home, while the man is counted among the best and most industrious." However, one learns the purpose of the piece (routine among weeklies) in this conclusion: "Perhaps if some more of Renfrew county's inhabitants would spend a few years living in caves it might purify them physically, morally and politically. We would recommend the cave as a cure for political corruption disease which appears to be so prevalent in that riding."

1909/10 Debaters. Sarsfield Brennan, J. Leclair, Mary Kelly—mascot, Bill Sarsfield, Harry Cameron, J. Parnell Duff, P.J. O'Brien, J.H. Lessard, Ed Leacy, J.J. O'Brien, Jim Dunbar, Harry Sarsfield, Leo Alphonse "Babe" Chaput, Emmett Duff and E.T. Durick. Courtesy Angus Kennedy.

1910/11 Pembroke Srs. Clockwise from top: Jim Dunbar, J. Parnell Duff, Percy Wilson, Harry Cameron, Graham Fenton, Joe Murray (president), Lindsay Fluker, Rowan Stewart, Gordon "Brick" Fraser, Frank Nighbor. Inside circle; clockwise from top: C. Warren (secretary-treasurer), commissioners, Jack Poff and Billy Wallace, Reg "Bedu" Morand, Gowan and Willard Beatty. At centre is the new Shield. Courtesy Champlain Trail Museum.

1910/11 Debaters. The same team as the previous season with the addition of Edward "Ted" Behan, top left corne; new mascot and Charlie Munro. Courtesy Champlain Trail Museum.

1911/12 Debaters. Top to bottom, left to right: P.J. O'Brien, Jim Cully, Dave Behan, Bedu Morand, Ted Behan, Cecil Giroux and Sarsfield Brennan. Jack Sarsfield, Tom Regimbal, Joe Bourke, Hum Lance, C. Ryan. Dan Durack, O'Driscoll Legge and Harold Duff. Courtesy Moodie Doering.

1910/11/12 Port Arthur Srs. Cameron and Nighbor on their second step to fame. Harry is third from the left, top row, with Frank extreme right centre. Courtesy N–W Ontario Sports Hall of Fame.

Left: Oliver "Dooney" Landriault, taken about 1912. Courtesy Marguerite Landriault, his youngest sister.

Below: 1913/14 Westmeath team. Standing, left to right: Joe Cecile, J. Alfred Dunn, Horace Ross, Norman Reid (manager), Alex Ethier, Eric Ross, Billie Carlson (goalie), Lorne St. Denis and Fred Lacroix. In front: Ed Nesbitt, Dr. Gardiner, Alex Laderoute, Joe Retty and Louis Ethier. Their second covered rink opened one year after McKay St Arena. Courtesy Noreen Desjardins.

1912/13 Renfrew Srs. Here
we have a good hockey
team, including those after
whom the famous 1920 tro-
phy was named. Top to bot-
tom, left to right: Bill Dean,
James Barnet, Johnny
Jackes, Dominic Ritza, Tom
Fishenden, Luke Imbleau—
Louis brother, Henry J.
"Harry" McLean, Charlie
Logan, Willard Box, Ian
McKinnon, Alf Anderson,
Norman Budd, Wilbert
"Bert" Parsons, Peter
O'Brien. Courtesy George
Fishenden.

1913/14 El Shadi. This club
operated for about fifteen
years but few pictures exist.
Top to bottom, left to right:
Solomon Owen Jones,
George Horricks, Robert
Clarence Coxford, Findlay
Huckabone, Lesley Smith,
Arthur Bromley, Delmar
Dobson, Lamour Small,
Cecil Tario, Bill Labow,
Walter "Welly" Tario, Percy
Smith, Dan Miller and
Ewart McMullen. Courtesy
Champlain Trail Museum.

Chapter 7

Reformation

1914/15 to 1918/19

A widely held opinion that assists somehow diminished goal scorer's accomplishments finally began to crumble. But recognition for the set-up man was reluctant and, briefly, he who scored got two points while his helper was given but one. Another world war would be upon us before two assists on a goal became anything but an anomaly.

Static line-ups were also slow to die. Many felt unrestricted substitutions would lead to devious tactics, while others argued "endurance-test hockey" was as easily manipulated. Nevertheless, increased NHA rosters led to all teams carrying ten or eleven men by the end of WWI. Naturally, the pace of the game quickened.

Games

1914/15

The IPU dissolved, which gave the UOVHL another chance. President Bates of Carleton Place became president and Arnprior came back on board. An application from Ottawa Aberdeens was rejected, which frustrated Renfrew officials as they had hoped that Aberdeens would improve the competition. Carleton Place's J.D. Innes donated a league trophy.

The Creamery Town had a point; while other teams in the league lost promising players to lucrative offers elsewhere, Rivers officials provided sufficient incentive to keep theirs. As a result they usually won the UOVHL championship, although this season they lost the Shield game to Buckingham, 3-2.

As an example of this imbalance, Pembroke Srs defeated Arnprior 8-1 and Carleton Place 8-2 but lost 14-2 in Eureka Rink. The County Town played two exciting games, both with Arnprior. Goals by Omer Landriault and Dan Durack offset markers from Charles Mulcahy and Ray Barnes in the Woollen Town, forcing overtime. They agreed to play five-minute periods until someone won. Five periods were played before Ernie Stavenow and Domenic Raby secured an Arnprior victory. In Pembroke, our heroes lost 2-1, the tying goal being disallowed

Actually, it was not a season to be proud of. Pembroke faced several protests over arriving late for away games and never being ready for home contests. Eventually, the club declined to attend a league meeting, this was ordered to post an $80 performance bond and submit the unpaid membership fee. They did neither.

The team couldn't even keep a date with Westmeath. They tied 4-4 in the first half of a two game Reid Cup series then failed to show up for the second game. Charlie Duff's

Renfrew club finally took the trophy from Westmeath. Meantime, Pembroke's shameful campaign ended with a 9-3 exhibition loss to Ottawa College, where Ted Behan was team captain. This happened despite the services of Renfrew's Box, Imbleau and McKinnon.

*****

In town action, the Allies, Presbyterians and Independents refused to let the stacked Debaters participate, then added insult to injury by announcing they were playing for the Munro Cup, a trophy the Debaters had won thrice in a row and therefore owned. The Debaters then organized a Federal League, with Shamrocks and Crescents, claiming their victor would challenge for that mug. Not blessed with great talent for a change, Debaters just won the league championship. Meantime, Gordon Fluker's Independents proved the best of the other bunch, although Gordon was already overseas. Surprisingly, Munro Cup trustees Jack Wallace and R.L. McCormick agreed they should play the Federal champs. Independents refused, so Debaters took their own cup without a struggle.

Lehman and Nighbor won a Stanley Cup in Vancouver while Cameron stuck with Toronto.

1915/16

Pembroke Srs did not apply for UOVHL membership, last of the originals to miss a season. Renfrew won over Arnprior, Almonte and Carleton Place.

But MacKay St Arena was busy anyway. Frank Garrow and Captain Joe Tessier leased the building and charged 25¢ to attend whatever game was going on, a fee that included public skating afterwards.

Pembroke had a Sr team: the "Royal Hockey Club," under president E.B. Leacy. They played several exhibitions, a win, tie and loss with Renfrew for instance—all of which were in support of the war effort and carnival in nature. Ted Behan was home from university often enough to play a few games, one of which he organized against a Red Cross team from Petawawa to which several Russian families at the camp were invited to attend. None had seen a hockey game and unanimously proclaimed it a great sport with nary a single claim of invention.

The Royals would have fared well in league play. CPR ticket agent Art Bourbon was an outstanding player but he returned home to Rockland, when his brother died. Future

stars Jack Anderson, Dub Murphy and goaltender Welly Tario saw their first Sr action and visiting Fred Thrasher participated in one game. The star was Sarsfield Brennan, who returned from St Paul as the season began.

*****

The girls' club played several benefits, one in Renfrew during which charter member Ella Coxford was accidently knocked unconscious for forty-five minutes. She recovered completely after a night in hospital.

Led by Dave Behan and Dub Murphy, Debaters again narrowly won town honours.

Hugh Lehman stayed in Vancouver but Ottawa enticed Frank Nighbor back east with $1500, a move that infuriated the Patricks'. This brought Frank and Toronto's Harry Cameron into the same league. The first time they met Harry rammed his stick up Frank's nose and Nighbor was carried off one side while Cameron was banished through the opposite door. Frank had nose trouble all season. Odie Cleghorn hit it with his stick and Gord Roberts attempted to remove the proboscis altogether. Despite repeated damage, Nighbor played every game, seldom leaving the ice.

1916/17

Pembroke Srs returned to UOVHL action. The six-team league, which included the 240th, the Creamery Town half of a battalion stationed both in Pembroke and Renfrew, played a ten-game schedule under President J.F. Honeycutt of Renfrew.

This edition of Pembroke Srs often sported three Landriaults, since Eugene had been added. Because of constant shifting of munition plant employees, Archie Dimmell joined brother George on the team. Archie scored four goals in his first game (their father, Charlie, died a few days later.)

The season began as usual. Almonte dropped out, then in. Arnprior cancelled Pembroke's first visit, no ice, then refused to play the return match until game one was in the books. Pembroke won by default. Actually, little went right for the league; hockey teams held a low priority with war-concerned railroads.

Renfrew, sporting several veterans plus fiesty newcomer Patsy Parker and superb goaltender Bert McAndrews, took first place and the Innes Trophy by defeating Pembroke 4-1. This final contest was refereed by Harry Cameron. There was no Shield game however. Renfrew and Hawkesbury debated between a sudden-death contest or H&H until it was too late.

Munitions employees–hockey players frequently used the sport to vent frustration. One Pembroke Iron Works versus O'Brien Munitions battle deteriorated to such an extent that referee Billy Wallace, generally not given to exasperation, quit, leaving Roy McVean to finish.

Martin's son Bill Ringrose was president of the Debaters and enjoyed the services of youngsters Anthony Merryfield and O'Driscoll Legge plus excellent goaltending by Peter Dunlevy (whose son Jack tended goal for the 52/53 Lumber Kings). Still they couldn't win the town league. That honour went to the Iron Works, with goalie Welly Tario and scoring star Michael J. Lee.

In mid-March, local fans packed MacKay St Arena, twice, to watch Nighbor and Cameron team up with several former team-mates against local competition.

*****

This year was the closest Frank Nighbor ever came to winning a professional scoring title. He and Quebec's Joe Malone tied with fourty one goals. The Pembroke Peach— Frank's most popular nickname at the time, played best hurt. He took several stitches in his hand while practising in Pembroke at Christmas then, heavily bandaged, scored six times in a 7-1 win over the Canadiens December 30th. Later he registered all Ottawa's goals in a 3-2 defeat of Toronto, shortly after Sprague Cleghorn had stuffed several inches of stick handle down his throat.

In Edmonton, the *Journal* praised Pembroke's Miss I. Coffey for "pulling off spectacular saves time after time." She was the goalie for Edmonton Victorias, said to be Canada's top woman's team—and you thought Paul was the first Coffey to star in that city!

Veteran *Renfrew Mercury* writer, Will Lee, wrote that "compiling an honour roll of scorers had to stop, it promoted individual effort and took away from combination play."

During a game in Cornwall, John Glascow struck Jay Stevens over the head with his stick. A few days later, Stevens pulled Glascow from his cutter and beat him unconscious. Peace and County Court Judge O'Reilly fined Jay $400, saying he "loathes and despises hockey; it is brutal and demoralizing and, furthermore, all the players should be at the front."

1917/18

With neither the UOVHL or LOVHL operating, hockey was left to shell plants, businesses, schools and boys clubs. Bear with me while I trigger local memories with line-ups from three teams.

PHS was coming into a period of Valley domination. This season's team featured Lawrence 'Nig' Jones in goal, Billy Williams's son Harry playing defence with Charlie Parr, centre Buzz Armstrong, wingers Betsy Bethel and Denny McMullen plus Bert Markus (schools still used rovers). Ed Rowan and Gordon Weinke were spares on this club that competed for the new Red Cross Cup, a challenge trophy won on this occasion by Renfrew High.

The very active girls team consisted of goaltender Gertrude Daly, Bessie Barrand, Mrs R. Small, Norma Billings, Keitha Fraser and Emma Fournier plus Irene and Ethel Ludgate. Westmeath boasted the star netminder; Julia Acheson was good enough to play on any man's club, had she not been born sixty years too soon.

El Shadi prevailed among the boys clubs. George Lemke, Clarence Coxford, George Horricks, Cecil Tario, Herbert Ritchie, Lamour Small, John Collins and Howard Fraser were the players; Ab Strutt and Dan Millar shipped out during the season's play.

With winter half gone, three local shell plants organized "Pembroke Munitions Hockey Club." Sarsfield Brennan, having more or less retired from playing, took up officiating, but the team was still potent with such veteran players as Neil Campbell and Montreal's Bill Mills. Goaltender Bert McAndrews, a native of Buckingham, switched allegiance from the Creamery Town and this group began by defeating the "O'Brienville Seven" 7-0, Archie Dimmell registering a hat trick. MP Herb Mackie dropped the first puck.

Though purely an exhibition season, Renfrew couldn't resist dressing old pro Tommy Smith for the return match, while Pembroke took along a guy called McCall, who turned out to be Jack McKell of Ottawa Munitions—shades of Skene Ronan. Like Ronan, McKell was suspended by the O&DHA.

Then Buckingham's Eddie Gorman, enroute to four pro seasons with Ottawa and Toronto, teamed up with fifteen- year-old Gordon Fraser to help beat Hull Canadiens 8-0.

Ted Behan and Jim Cully were by this time at McGill;

they brought their team to town and won 5-3, the fifth visitors goal being scored by one Rooney and assisted by Behan. The first assist awarded in a game involving Pembroke.

When Ottawa Aberdeens earned a 2-2 tie at MacKay St Arena, they brought regulars Rene and Aurel Joliat. Aurel scored both goals. All that tiny left winger ever did was become a legend.

Munitions finished 8-2-2.

In Ottawa, a military "press gang" detained every eligible looking lad they saw until he could produce an exemption certificate; these documents were routinely published for all to see. Forgetting their papers, several Renfrew hockey players were prevented from even stepping on the ice until team officials produced a $1000 bond; they were held again after the game until proof of exemption was provided.

Goodbye NHA, hello NHL. With Toronto Arenas, Cameron suffered through several fines and suspensions to win a Stanley Cup, defeating Lehman and his Vancouver Millionaires. Nighbor, stationed in Toronto with the airforce, wasn't cleared to play until the season was half over. Arenas owner Charlie Querrie tried to buy Frank for $1400 but the Senators would not agree.

1918/19

Under president E.A. Fox, Pembroke Srs adopted the name "Arenas" and were ready to play but a UOVHL didn't develop. The weather wasn't great either. No sooner did sixteen-year-old Lawrence "Nig" Jones get his first exhibition start in goal than mild conditions stymied proceedings till March, at which time Luke Imbleau came up from Renfrew for a game. They played two or three times, giving youngsters Denny McMullen, Buzz Armstrong and Wilf Cecile a shot.

PHS Srs were the 18/19 story. Nig Jones, Frank Deloughery, Esmonde Munro and Stewart Hunter joined McMullen, Bethel, Markus and Armstrong for a great start but then suffered with everyone else through the mildest winter in thirty-seven years. Before conditions softened they tied RHS twice; all cup challenges taking place on the holders' ice. In March, they tried again, warming up with a 7-1 win over Arnprior Alerts then riding two brilliant goals by Betsy Bethel to a 5-2 Cup victory, thus switching venues for future challenges. When RHS attempted to take it back, Willy McGuinty and Roy Ludgate had graduated from PHS Jrs and they were prominent in the successful defence, 6-2 win.

Brimming with confidence, PHS went into the Capital and defeated Ottawa Collegiate 3-1. When Renfrew tried again, Brennan and Orin Frood refereed the 3-1 PHS victory, insuring the Red Cross Cup stayed in Pembroke over the summer. Even Arenas, despite having Hum Lance back from the north and enjoying the services of Harold Duff before he moved to Ottawa, could only manage one narrow win in two tries against their younger brethren.

Suspended right off, Harry Cameron was traded to Ottawa where the defenceman scored fifteen goals in twenty games. Teammate Frank Nighbor recorded seventeen in the first NHL campaign with forward passing in the neutral zone. Frank had a difficult year, opening an insurance business with partner Dave Behan, later an ailing mother, and his sister Edith passing away in Detroit. Lehman was so-so, the one season in which no Stanley Cup was awarded; Montreal and Seattle quit mid-series when the Canadiens star Joe Hall died of influenza in a Seattle hospital.

Participants

Canadians didn't see the blatant manipulation of professional athletes in WWI that developed during the Second World War simply because pro sports hadn't escalated to the required level. Imagine the slight of hand required to protect todays million-dollar babies!

Varicose veins got Frank Nighbor rejected by the air corp, but he persisted, and made ground crew in 1917, though he never went abroad. Harry Cameron worked in shell factories during the off season and Warren Paving kept Hugh Lehman busy.

Local athletes enlisted in numbers. After breaking his leg during a motorcycle accident in England, Brick Fraser went on to lengthy service with #1 Tunnelling Co., a favoured means of penetrating enemy lines. Basil Morris, son of Jim Morris, laboured for the same outfit till taking up flying; Basil died trying to land his tattered plane. His brother Ramsay suffered severe eye infection at the front and spent time in an English hospital. Billy Williams's son Welland was wounded in the Regina trench and found himself down the hall from Ramsay; their mothers visited them there. A superb athlete, Welland survived Ypres and the Somme only to fall in the horror of Vimy. Major W.C. Weaver found his tag a year later and sent it to the family.

Billy was town solicitor and legal council for the railroad at that time, while another son, Murray, was with 68th Battery in Toronto. Mayor Jim and Sheriff Alex were brothers to Dr Osborne Morris of B.C. All three served the war effort one way or another.

Milt Horn of the 21st (Princess Patricias) was left behind thanks to a bout of pleurisy, then pneumonia. Finally, enroute to France, he collided with his brother Archie on a London street corner, Archie being homeward bound to recover from trench fever. Following hostilities, Milt returned to the Department of Lands and Forests, married Annie Sikorski in 1928 and moved around until settling in Sudbury, where he died November 18, 1954 at age seventy.

Allan Wilson started similarly. He enlisted immediately but was left behind in Kingston with blood poisoning. Allan recovered, won every event in a military carnival, then took pneumonia. He caught up in England (where his lacrosse team won a title) and reached the front by spring! Soon a Major with Canadian Forestry Unit, Wilson built sawmills for making trench supports, within spitting distance of enemy fire (Lieutenant Tom Hale received a Crois de Guerre from the French government for reconnoitering while doing the same thing.) At one point, Allan wrote to William Beamish's parents, telling them he'd seen Bill in hospital and the lad was coming along fine. Unfortunately they knew nothing of Bill's wounds, as official word did not arrive until a month later. Things like that happened often; Sergeant Mitch Dempsey was reported first missing, then dead, before coming home with a DSM. Wilson was also at the bedside of J. Everett "Zip" Anderson when he died of spinal meningitis, the result of wounds. Zip was the first native son who enlisted in Pembroke to die, almost two years after hostilities began. Zip and his brother, you're right, Zap, were active in the town league.

Lindsay Fluker lived in Dunnville when he enlisted, following brother Gordon to battle. Gordon remained unscathed but Lindsay was wounded two months before armistice. Their sister, Queenie, perhaps the most popular young lady in town, married Rev. A.B. Ranson in 1917 but died a year later in childbirth.

Recall Charles Thorpe's one disastrous game? In Halifax to join the navy, he died of a broken neck after falling down a railway embankment.

Others were: Randolph and Emmett Spooner (coming up in our story), Harold Duff, Dave Behan, Jim McAlindon, Andrew Irving, George Dunbar, Jim Coxford,

Jack Sarsfield Jr., Dr Gordon "Curly" Campbell and Lorne Ranson, who returned to Winnipeg with a French war bride. Dan Durack enlisted but failed the medical, taking a CPR job in Regina.

Of nineteen Pembroke boys who joined the first contingent, five survived, one a POW. A year after twenty-one Renfrew lads joined the 21st Battalion, every man was either dead or wounded. Five Fishenden brothers enlisted; two paid the ultimate sacrifice.

Calvin Rowan Stewart left the Quebec Bank and joined up in 1914. Police Magistrate James Stewart's son was gassed and wounded before coming home to a job in Iroquois Falls. He married Kathleen O'Neill there, then returned to the Department of National Defence in Petawawa. Active in the Great War Veterans Association and charter member of its successor, Canadian Legion, Rowan died the day before Christmas, 1961.

Herb Mackie was almost forty when war broke out. He became a staff officer with the Soviet forces and purchased equipment for them in North America. Russia's shell requirements were tested at Petawawa; Mackie supervised construction of the trial field and several Russian families lived there.

Lieut. Col. Lennox Irving had long since retired as C.O. of the 42nd Regiment, but even he returned to duty. When he was refused active service, Sir William Otter appointed him commandant of the poorly equipped POW camp that housed seven hundred Austrians at Petawawa. But a stall order kept Lennox at bay until an officer of the proper political persuasion could be positioned. Irving hung tough though, becoming second in command of the 240th Battalion and actually made an appearance in France. Meantime, his recruitment speeches featured such patriotic fervour that soldiers felt guilty coming home wounded!

The long-time bachelor married Renfrew's Grace Barnet at war's end. Irving closed his law office there in 1925 and retired, first to California then Victoria where he died in November of 1938 at the age of seventy-five. Brother Edward was living in Brockville at the time.

Ted Behan and Jim Cully became stars at McGill, as did Bert Markus at Toronto U. Archie Dimmell returned to Arnprior and George moved to Capreol. Neil Campbell married Myrtle Horn and moved to Toronto, both suffering serious injuries in a car accident a month later. After a long recovery period, the couple moved to Cobden where Neil lent a hand organizing various sports.

Roy McVean worked in munitions plants from Montreal to Hamilton during WWI, returning to Pembroke when Eddy Match Company set up shop in the mid 20s. The machinist was offered a pro hockey contract in 1910 but his father had just died and he elected not to leave his mother. Roy never married and lived in the family home on Renfrew St till the day he died, November 9, 1963.

Life wasn't dull for Sarsfield Brennan, on or off ice. First, it was he who discovered a fellow workman killed by a collapsing lumber pile. Then, in 1918, he was the only witness when deaf Louis Perrer stepped in front of a train. The next year, while working in Forest, Ontario, Sarsfield nearly died of influenza; his father and sister were not as fortunate. That sent him to Edmonton, there "to seek restoration of health and probably remain permanently." Within months the itinerant bachelor was back, becoming a shipper with Pembroke Lumber Co. Mr and Mrs Tom Brennan's boy moved to Ottawa in the late 20s and was seventy when he died there in February of 1961.

Sixteen-year-old Gordon Fraser joined Hum Lance in Port Arthur for 18/19, beginning a career that included two years with Lloyd Turner's Calgary Tigers, three PCHA campaigns in Seattle, two in Victoria, then a season and a half each with Chicago and Detroit. Gordon split a year between the Canadiens and Pittsburgh before finishing with Philadelphia in 1931. At that point he remarried and settled in London, there to coach the Tecumsehs before guiding Baltimore Orioles up to WWII, at which time he switched to working in shell factories.

Hired by Fort Frances Canadians to build an Allan Cup contender from purely local boys in 1946, Gordon's club improved steadily through 48/49, after which he retired from coaching. It was essentially the same team that coach Joe Balzan and captain Sambo Fedoruk succeeded with in 1952. Fraser, an avid golfer, passed away in 1964.

Gordon Fraser was part of an interesting hockey story while in Calgary. Alberta's top teams were amateur to 1920 and from 1922 they joined the professional WCHL. That two-year interim, Fraser's time, was filled by a league called "The Big Four," consisting of Calgary Tigers and Canadians plus Eskimos and Dominions of Edmonton. Declaring itself amateur, this group drove PCHL president Frank Patrick to distraction. Patrick had a deal with the NHL giving him rights to all pro players west of the Lakehead, so he offered $1000 to whoever could disprove his assertion that all Big Four players were making a living

at the game. Naturally, no one claimed the money. Patrick never got a player out of it but he did force the renegade league to pay provincial entertainment tax, from which amateur leagues were exempt.

Solomon "Hum" Lance played three seasons at the Lakehead before failing a tryout with Ottawa Senators. Victorias thus enjoyed his services for 1920/21. Next, Hum played a year in the town league then disappeared, reportedly to the Chicago area. Max Lance lived a long life in the Ottawa Valley, never hearing from his brother again.

Though he didn't play for Pembroke, a few words about Lesley Bertrand Lindsay are in order. Born July 23 1881, Lindsay moved from the Guelph area to Ottawa at an early age, learning goalkeeping there. He married Renfrew's Maude Louise Villemaire in 1908 and the couple raised nine children, six of them boys. Bert maintained a home in the Creamery Town while continuing his pro career, interrupted by military service, with Edmonton, Victoria and the Wanderers before finishing up in 1919 at Toronto. He coached Renfrew Jrs and Srs until accepting a machinist position at Toburn Mines in Kirkland Lake during the dirty thirties. Lindsay retired in Sarnia and passed away November 11, 1960. Yes, one of those sons is Detroit Red Wings Hall of Famer, Robert Blake Theodore "Terrible Ted" Lindsay.

The Landriaults: Born in Ottawa September 22, 1868, Theodore "Tom" Landriault moved to Pembroke at eighteen as an apprentice barber. Josephine Legère was the same age when she walked into Tom's shop for an emergency trim; he took forever to do the job then refused payment. They were married in 1888. Joseph was born in 1889 and Marguerite in 1910, book-ends of an even dozen. While Oliver, Omer and Eugene were the hockey players, Bertha, eldest of four girls, married Louis Kahl and two of their boys made a mark in the game after WWII.

Tom bought the Pembroke House in 1908 then sold it to purchase the Mackay House during WWI, an establishment he retained until 1943, six years beyond the death of his wife and a decade previous to his own passing.

The Landriaults are a fine example of how surnames were toyed with. When Tom took possession of his first hotel, he brought brother Oscar up from Ottawa to lend a hand. Oscar eventually took over a livery business of Tom's and then became driving licence vendor, something the avid hockey fan continued to do until his death in 1954. Tom was a product of his father's first marriage and Oscar came two wives later, making the boys one-third brothers, I suppose. Anyway, the younger semi-sibling was visiting in Ottawa one day when a relative told him Landriault was supposed to be minus the last two letters. Oscar switched immediately and, to this day, we have Landriaults and Landriaus, all from the same clan. (Renfrew's Dave Lorente tells me in his family a priest baptized six members, spelling each one differently on the certificate!)

Of the brothers, Oliver "Dooney" Landriault reached the highest level of hockey competition, with Port Arthur and St. Paul, before taking a CPR job in Toronto. He died at seventy-two, in 1965.

Omer "Schauf" Landriault played for twenty years, much of the time in Temiskaming. A confirmed bachelor who died in 1966 at seventy-one, Omer also had trouble with names. Believing his second handle to be Leonard, he signed O.L. Landriault until receiving a birth certificate late in life, when he discovered his middle name was Ernest.

Eugene "Ching" Landriault joined the army at nineteen, in 1917. He came home, played a season in Peterborough with Dub Murphy, then suddenly died during the winter of 1920. A year later, when one of Ching's military buddies arrived to visit, the family finally learned of a probable cause. While training in Kingston, Ching was found by an army doctor, unconscious, having been kicked in the chest by a horse. Before leaving the service he was told something growing in there would probably kill him one day. Oh yes, it was a Dr Landriault that found him.

Lastly, Hugh Matheson Fraser, whose brief story was more difficult to trace than any in this book. The problem was the Frasers in general. Pembroke sported three unrelated Fraser families; two large ones and one medium sized. Five of those Frasers were "Hugh" and the one in question compounded my problem by disappearing.

Anyway, this superb hockey player was the son of renowned carriage maker Hugh Fraser. After 1908/09, young Hugh became first a salesman, then surveyor, in Moose Jaw, Sask. He tried several times to enlist, even enduring numerous unspecified operations to pass the medical. Eventually, he succeeded, only to be discharged following an eye injury. Hugh made brief appearances in Pembroke but had actually moved to be near his three sisters in Bloomfield, Prince Edward County. There, during February of 1919, at the age of 31, Hugh Fraser succumbed to influenza, just weeks after his brother James was taken by the same disease and two years past the death of his father.

Adjuncts

When war broke out, the little summer training base at Petawawa became a temporary home for 12,000 troops and 6000 horses, creating tons of raw sewage that was dumped into the Ottawa River a few miles upstream from Pembroke's intake pipe. But the soldiers were more concerned about beer, as it was a forbidden commodity. Major Leonard was demoted after allowing his 6th Battery boys to smuggle some in.

Canada recruited by battalion, none of which faced embarkation until reaching full strength. Thus thousands of troops marked time here, while those at the front cried for relief. That forced conscription and created Selection Tribunals, the local version made up of T.H. Moffat, Billy Williams and Lennox Irving, a group facing the unenviable task of saying "yes" or "no" to hundreds of exemption applications.

Munitions plants sprang up (some blew up) all over; at one point Pembroke and Renfrew sported three each. Take inexperience, add urgency, stir in capitalistic independence and flavour with unabated opportunism and you've got a product that frequently reached foreign shores 90 percent defective. Canadian WWI shell plants should be compulsory study for all students, with *A Canadian Millionaire* by Michael Bliss one of the textbooks.

Though Patriotic Fund drives generated friendly competition between communities, nationalistic fervour often soared beyond reason. Young males not either fighting or growing food were frequently subjected to mental and physical abuse. Young females were expected to contribute wherever, freely. Everyone best hold their tongue, for comments once laughed off could now land one in jail. Area incidents drew national attention but it was only after the *New York Times* headlined a story about local youths holding off military police with machine guns, "Sedition Running Rampant Through the Valley," that Mayor W.R. Beatty produced documents proving Pembroke had one of the highest enlistment percentages per capita in Canada, somewhat reducing the rhetoric. By then offices of *The Deutsche Post*, a German-language newspaper published by E.B. "Christy" Christiansen, had been damaged so often that Christy closed down. There are those who still insist he was sending coded messages. To the man's credit, he remained in Pembroke and the fourth estate throughout his life, earning many friends.

For the young men, and volunteer nurses, going to war was an exciting adventure. When reality arrived with the casualty reports, enthusiasm was merely replaced by a stiff upper lip. Pembroke native Jack Campbell, working in Edmonton when hostilities commenced, was wounded at Langemarck. His letter is a fine example.

Dear Mother:

I suppose you will be worrying to know how I am . . . I am feeling fine and none of my wounds are serious. I got my first wound in the back at about ten friday morning and got the other one in the forehead shortly after and when I got the one in the thigh at eleven I had to give up fighting . . . a shrapnel graze in my side I did not know I had until we got on the hospital train . . . [almost two days of travel, waiting, and makeshift medical care later] . . . we got in here [Cardiff] at eleven last night and the way every person uses us is grand . . . I will not be able to go back to the front for months as you are no good there unless you are strong on your legs . . . I only hope I will never have to go through the same thing again, but if I have to I will only have to . . . write and tell Lizzie and Agnes as I suppose they will see my name in the papers among the wounded.

Your loving son, Jack.

Here's part of what a thirty-four-year-old Gananoque mother of ten children had to say after her spouse was killed. "I am better satisfied with a dead husband that was brave and manly than I would have been with a living one who was cowardly."

"I would like to try to describe to you the general life as I see it around me," wrote Private Ernest Wilson, "but the censor is a jealous god and watches all one says so closely and with such a fierce scowl that one naturally shrinks from breaking any laws he may see fit to make." Coded comment, perhaps?

Sergeant O'Reilly went over with the first contingent. Gassed and wounded at Hill 60, he recovered consciousness in hospital four days later. Three months after being invalided home, the shattered soldier required half a year in Kingston Psychiatric Hospital. Once recovered, he could only tolerate a month at Pink's Foundry before rejoining his outfit!

Martin Dunlevy, Peter's brother, was killed while carrying a wounded man; the little guy had great difficulty convincing authorities he was old enough to sign up.

William James McInerney spent years at the front, came home wounded, then drowned while swimming. A bullet passing through the shoulder, collarbone and jaw, lodging in his tongue, put Weldon Beatty in hospital for months; he went on to Vimy, and Mons, then home. Sergeant Major P.S. Flinter earned "Canada in Flanders" praise. Jack Bowden's cousin, Private W. McFadzean of Belfast received a posthumous Victoria Cross for sacrificing himself on a grenade in a crowded trench. Private Andrew Vaillancourt of Allumette Island was similarly honoured afer saving the life of his Colonel, except Andrew landed home for Christmas.

Armistice came as a surprise. People who had expected the war to be over in three months were now thinking it would go on forever. Enlisted men came home heroes but conscripted soldiers, wounded or not, faced at least derogatory remarks. Town council even wanted to bestow bronze medals on a "selected basis," excluding those, for instance, who "practiced safety first in Britain." They regained their senses after councillor James H. Kelly delivered a brilliant speech on rationality and justice.

Jim Morris released his Pembroke and area casualty list, ninety-three fell in battle. The Great War Veterans Association and Dominion Day were born and the armistice treaty was described as "leaving no opportunity to renew the struggle."

The December 17, 1917 federal election caused a stir in Pembroke, shoving even the Halifax explosion to back pages. Lieut. Col. Gerald V. White returned from the front expecting to carry the Unionist banner only to find Herb Mackie had the nomination all sewed up. Herb won too, defeating Grit Norman Reid. White returned to England where the King eased his pain by making him Commander of the Order of the Empire.

Meanwhile, MPP Edward A. Dunlop toured the front, even crawling in mud occasionally.

Some prominent Citizens died of natural causes during the war. Lumberman Robert Booth was seventy-eight when he succumbed in 1915; his older cousin, J.R. Booth, attended the funeral. Former Mayor, MP and MPP Thomas Murray passed away that same year, as did Bishop Lorraine. Renfrew's M.J. O'Brien almost died of peritonitis, but recovered. Toward war's end, Robert Booth's former partner, Alexander Gordon, died at eighty-one and Pembroke's first postmaster, Alexander Moffat, passed away at eighty-eight. Ben Hollinger, who discovered gold while operating on a $35 grubstake, was just thirty-four when he fell from his chair at the breakfast table.

Patrick Sexton Cardiff died of pneumonia in Salem, Oregon, April 20, 1917 at the age of fifty-three. Never heard of him, you say? Well, all this native of Wilberforce township did was fight John L. Sullivan to a six-round draw in Minneapolis, January 18, 1887. Perhaps you remember him as Patrick Carden. Then you may also recall the crowd flew into a frenzy, convinced Patrick had won easily. He probably would have, had he known Sullivan broke his hand in an early round.

Anyway, Carden–Cardiff learned to box in Chicago and earned his shot at the big fellow by defeating Jake Kilrain and Charlie Mitchell, among others. Following his ring career, the lad born of a French father and Irish mother operated a liquor store and gymnasium in Minneapolis before becoming a Portland, Oregon police officer. Patrick was in the moving business at the time of his death; he and wife Nellie raised three daughters. Sullivan himself died in 1918 of a heart attack, at fifty-nine.

Others died by accident. Etienne Groslouis, fifty-five, became Pembroke's first traffic fatality when he stepped off a downtown curb and was hit by a Ford. Mr and Mrs John Tracey of Eganville lost three teenaged sons when they tried to rescue one another from the Bonnechere River. Their bodies were found clinging together. And forty-five-year-old Allan T. Fraser, chief CNR engineer west of Winnipeg, was killed by a snowslide at Mount Robson, B.C.

James F. Munro, forty-seven, died November 12, 1919, in the first plane to visit Pembroke. The "Victory Loan Aeroplane" was on a publicity tour. James, hitching a ride to Ottawa, died with pilot Harry Dobbin when they crashed in fog near Eganville. J.W. Munro brought James up from Fitzroy Harbour at sixteen and taught him masonry. By 1902 he was in business, his eventual credentials including directorships with Lee Mfg., Thomas Pink Ltd., PELC; president of Massey Lumber and Pembroke Iron Works; founder of Pembroke Realty; owner of Pembroke Woollen Mills; builder of the Munro block and many houses; purchaser of Tom Murray's home—which he made into a showpiece, and municipal politician. He left his wife Margaret (Little) plus children Esmonde, Charles, Hugh and Iveagh.

Pembroke Machining Co. night watchman Joe Dow was found one morning, shot in the head. A rifle was leaning against an office chair, butt up. Since everyone liked Joe, police decided he must have shot himself accidently. When the *Perth Expositor* headlined "Murder Mystery in Pembroke," the *Observer* wondered how it could say such a thing when there wasn't even an inquest.

Some died by design. When William Bennett killed Bruce Leitch in a fit of jealousy at Sand Point, he was sentenced to hang April 17, 1918. Thanks to a lengthy petition, the sentence was commuted April 10, but by then Bennett had blinded himself in a suicide attempt.

Later that same year, Adolph Gohr was charged with murdering John Bohn at Golden Lake. Gohr had been living with Bohn for six years, running off occasionally with the man's wife. A military deserter, Adolph had been arrested but escaped back to Bohn's, who wouldn't let him in. Two days later John was found with two bullets in the back of his head. Defended by Peter White, K.C., Gohr was found not guilty despite having threatened to kill Bohn, the fact that the bullets were from a rifle like Gohr's and Bohn had lived long enough to tell his son who did it. The moment Gohr walked out of court he was arrested for desertion, receiving fifteen years of hard labour in Kingston penitentiary.

On July 8, 1919, the mangled body of tobacconist Michael Legge was found next to the CPR line. Legge feared trains and avoided the tracks. He always carried a wad of money, it was gone, and a blood stained knife lay nearby. But, as in Gohr's case, matching bullets with guns and blood stains with victims was not yet possible. An inquest declared Legge's death accidental. The frustrated family hired a detective to follow the last man Michael was seen with. Weeks later, convinced he had enough on Mexican Jack Calder and Mike McNeill, the private eye had them arrested, but police found his evidence weak and released the pair. Forty-two years later, knowing he was dying, Clifford O'Brien confessed to the murder. O'Brien was exonerated in court then passed away shortly thereafter, in a hotel room within sight of where Legge had died.

Hundreds succumbed to Spanish influenza, especially during the summer and early fall of 1918. Still, humour was found where available; believing camphor warded off the deadly disease, many people wore a cube around their neck, claiming it made them feel more camphorable.

Martin Ringrose had been West but returned unimpressed; he tried to buy the McPhee House in Arnprior but failed, then bought Dr Irwin's drug store on Pembroke St, a deal that included Beal's Marble Works plus Beamish's Furniture and Undertaking Parlour. Ringrose moved into the building and began renovating while attempting to buy the Leland Hotel, a roofless structure thanks to a 1915 mid-summer storm that put nine foot waves on Allumette Lake and brought down both of Pembroke Lumber's seventy-foot smokestacks. J. Parnell Duff and Geraldine Sauve were married that day, prompting a whirlwind romance label. The town hall clock quit about then too. It wasn't fixed for a year and as soon as it was, another big blow fetched it down, within inches of someone walking beneath. Some said it was an omen, it being built in Germany.

Martin didn't buy the Leland either; he and son Billy bought an old printing press in New Liskeard and resurrected the *Cobden Sun*. Once operating, they turned it over to former *Lanark Era* publisher D.C. McFarlane and moved across river to Campbell's Bay, there reviving the *Pontiac Advance*. Billy stayed with that but dad moved on.

Mayor Morris and Chief Butler never saw eye to eye from day one. Pembroke had a fair share of hobos when the war began so Butler took to physically depositing them about the countryside, in the often vain hope they'd not return. Morris found this unsatisfactory and, when a farmer's barn burned near one of Butler's boomerang deposits, the Mayor demanded the Chief's resignation. He got it, but gave it back following an "independent investigation." Butler quit later anyway.

The Mary St bridge was condemned, again. As for the other one, well—as soon as we get this war behind us . . .

Eugene "Charlie" Giesebrecht ran a jitney service between Pembroke and Petawawa. One day, he backed into the river, thoroughly soaking his load of servicemen and dampening Charlie's pride.

Suddenly, a thousand birds fell dead off a hydro wire over the Muskrat River bridge. No one ever determined the cause. Foul play?

Would you believe a pine cut in Quebec by Colonial Lumber Co. that stood 128 feet high, measured 54 inches in the stump and produced 3648 board feet of lumber?

The new Police Chief Harry Carroll of Pembroke suspected Fong Deen (Oriental Cafe) and Fong Que (Minto Cafe) of importing opium. Sure enough, he and Ottawa's Inspector McLaughlin found quantities of the poppy seed product in both locations. Deen and Que paid $50 fines and chalked it up to experience. However, while Que laid low,

Deen ordered a fresh supply immediately. But Carroll watched the post office and, when Deen arrived to pick up a suspicious looking parcel, he and McLaughlin were waiting. They paraded Deen before Police Magistrate James Stewart. The hour was late, so Stewart doubled the fee, whereupon Deen extracted a huge wad from which he peeled off two fifties and a fiver to boot, departing more pained from the loss of merchandise.

Renfrew Mercury: "He was the victim of a stroke, which proved fatal a few days previous to his death."

Son: It's a hot day, dad. Buy me some ice cream.
Scrooge: I'll tell you some ghost stories and your blood will run cold.

Mrs Jones: I'm going to console Mrs Brown. Her husband hanged himself in the attic last night.
Daughter: Be careful, you tend to say the wrong thing.
Mrs Jones: Don't worry, I'll stick with the weather.

Mrs Jones: We've had lots of rain lately.
Mrs Brown: Yes, I haven't been able to get my clothes dry.
Mrs Jones: Try hanging them in the attic.

"Blazes"

Shortly after WWI began, Pembroke averaged a fire a week for some time, but most were put out with little damage. Businesses supporting the war effort seemed most vulnerable but an arsonist was never convicted. Copeland Hotel outbuildings went up in smoke during the stretch and Pembroke Lumber Co., situated virtually downtown, suffered severe damage. Having picked up Magistrate Stewart along the way, George Dunbar was rushing to the sawmill fire when he swung his Ford to miss a fire truck, ran over a manhole cover and flipped like a pancake. Citizens running toward the initial problem stopped to help at this more recent event but both men crawled out unscathed and continued on foot.

Then Cecile's Windsor Hotel lost all its outbuildings and a quartet of steeds. Why Tom didn't switch to "Inn of the Four Horses" and have their ghosts roam the premises is beyond me.

An August 1916 fire that swept the Matheson–Cochrane district, taking four hundred lives, hit Pembroke and area particularly hard. Mr and Mrs Joe Dupont of Allumette

Island lost their son, his wife and two grandchildren. Mr and Mrs Thomas Little, while visiting their niece in Pembroke, Mrs James Munro, reportedly picked up a city daily to learn four daughters, one son, one son-in-law, eleven grandchildren, their home and possessions were all lost. I can't help but wonder how much shock a human being should be asked to withstand.

Colonial Lumber Co. saw it's sawmill reduced to ashes in the spring of 1917. Diligence on the part of firefighters prevented the particularly savage blaze from spreading downtown; Pembroke Lumber double-shifted to cut both companies' logs while Colonial rebuilt.

Unfortunately, that was a mere warm-up for Tuesday, June 18, 1918. A fire started in the storehouse of Bernard Leacy and Co. and, aided by a stiff wind that carried pieces of roofing as far as Douglas, took out almost everything between Albert and Agnes Sts, on its way across Pembroke, Renfrew, Isabella, Mary and what is now Welland St before dying out on the Hogsback. Over forty private homes and as many businesses were destroyed, including banks, theatres, restaurants, town offices, a flour and feed, Ringrose's Printing Shop and part of Pink's huge operation. The Presbyterian Church caught fire twice but was extinguished. Huge trees helped protect the Cathedral and Convent while fire walls saved Dunlop and Co., Fenton and Smith and Hotel Pembroke, the latter surviving until it burned in 1991.

Fire Chief J.M. Taylor and his crew performed yeoman service, aided by the Renfrew brigade. Herb Mackie prevailed upon his military friends in Ottawa to ship up fifty tents and J.W. Smith arranged for some GTR boarding cars to accommodate the homeless. There was no looting and every safe had protected its contents, including one that survived the 1908 fire. Several people sold and left town after this one.

Markus and Co. took charge of the clean-up, which began at once despite discouraging material shortages. New building regulations came into effect and improved fire-fighting equipment was purchased.

Then, at 4am on July 4, Thomas Pink's Tool Mfg. and Shell Plant went up in smoke; the only reason it didn't spread to Pembroke Lumber and the adjacent Dunlop homes was a combination of calm weather and insufficient connecting fuel. With the war still on, Pink's employed 250 people and Pembrokeites were furious, remembering earlier attempts to burn Superior Electrics, a new firm resid-

ing in the Lee Mfg. building and manufacturing shell cartons. But Pink's rebuilt, bigger than ever.

Finally, at 4am on a warm mid-August night, fire #3 broke out. It seems one of Oscar Landriau's livery employees ran out of gas for his Ford and attempted to siphon some from Oscar's Overland. The clever fellow lit a match to see how he was doing. Awakening, people noticed a glow midst the incinerated section of town and wondered what was left there to burn. Oscar's Overland, for one thing . . .

The Wild West Comes East

November 1914. Following a lengthy stakeout, Peter Whiteduck and Anthony Jocko were caught stealing from GTR boxcars near their Golden Lake Reserve. Jocko had been arrested for a similar offence in 1911 and again after he and Pat Partridge sold twenty-nine stolen mink hides to an Eganville buyer for $94. Whiteduck carried no record.

Sunday evening, November 29, 1914. In the Pembroke gaol, Anthony persuaded Peter to help him break out. They convinced turnkey Robert Coxford their toilet didn't work and bludgeoned the guard to death while he was guiding them to another one. Other prisoners banged on the bars, fetching gaoler Brown, who was also set upon and left for dead. Lifting keys, the pair made an escape up William St into White's Bush.

Brown was able to crawl for help. Sheriff Alex Morris responded to the much maligned fire alarm, as did a large segment of the population, most of whom were immediately deputized and sent home for weapons. Those that didn't own guns bought out the two hastily opened stores that sold them.

Meantime, Morris and the most readily available segment of his instant army commandeered GTR transport and systematically scoured the Reserve; those slower to arm ran off in all directions. Finding neither man, the posse picked up Paul Benoit; he was a routine suspect in anything untoward and better than coming home empty-handed.

Monday. The pair were spotted and shot at. Though separated, they escaped. Peter Whiteduck made his way to presumed friends, was given a bed and fell asleep exhausted. He awoke looking up the barrels of several rifles. With lynching a distinct possibility, Morris smuggled his prisoner to gaol. By then, Anthony Jocko's brother Seymour and Tom Sarazin had also been arrested.

Five days later, the mob circled a residence near Killaloe

and waited. At dawn, Anthony Jocko emerged, spotted movement and ran, being felled by rifle fire as he climbed a fence. Mortally wounded—he died thirty hours later in hospital—Anthony asked why they didn't repeat the method used on Peter. We thought you were armed, he was told.

Seymour Jocko got thirty days for receiving stolen goods. Paul Benoit was aquitted of the same charge. Tom Sarazin also went to trial but was discharged when the arresting officer couldn't be found. Peter Whiteduck awaited spring assizes.

May 15, 1915. Chief Justice Sir Glenholme Falconbridge began sharply at 9 am and by 2:30 the case was heard and jury charged. Gaoler Brown had recovered enough to testify. Peter claimed simply to be a follower, responding to Anthony's wishes. Falconbridge didn't buy that and, when the jury came back at 5:15, hung, he bristled, telling them to return with a verdict by 6 pm or else. When the jury was still hung then, the judge declared amazement that "twelve intelligent men, in light of evidence submitted, should not be able to reach a verdict in five minutes." A second trial was ordered for the fall assizes.

November 1915. Peter Whiteduck appeared before Mr Justice Middleton. The lawyers were the same: R.A. Pringle of Ottawa for the Crown and T.M. Costello of Renfrew for the accused. Except for one witness, described as "of little consequence," it was a carbon copy of trial one, including the outcome; ten said guilty, two didn't think so. Despite efforts for a change of venue as a hastening procedure, Whiteduck faced a third trial in Pembroke.

June 1916. Seventy-two prospective jurors were boiled down to twelve good men and true. This time, they had options: murder, manslaughter or not guilty (Peter had pled guilty to a jail-breaking charge). The jury quickly opted for manslaughter and Peter Whiteduck was given thirteen years in Kingston penitentiary; he died there of TB the following summer. Peter's wife predeceased him by six years and four children from the marriage were in an Ottawa home.

Tobias Boland replaced turnkey Robert Coxford. Shortly after Anthony Jocko was killed, his mother died of a fall. In 1918, Anthony's brother, who called himself Jocko Commanda, was killed by a rifle shot while building a canoe with his son.

Chapter 8

REGENERATING

1919/20 to 1921/22

Most hockey leagues restricted teams to dressing ten players. Minor penalties were set at two minutes and majors at five, rather than the old system of leaving penalty time at the referee's discretion. No substitutions were allowed, except in the case of match penalties, after which a player could be replaced when his team had played short-handed for twenty minutes! Now that's a penalty!

Games

1919/20

Pembroke Arenas, under president P.R. Morin and manager Walter Chambers, joined with Arnprior, Almonte and Carleton Place in a revived UOVHL. Through a Central Canada Hockey Association (CCHA) affiliation, league winners finally had a shot at an overall Valley title. Survivors of a UOVHL–St. Lawrence League series would meet Ottawa's best for the new Beach Trophy.

This format crippled Shield competition, which was never properly figured into the equation. While a UOVHL–LOVHL series usually occurred, the *Citizen* never came up with a third Shield until 1927/28, when the

league temporarily switched from Sr to Intermediate classification. The second Shield had mysteriously disappeared during the war.

Renfrew, though belatedly unable to ice a team, donated the Anderson-McKinnon Cup for UOVHL champions. Honouring not only Alfred Anderson and Ian McKinnon but Bill Fishenden and Cameron McKay, all lost in the Great War, this well-intended trophy survived two rocky decades before fading from competition, surfacing years later at an auction. Bought for one dollar, the ornament, doorstop and ashtray eventually became home for an ivy plant.

Though Archie Dimmell returned to Arnprior,. Pembroke gained one of the famed Mulvihills. Michael, twenty-four, set up a dental practice in Pembroke then met Eileen Murray, Tom's daughter, and they married in 1922. Otherwise, the team was local. Nig Jones, who wore a mask, preceeding Jacques Plante by forty years, began the six-game schedule back-stopping the Arenas to a 3-2 win in the Woollen Town. Mulvihill notched the winner, while Dimmell was held scoreless.

Rowan Stewart scored once during his brief comeback, a 5-1 defeat of Almonte. Pembroke lost the return match 1-0 then went down 5-1 in Arnprior, though the latter game was ordered replayed because either Bert Burke or Gray Brunet played under an assumed name. Arenas took both games from Carleton Place, one when Jack Anderson scored in overtime for a 1-0 victory. Pembroke was at 4-1 with the replay still to be go.

Arnprior, manned by goalie Russell Whyte, Dimmell, Domenic Raby, Anatole Daze, Charlie Mulcahy and Bill Mulvihill, needed either a tie or a win to force another game. But Dub Murphy led Pembroke to a 6-4 victory, taking the first Anderson-McKinnon Cup.

St Lawrence champion Brockville won the two-game, goals to count series 15-4, 3-3 (18-7). Ottawa Munitions then clobbered Brockville almost as badly, taking the first Beach Trophy.

Arenas then played a Shield series with Aylmer, Que. Denny McMullen scored twice in the 4-4 opener at MacKay St Arena but goaltender Harold Quinn came up stingy in game two; Aylmer prevailing 7-1 (11-5). Ottawa's Billy O'Hara refereed almost every game Pembroke played.

*****

Having added Vic Ryan, O'Driscoll Legge and Des Irwin, PHS put down two Red Cross Cup challenges from Renfrew to maintain possession. I have no idea who won the town league but looking over a GWVA roster it's hard to imagine them losing even one game.

Ted Behan and Jim Cully led McGill to a Canadian University title, defeating Toronto Varsity 5-4 in the final.

Hugh Lehman enjoyed one of his better seasons in Vancouver while Harry Cameron continued a nomadic existence; going from Toronto to Wanderers to Toronto to Ottawa to Toronto to Canadiens in less than two seasons. Harry then told Habs management to arrange a trade with Quebec in order that he may complete the cycle—they shipped him back to Toronto.

Playing through his usual assortment of injuries, Nighbor led Senators to a Stanley Cup. With the Black Sox baseball scandal on everyone's mind, Frank made several speeches over the off-season defending hockey's honour, saying "If the time ever comes when I have to lower myself to such an extent as to 'fix' games, I shall hand in my uniform and retire."

1920/21

Renfrew almost missed another UOVHL campaign, coming in at the last minute. Under president W.J. Hughes of Carleton Place, the league drew up an eight-game schedule. Again, Moran accepted Arenas presidency.

Jack "Lip" Anderson and Luke Imbleau led Renfrew. Almonte featured slick young forward Ray Edmonds and solid goaltending by Harry Houston, while Carleton Place could not boast a star but several youngsters held promise. Jones and Tario shared back-stopping duties for Arenas while blue-liners Mike Mulvihill and Dave Behan rated second to none. The defensive hockey rarely produced more than five goals a game.

But Arnprior, already strong and having added Dinny Barnes and Jack Gardner, held off County and Creamery Town bids to take the Anderson-McKinnon Cup. They lost the Beach series to Ottawa Gunners and a Shield round with LOVHL champion Hull never developed.

*****

PHS retained the Red Cross Cup a third season, taking permanent possession. New stars were goaltender Mervin McConnell, Milton Kidd, Ivan McDonnell, Dick Williams and Fred Radke. The Radke family later moved to Toronto where their three sons became well-known in sporting circles.

Town hockey was divided into Intermediate and Sr levels, headed by Dave Behan and Wilbert Behan respectively. Pats won the younger group while Father Holly's SCBC took the brand new Behan-Nighbor solid silver Sr trophy. A flood of good young players were appearing now, including Cecil Gallagher, Hubert Whyte, Harry Oshier, Gordon Anderson, Jim Kenny, Lorne Wilson, Anthony Merrifield, Duff Groslouis, Roy Ludgate, Dan Vondette, Joe and Wilfred "Pop" Fournier, and John and Joe Sparling.

An SCBC Jr team played in Arnprior one night and won 4-3, thanks to a hat trick by Dave Trottier. So impressive was Dave's performance, a female Arnprior fan knocked him cold with a 2x4!

The season highlight was an exhibition at MacKay St Arena between Ottawa Senators and Toronto St. Pats, allowing local fans to see Nighbor and Cameron face each other. When the advance ticket window at Van Gene's Music Shop did not open on time, an impatient crowd broke in; Chief Harry Carroll required recruits to restore order. Senators prevailed 8-5 before a packed house.

1921/22

Pembroke dropped the name "Arenas" in favour of just "Srs"; no one used the fancy handle anyway. However, after losing the home opener they went to Almonte from where a Factory Town scribe, reporting for a County Town newspaper, wrote "Pembroke struck a snag when they visited Almonte tonight. The Lumber Kings bit off the short end of a 4-1 score, and were completely eclipsed in every period by the fast playing locals." This is the first time I found a Pembroke team called "Lumber Kings" in print. Even then it was unofficial, like Renfrew Millionaires, and the team actually re-adopted "Arenas" the following year.

Jones played only in the town league, allowing Tario to take over in goal. Other than Jack Anderson, back from a season with Hamilton Tigers, Dub Murphy and Omer Landriault, few of the players had any Sr experience. Bethel played one game and was injured. Though Pembroke beat powerful Carleton Place once, 4-3 thanks to Anderson's hat trick, the team could register only two wins and the second was tainted. Almonte arrived with an ineligible player and, denied his services, trailed 1-0 after twenty minutes. Headed for the dressing room, visiting players tangled with an inebriated fan and refused to appear for further play; Billy O'Hara had no choice but to award Pembroke two points.

After losing the final game 6-1 in Arnprior, Pembroke Srs elected to stay over in the Burns Hotel, an aptly named establishment because it took fire, driving several "scantily clad" players over a balcony.

Carleton Place won almost every game enroute to the Anderson-McKinnon Cup, an anti-climactic occurrence through no fault of the winner. Set for a two-game final with Arnprior, a first in UOVHL play, O&DAHA officials suddenly advanced the dates by two days, conveniencing the city champion as usual. Arnprior refused to adjust, forfeiting the series. The fine Carleton Place team, staffed by future pros Percy "Babe" Morrison and William "Bat" Phillips plus Wilf Beck, Sandy Machlem, Bill Follis,

George Fleming, Joe Moore and goaltender Ivan McIntosh, then lost the Beach round to Ottawa Gunners.

Pembroke Srs won five post-season games in a row, concluding with an exciting 6-4 triumph over Gunners, March 20, 1922.

*****

Even with Hum Lance in nets, SCBC wasn't strong enough to prevent Jim Findlay's El Shadi club from taking the Behan-Nighbor Trophy. The town league was once again a single division, in which brothers Hubert and Russell Whyte both tended goal.

A new Renfrew County high school trophy was donated by the Great War Veterans Association. Only Arnprior and Pembroke competed, PHS taking the final game 4-1. Jim Mulvihill kept goal for both AHS and the Sr team; some of his up-and-coming mates were Willie Close plus cousins Anthony and Ollie Mulvihill. PHS saw Lloyd Ludgate join brother Roy, and Jack Bowden came on board. Defenceman Dick Williams, 160 lbs soaking wet, was heaviest on the team.

Pembroke Alerts began the most prominent decade of ladies hockey in County Town history, invariably on behalf of charity. Organizers throughout that period included Isobel Fraser, Mary Kossatz, Dorothy Walker and Jennie Wilson.

Cameron and Lehman met in the Stanley Cup round, Harry's St. Pats prevailing. Vancouver earned the opportunity by defeating Seattle, where Gordon Fraser had one of his best seasons. Injuries finally kept Frank Nighbor from playing; he participated in only eight games, a problem elbow, courtesy of Sprague Cleghorn, the major reason. This time, and each year for the rest of his career, Frank threatened to quit, convincing neither himself nor anyone else.

Participants

Players really began moving around. Jim McAlindon and Harold Bresnahan found both the game and employment in Temiskaming, a pulp mill community that seldom iced a team without Upper Ottawa Valley representation. Jim later opened his own plumbing business in Cochrane. Milt Horn resigned as assistant town engineer and joined the

Highways Department in Brockville. O'Driscoll Legge enrolled in dentistry at McGill, just as Drs Ted Behan and Jim Cully were graduating. Lindsay Fluker won an NOHA title with Iroquois Falls. Harry Williams enrolled at Belleville Business College and, finally finding a subject he liked, graduated from the surveyors course with honours. Ramsay Morris opened a law office in Leamington. Dave Trottier enrolled at St. Alexanders College, Ironsides, Que. Michael J. Lee moved to Foleyette, Ont.

Richard Gournalle "Betsy" Bethel, a son of druggist William Thomas Charles Bethel who became an optometrist, gave away his sister, Helen Gournalle Bethel, at her wedding. Aside from the lengthy appellations, how often do you see a brother and sister with identical middle names?

Dr Fred Delahey, desperate to get son Charlie's mind on education as opposed to whatever sport was going, enrolled the youngster in Trinity College at Port Hope, twice, but he wouldn't stay.

Dave Behan played, coached, managed, held executive positions and organized sporting events while still finding time to attend games or horse races anywhere between Montreal and Toronto almost every weekend!

Hum Lance would have been the 1921/22 Srs goalie but, having played minor-pro hockey, required amateur reinstatement, which didn't arrive on time. He disappeared that summer. It will never be known whether having recently patented a cigar-making machine had anything to do with it.

Allan Wilson moved with the Forestry from Hatfield, England, to Swa, Burma, where he supervised construction of a sawmill and fourteen miles of elephant-replacing railroad.

Bob Trapp was born in Pembroke on December 19, 1898 but he left at an early age, never to return. In fact, Bob forgot the area so completely he addressed a card to his nephew: Stan Trapp, Pembroke St., Ottawa—and Stan got it! Anyway, Trapp's pro career included four WCHL seasons at Edmonton, one WHL campaign in Portland, then two with Chicago Black Hawks. Tulsa opened a new arena in 28/29; the defenceman moved there and played several seasons of sixty-minute games before retiring. Trapp coached in Niagara Falls N.Y., New Haven, Providence, Fort Worth then Kansas City, where he settled, passing away November 17, 1979.

Lastly, a marginally peripheral participant note:

Being an avid hunter, Frank Nighbor was thus membered in the school of accounting unhindered by accuracy. He was standing watch this day, on the shores of rigid water. A deer, seeking space to throw on afterburners, found ice to its liking and made haste forthwith. Unfortunately, the fleet venison had no way of knowing it was trodding on said human's element. Frank laid down his weapon and commenced hook-checking, forcing his quarry into submission, theory being he had no wish to put holes in the hide.

Adjuncts

The economy was booming. Gas went to 50¢ a gallon, 11¢ higher than the post-WWII price; sugar sold for 30¢ a pound and trappers got $60 for a beaver pelt. Several new sub-divisions sprang up in the County Town and Pembroke St got a facelift. Warren Paving (with Lehman) put down the surface and thirty-eight new lamp standards earned main street a "Great White Way" handle. The community also corrected some confusing street names. There was both an E–W and N–S Elizabeth, so the former became Welland. There were also two William Sts, one of which was renamed Moffat. Did you ever wonder why Herbert St curves past E.A. Dunlop's mansion? Edward Dunlop offered to spend $500 improving the little park opposite if council would permit a bend in the road, giving him more yard to the south of his building. So be it. Incidentally, Dunlop bought Pembroke's first "wireless receiver." The first program heard was a church service from Pittsburgh so Edward sent the minister a donation. Within weeks, there were so many radios about that people began demanding the government ban the menace.

Naturally, as roads improved, speeds quickened. Dr. J.B. Galligan who earlier cranked his car while in gear, allowing it to jump through Sam French's barber shop window, drove the twenty-five miles to Eganville in an incredible time of one hour and forty minutes, drawing gasps all round.

Fire Chief M.J. Neville got so fed up with cars passing his fire engine he asked council to make the practice illegal. Actually, Neville was only "acting chief"; he and Billy Bogart both quit when outsider C.S. Blackler was hired for the now paying job without giving either of the old hands a shot at it. That caused quite a scene, putting residents in mind of several years earlier when, after deciding firemen should get 25¢ a practice, 50¢ a meeting and $2 a fire, meetings developed with amazing regularity and every little flame got royally doused!

Police Chief Harry Carroll resigned too. Daniel MacLachlin, former bodyguard to King Edward, Scotland Yard detective and veteran of the Collingwood and Niagara Falls police forces, was given the $1500 a year position.

W.H. Bone sold the *Standard* to Tom Whalley and moved to Ottawa. *Observer* publisher Dan Jones served a term as mayor while his predecessor, Martin Ringrose, built a three-storey hardware and general store on the corner of Douglas and Tecumseh Sts in Windsor. Bill Ringrose soon sold the *Advance* and joined his ailing father.

Capt. Wm. Murphy, battling low-water docking problems and recovering from being severely crushed by a load of shifting wheat, was given a hard time by the non-Liberal government over his normally automatic five-year ferry licence. He survived it all.

Born in Chelsea, Massachusetts, Bill Roland gave up a long vaudevillian career and became a Pembroke theatre manager in 1913. Shortly thereafter he married Walter Beal's daughter, Edna. The County Town boasted three theatres during Bill's time and he often tended them all. In 1921 he was hit by a shunted rail car, breaking his arm. No sooner was it healed then he fell and broke it again. Roland succumbed to Bright's Disease in April 1924. By the darndest coincidence, Billy Boston died in Los Angeles a few months later. You see, Boston was born and raised just outside Pembroke, had operated the Casino Theatre before Roland did but quit that job to become a vaudevillian! Furthermore, when Bill Roland died he left one blood relative, a sister—who lived in Boston.

Roland's most prominent peer was Joseph Hubert Bruck, who passed away at sixty-two in February 1948. The Luxembourg native arrived with the CNR builders before WWI and either worked for Markus Construction or managed theatres until moving to Ottawa in 1936. He retired in Pembroke after WWII.

Retired Imperial Bank of Canada general manager, Pembroke's William Moffat, died in 1921 at sixty-seven. And third-generation postmaster William Alexander Moffat was sixty-one when he passed away in April 1922. Every business closed for the funeral.

Walter and Ellesworth Smyth opened Pembroke's first dry cleaning plant . . . Pembroke council held a Citizens picnic at Giroux Park (Bell's Shore) to garner public opinion on purchasing the 1300-foot riverfront property. They eventually bought it and Riverside Park was born . . . The largest County Town commercial transaction to date was when MacGuire, Patterson and Palmer (Pembroke) Ltd. bought Pembroke Lumber Co. plus the timber limits and Pembroke Iron Works. This created Canadian Match Co.

Chautauqua Days came to town, twice . . . the whole county voted dry (except Pembroke), licencing bootleggers for another term . . . The gaol went without an inmate for a record one full month . . . January 1921 saw a temperature change of 70 degrees in twelve hours . . . 1922 licence plates went to 23¢ each because they had to be a better product, all the 1921 plates peeled.

When Searchmount Lumber Co. formed a three-team baseball league four axe handles and a plow-share north of SSM all but one player came from Pembroke; Sarsfield Brennan made regular reports.

After a sheep jumped through the *Standard* office window, *Observer* editors did not suggest they knew which publication fleeced its readers.

Did you hear about the fellow that stuck his head into a train compartment and asked for whiskey because a lady had fainted? Then he drained the proffered flask, saying it always upset him to see a woman pass out.

Granddaughter: I won't wash my face.
Grandmother: Naughty, naughty. When I was a little girl I always washed mine.
Granddaughter: Yes, and now look at it.

MP Herb Mackie decided not to run again in 1921. One of his last official acts was raising a $3850 grant to replace that unfortunate clock; the new four-sided beauty was "visible from practically all parts of town." Mackie had spent much of his last term as a British trade–USSR go-between but lack of official English recognition made Lenin less than co-operative. That didn't stop Herb from blaming the old Czar for five thousand deaths a day while he spoke far and wide on behalf of Russian relief. Claiming more crime existed on New York streets than all the USSR, he raised piles of money, and *Financial Post* hackles. The second son of Tom and Jessie (Shaw) Mackie married Delia Shannon, daughter of Mr and Mrs Pat Shannon. They had no children and Herb died in his Ottawa home January 9, 1947 at seventy-one. The Prime Minister and several cabinet ministers attended the Pembroke funeral.

Sergeant Major Percy S. Flinter was born in England. He served in India, Egypt, South Africa and Siberia before retiring. Flinter was working at Pembroke Shook Mills when war broke out so off he went again, only to be shell-shocked and gassed. He recovered and returned home. Through all this, Percy earned the Soudan Medal, Khartoum Medal, Queen's South African Medal and Four Bars, King's South African Medal, Allied Medal, General Service Medal and a DSM. One evening in April 1920, he bid his wife adieu as she left for the theatre with friends, tucked his ten and twelve year old sons in bed then retired himself. The kitchen was in flames when Mrs Flinter came home, her family dead of smoke inhalation.

Sheenboro's Dan Sullivan could be difficult. The thirty-eight-year-old farmer-trapper who lived alone routinely took on a snootful then got in enough trouble to fetch Pontiac County Sheriff B.J. Sloan. Dan told the sheriff during one of those times, if it ever came down to it, he'd never be taken alive.

November 1921. Again, Sloan was paged at his Campbell's Bay office. With his deputy and son, William, the lawman began another tedious trek upriver but their vehicle broke down, necessitating an overnight stay in Chapeau. Next morning, they found Dan armed and barricaded behind his bed. During the room-wrecking melee that followed, B.J. suffered a wound to his nose and William's wrist was injured. Nonetheless, Sloan was able to man-handle Sullivan toward the car, telling his son to shoot if necessary. While being cuffed, Dan slugged the sheriff. William fired low but Sullivan stumbled, taking a bullet in the kidneys; he died within minutes. Next evening, by the light of the moon, neighbours buried Dan Sullivan on his own farm. An investigation exonerated Sheriff Sloan and his son.

1914/15 Debaters. Top to bottom, left to right: Omer Landriault, Emile Martin, Bill Leacy, J.J. O'Brien, Angus Bedard and Jim McAlindon. Art Bourdon, Bill Ringrose, E.J. Lamothe and M.B. (Harold?) Duff. Jack Sarsfield, Dave Behan, Dan Durack, Bedu Morand, Hum Lance, Tom Bresnahan and Tom Murphy. Courtesy Ted White.

Pembroke town council 1915. Many of these council members appear in this book. Council consisted of a mayor, reeve, deputy reeve, plus three councillors each for east, centre and west ward. Here we have Harry S. Bowden, Henry Harwood, Daniel A. Jones, Andrew Hamilton, August Woermke, Bill Bromley, Dr Harry Irwin, Jim Morris, Tom Moffat, Bill Hunter, Willard Beatty and Arthur Leroy Eastcott. Courtesy Moodie Doering.

The Pembroke Electric Light Co.

LIMITED

will supply

HYDRO ELECTRIC POWER

to manufacturers and others desiring the same in large
blocks at prices as low as **$12.00 per H.P.** unrestricted
service.

DUPLICATE GENERATING UNITS.
PRESENT INSTALLATION, 1500 H.P.
10,000 H.P. AVAILABLE.

The Pembroke Electric Light Company, Limited

*The photographs on pages 94 to 105 are
from a booklet entitled "Canada's Next
City," dated June 1, 1915.*
Courtesy Moodie Doering.

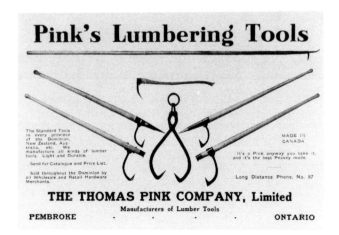

CARNEGIE PUBLIC LIBRARY

THE GENERAL HOSPITAL

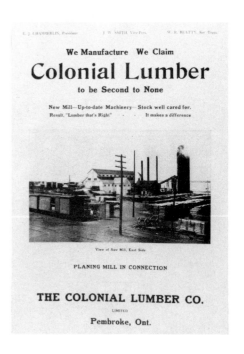

96

W. A. HUNTER.

W. E. WHITE, K.C.

SAMUEL HUNTER.

EDWARD CLARKE.

T.A. Sammon, Proprietor.

98

PEMBROKE'S PROMINENT MEN

MR. PETER WHITE, K.C.

MR. JAMES F. MUNRO.

MR. G. V. WHITE, M.P.

MR. J. M. TAYLOR
Fire Chief and Prominent Odd Fellow

MR. WILLIAM B. MARKUS.

BISHOP LORRAINE

POST OFFICE

ST. COLUMBA'S CATHEDRAL

GRAND TRUNK DEPOT

MR. CORNELIUS CHAPMAN.

MR. A. J. FORTIER.

MR. ALEXANDER MOFFAT.

MR. JOSEPH BOURKE.

MR. ALEXANDER MILLAR.

MR. THOMAS PINK.

MR. THOMAS CLARKE.

MR. ALEXANDER McDONALD.

MR. THOMAS MURRAY.

MR. W. C. KENNEDY.

MR. MICHAEL HOWE.

MR. WALTER BEATTY.

COURT HOUSE

SEPARATE SCHOOL

HIGH SCHOOL

Scene after the June 18, 1918 fire. Courtesy Bill and Mabel Parr.

Top left: Eugene "Ching" Landriault, taken about 1919. Courtesy Marguerite Landriault.

Above: Hugh Lehman. Courtesy Champlain Trail Museum and Hockey Hall of Fame.

Left: Dave Behan and Frank Nighbor, business and sport partners, taken in August of 1921. Courtesy Champlain Trail Museum.

1919/20/21 Pembroke Srs. Top to bottom, left to right: Emmett Spooner, Richard Bethel, Dr Harry Irwin, P.R. Moran, Cecil Tario, Jack Anderson, Wilf Cecile, Denny McMullen, Dr Michael Mulvihill, Omer Landriault, Dub Murphy, Dave Behan, Lawrence "Nig" Jones, J. Fred O'Leary, Walter J. Ross, Jack Sarsfield, Buzz Armstrong, Welly Tario. Courtesy Buzz Armstrong.

1920s. Charles Rattray, frequent sports executive. Courtesy Carol Doran, his grandaughter.

Frank Nighbor in Senators uniform. Courtesy Frank Nighbor Jr.

1920/21 PHS. This club consisted of Harry Williams, Mervin McConnell, Sid Thomson, Roy Ludgate, Vic Ryan, Allan McDonnell. Fred Radke, Ulysses J. Flack, Denny McMullen, Charlie Dunlop, Lorne Wilson. Courtesy Roy Ludgate.

1920/21 SCBC. Tom Carmody, Victor Ryan, Adolph "Duff" Groslouis, Wilfred "Pop" Fournier, Roy Ludgate, John Hunt, Dan Vondette, John Carmody. Anthony Merryfield, Harry Oshier, Father Tim Holly, Joe Fournier, Parnell Duff. Courtesy Roy Ludgate and Joe Houlihan.

1921/22 PHS team. Harry Williams, Bert Armstrong, Sid Thomson (manager), Jack Bowden, Dick Williams, Roy Ludgate, (captain). Ulysses J. Flach (principal), Merv McConnell, Mr. J. Milhausen (teacher). Lloyd Ludgate, Allan McDonnell. Courtesy Pembroke Observer.

1921/22 PHS girls team. Margaret Wilson, Sid Thomson (manager), Bessie Anderson, Allan McDonnell (coach), Janet Jones. Marguerite Gourley, Jennie Wilson, Dorothy Walker. Isobel Fraser, Sybil Workman. Courtesy Pembroke Observer.

Chapter 9

GROWING

1922/23 to 1924/25

Everyone wanted sports and the games were there. Lacrosse enjoyed unprecedented popularity, baseball boomed and high school football was the rage. Now this newer game of hockey, developmentally delayed a decade due to war, was finally coming into its own.

Of several rule changes discussed, few were tried and none survived. One short-lived gimmick was a black forward-pass line drawn across ice twenty feet in front of the goal "to get the puck out of corners."

Games

1922/23

An early team meeting report began "The Arenas hockey club met and . . ." Obviously the name "Lumber Kings," was never official. Robert Coxford headed an operating committee that included Roy Kennedy, Frank Cohen, Charles Rattray, J. Parnell Duff, Tom Benson and J. McQueen. Omer Landriault was named team captain and therefore "coach." Elmer Sparling and Jack Campbell

teamed up to lease MacKay St Arena and actually ran it for several years, eventually donating a trophy for town league competition.

Former Pembroke Srs president P.R. Morin, by then living in Ottawa, was elected O&DAHA president, a position of declining authority as the secretary, Cecil Duncan, was slowly taking control.

The usual UOVHL organizational problems saw Arnprior quietly try to organize an intermediate group directly under OHA authority and Carleton Place threaten to join the Rideau League but, after Almonte dropped out, they settled in again with a twelve game schedule. Another first: a best-of-three championship with the third game on neutral ice. Also, for not showing up for the final game the previous spring, Arnprior forfeited its $50 deposit to Carleton Place.

Pembroke Srs had never actually received the Anderson-McKinnon Trophy won in 1920 nor, apparently, had the other two winners. Incredibly, one stipulation for this so-called league trophy read "60% of receipts from the final game go to trustees for promotion of senior hockey within the town of Renfrew." A debate had raged since day one on this subject and, though trustee A.W. Baird eventually convinced his peers to drop "within the town of Renfrew," there is no record of the trophy being presented, to date.

The Arenas played two pre-season games at Christmas, virtually annual events allowing Pembroke fans to see otherwise unavailable players. This time it was Dr Ted Behan and Dr Jim Cully, the former having a temporary practice at Timmins and Cully interning in Montreal, Wallace McKay and Betsy Bethel, who were home from school. Roy Ludgate missed the season, being in B.C. with his brother, Herb. The first game was with Sudbury, where Wilf Cecile played most of the season. The second ended in a 2-2 deadlock in North Bay; a credible score in that the Bay sported Henry Maracle, Leo Bourgeault, Jack McVicar and Shorty Horne, all eventual NHLers.

When the regular season opened, goals by Anderson and Armstrong gave Pembroke a 2-1 victory over Renfrew. The visitors protested, claiming the goal creases were "inadequately marked" and that neither Buzz Armstrong or Emmett Spooner had amateur cards. Though Spooner missed only the next game and Armstrong never missed a stroke, it was upheld by the league and a post season replay ordered, if necessary. Then the Arenas went to Carleton Place, where Omer Landriault put Fred Murphy out of commission with a wicked check and a Buzz Armstrong–Lloyd Devlin fight precipitated a full scale brawl during which Jim Kenny suffered a severe cut over one eye. The Arenas lost 6-3, but Tario shut Carleton Place out 4-0 in the return match.

Standings were Carleton Place 4-2, Renfrew 3-2-1, Pembroke 3-3 and Arnprior 1-4-1 at the half. Then Arenas first true coach came aboard; old pro Horace Gaul had been handling Ottawa St. Pats but agreed to work with the lightest UOVHL club. This created tremendous interest and fan attendance at practices matched that of games.

Local events were cancelled when Pembroke visited Renfrew for the initial "coached" contest. Jim Kenny, a reluctant-to-pass defenceman, benefitted most from Gaul's tutelage, scoring twice in the 4-1 victory, a feat he repeated when the Arenas upset Carleton Place 4-2 a few nights later. But Carleton Place, led by eventual Maroon "Bat" Phillips, took the return match 7-5.

Lorne Wilson debuted in the season's best game. A Renfrew visit produced sixty minutes of end-to-end action before the home team prevailed 3-1. Tario starred.

Arenas ended the season by taking a pair from Arnprior

while Renfrew, led by Clarence Moore, surprisingly did likewise to Carleton Place, making it necessary to replay that disputed contest. That occured in Carleton Place, February 14, 1923. Emmett Spooner gave Pembroke a 1-0 lead but Moore's goal forced overtime, in which Anderson scored giving Arenas the victory.

That win meant the Creamery Town had to determine second place by replaying the tie with Arnprior. Renfrew won 3-2, knocking a disappointed Carleton Place club to third and out of it.

The Pembroke-Renfrew championship series demonstrated all elements pertinent to hockey of the day, good and bad.

Game One: Pembroke, Monday, February 19, 1923. Omer Landriault scored on Harold Eady following a rink-length dash. Later, Jim Kenny did likewise. Then Renfrew rang one off the crossbar which referee Billy O'Hara called a goal despite lengthy home-team protestations. After Welly injured his thumb, Nig took over and preserved the 2-1 victory.

Game Two: The following Wednesday, in Renfrew. Five hundred Arenas fans paid the railroad $1.65 each to enjoy with eight hundred Renfrew supporters an enormous struggle on superb ice. Late in the scoreless contest, Renfrew's rising star Alton Dick, who was deaf and therefore called "Dummy," scored a disputed goal. Pembroke couldn't match Renfrew's argument of two nights previous so the marker stood, forcing overtime, as the total goals of both games was tied.

This was supposed to be a best-of-three. At least everyone there, except referee O'Hara, thought so. Both clubs were already playing under protest; Pembroke claiming Moore, who had played the previous year in Temiskaming, was ineligible, and Renfrew insisting Dave Behan, who was spare but never played, had no amateur card. Besides, the host club claimed the Arenas had arrived late. O'Hara could find nothing in the rule book about late arrival penalties and he had a telegram from the Registration Board secretary verifying Behan's status. Billy couldn't make an immediate decision about Moore but he did insist on overtime. They played thirty minutes without a goal so O'Hara declared there'd be a third game after all.

An emergency UOVHL meeting saw all protests thrown out and a third game ordered, in Dey's Arena, February 23, 1923.

Game Three: Another dandy. With seven minutes to go,

116

Buzz Armstrong took a pass from Kenny and fired a clean marker behind W. Jolicoeur. Jones, the Pembroke goalie, allowed nothing, securing Pembroke's second Anderson-McKinnon Trophy, in theory anyway. A huge number of fans carried the players off ice; anytime Renfrew is beaten six out of eight games it's cause for extended celebration.

Arenas met Hull in the Shield round. Spooner and Armstrong gave Pembroke a 2-2 moral victory in the Quebec town, where Leth Graham and Jess Ketchum officiated, but Hull prevailed 3-1 (5-3) at MacKay St Arena, thanks to superb goaltending by Kick McCann. With Spooner and Kenny injured, Gaul used Lorne Wilson and Dave Behan, the latter going sixty minutes despite not having played for two years. The difference in this game was Hull's liberal use of spares while Horace Gaul never went to the bench.

Shortly thereafter, Renfrew advised Pembroke it had yet to win the Anderson-McKinnon. County Town officials asked how that could be. In order to win the trophy, they were told, it was necessary to play three games, the last on neutral ice. Was that not precisely what took place? No, insisted Creamery Town authorities, the third game played didn't count; it only determined who advanced and had nothing to do with the trophy itself.

By now you'll believe this: the UOVHL upheld that view and instructed Arenas either to play another game or forfeit their $50 deposit to Renfrew. Let's just say the issue simmered all summer . . .

Post-season matches included another old vs new battle in which Cameron, Horn, McVean and Billy Wallace participated and Jack Poff managed twenty minutes in goal, his first donning of the pads in fourteen years.

Sparling and Campbell gave the boys a banquet and secretary Roy Kennedy announced that, despite giving hospitals $180, Arenas came out of their $3600 budget $187.77 in the black.

*****

Calmax, Independents and El Shadi, using all available players, drew huge crowds to their once a week town-league games. Favoured Calmax, with Nig Jones, barely prevailed over Independents, where goalie Mel "Fats" Larwell was sharp. Other championship team members were the Williams boys, Lorne Wilson, Jack Bowden, another Anderson, named Boyd, and Charlie Delahey, home under his father's watchful eye.

Though PHS still had Dick Williams, Bowden, Carmody, Buzz, Fats and Charlie, they suddenly couldn't score, going winless. Led by Ollie Mulvihill, who got six in a 7-6 defeat of PHS, Arnprior High School took top honours.

Helen Kelly and May Campbell sparked coach Jack Anderson's Arena girls to far more wins than losses.

The last game in MacKay St Arena was played April 12, on excellent ice. It was a strange year for weather. Murphy was running his ferry on April 8 but on April 18 they were hauling logs across on sleighs!

Ted Behan had a great season in Timmins. He scored five in a 7-5 victory over Lindsay Fluker's Iroquois Falls team and when they met in NOHA play-offs, Ted notched an overtime winner at 4am! The game was not that long, but Timmins didn't arrive until 1am.

Cameron tailed off in Toronto but Lehman enjoyed one of his best Vancouver years. Nighbor was never better, leading the Senators past Edmonton and Hugh's gang to a Stanley Cup. Returning home, the team stopped in Pembroke, where coach Petie Green said, "Ottawa won because Nighbor was there . . . imitators of the Ottawa system failed simply because they could not bring out a man like Nighbor."

1923/24

Robert Coxford and Roy Kennedy held their executive positions and sporting goods store owner Cecil Bailey came on board for the first of many times. J. Parnell Duff became manager and Dave Behan coach.

Ted Behan moved to New Haven; Jim Cully joined him and they both had exceptional seasons. Charlie Delahey began with Brockville's Albert College and finished at Upper Canada College. Roy Ludgate returned to Temiskaming and Lindsay Fluker continued with Iroquois Falls. Bedu Morand considered unretiring but changed his mind. The team expected Wilf Cecile back but he played in Shaunavon, Saskatchewan instead. However, Jack Anderson gave up a notion to extend a Banff holiday over winter and Denny McMullen returned from Renfrew.

A four hour UOVHL meeting November 21, 1923 saw the league reverse its decision and order Renfrew to return Pembroke's $50. When the ODHA agreed, for a change, Arenas eventually got the money, but no trophy. Arnprior dropped out while Munitions and Almonte applied to join the league. Munitions, playing out of Carleton Place, was accepted but the league decided Almonte had insufficient players. Then Renfrew pulled out, after it was discovered they had been negotiating with Arnprior and Almonte to form another league. When asked, Arnprior said they hadn't quit, they'd been shoved. The ODHA met on the subject and a two-division UOVHL was born: Pembroke, Renfrew, Arnprior and Almonte, and Carleton Place, Perth, Smith's Falls and Munitions. There would be twelve games. To save money they decided on local officials; twenty-nine-year-old Luke Imbleau and Lip Anderson handled most Renfrew games while Billy Wallace and Dave Behan, with help from Dr Mike Mulvihill, did likewise in Pembroke. Dave Behan refereed games for teams which he also coached for many years, with rarely a complaint.

Pembroke opened by blowing a 2-0 lead in Renfrew with five minutes to go, losing 3-2. After splitting a pair with Arnprior, Omer Landriault and Jack Anderson suddenly took off for Temiskaming, giving Des Irwin a chance to play. But it was Buzz Armstrong who insured Renfrew didn't repeat the opening night performance; he fired all his team's goals in a 4-1 return match victory.

However, neither Buzz nor Jim Kenny liked to pass, a tendancy that drew the ire of fans. When Almonte visited with just six players and only Charlie King of star quality, they won by concentrating on the puck carrier. Arenas never threw a pass all night. Behan was so incensed he suited up for the return match, scoring an overtime winner.

Dave continued to play and Arenas began throwing the puck around, taking five shots on Harold Eady for every one Renfrew fired at Tario in the next game. Pembroke won 4-1 while Buzz and Jim discovered they could both pass and score, sharing the goals. Bill Mulvihill played well and defenceman Dick Williams, enjoying his only full season of Sr hockey in Pembroke, steadily improved.

Then, a dark spot appeared on Arenas' rather proud history. Locked in second place, the team took few regulars to a meaningless final game in Almonte. Fats Larwell and a collection of high schoolers were hammered 16-6; a match ignored in local papers but the *Almonte Gazette* rightfully tore strips off the visiting team.

The Renfrew-Pembroke title round was a two-game total goal affair. They met first in MacKay St Arena February 18, 1924 where fourteen hundred fans watched McMullen feed Armstrong for the game's lone goal. Tario earned the shut out.

Game Two in Renfrew began at 11:20pm, thanks to a snowstorm. Actually, that's when the train arrived; proceedings got underway at 12:21am, but not a soul complained given the quality of play. When referee Jesse Ketchum disallowed an early Pembroke goal, manager Duff's argument got the umpire changed but didn't preserve the marker. McMullen tied the game four minutes after Bob Perry gave Renfrew a 1-0 lead. From that point Tario had perhaps his finest hour. The 1-1 final score gave Pembroke the round 2-1, and division title. The old rivals had met six times, Pembroke holding a 4-1-1 margin and 13-6 edge in goals.

Munitions, led by Happy Hooper, ran away with the other division then buried the Arenas 3-1 and 11-3. Hotel Pembroke hosted both clubs to a banquet at which no trophies were awarded. The Arenas finished the season playing a H&H with Temiskaming. Since Peter Dunlevy, Emmett Spooner, Anthony Merrifield, Roy Ludgate and Jack Anderson were all with the mill town, you couldn't tell one team from the other. Louis Berlinquette, having returned from Saskatoon, refereed both games.

Helen Kelly, the cheery chick from Creighton Mines attending school in Pembroke, was elected president of the girls Arenas. Bill Labow and Bill Mulvihill coached them through several games, one being a 7-0 loss to Ottawa Alerts, a team that sported one Shirley Moles, described as being the equal of most male players.

Arnprior and Renfrew high schools peaked while PHS hit bottom.

El Shadi withdrew from the town league, organizing a Jr club called Tuxis that competed mostly in Pembroke, transportation being such that even a trip to Beachburg required billoting. Dave Behan held the three-team town league chair, Calmax taking the Behan-Nighbor Trophy despite losing star performer Jack Bowdens to Renfrew.

A CNR club won the first Industrial League title.

Lehman spent another season in Vancouver while Cameron switched allegiance to Saskatoon Crescents of the WHA.

On March 11, 1924, Canadiens defeated Senators 4-2 in Ottawa, taking the Stanley Cup. During the game and before 12,000 fans, Gov. Gen. Byng presented the first Hart Trophy, donated by Dr D.A. Hart of Montreal, to Frank Nighbor. Though not one of Frank's better seasons, he still won the sports writers vote over Sprague Cleghorn by a single ballot, 37-36. The new award was displayed in E.B. Leacy's store window all summer.

1924/25

Arenas gave some thought to hiring a coach and allocated $500 for the purpose, but, after considering former Ottawa pro and Queen's mentor R.H. Lowrey, decided they couldn't afford one after all. So Dave Behan became team president, manager and coach, not to mention heading up the town league. The year held promise; Peter Dunlevy came down from Temiskaming and Jim Cully returned home but Wilf Cecile seemed determined to play anywhere but in Pembroke; he suited up with Arnprior.

Renfrew's Tom Costello became UOVHL president with Dave Behan his vice. Though Almonte dropped out the schedule remained at twelve games, with a re-established residency date of December 15.

After the annual Christmas-New Years exhibitions, Emmett Spooner decided to come on board. Pembroke opened in Renfrew, where Bert Lindsay was now coach, and got roughed up 8-3. Clarence and Harry Moore dominated a game leniently officiated by inexperienced Domenic Raby.

With Dr Cully and Gordon Anderson, Arenas were strong defensively but had trouble scoring. After losing six of seven games, Behan went out and got new red and white sweaters, switched from Tario to Dunlevy and shuffled line-up positions, before meeting Lindsay's powerhouse. It worked; Cully scored twice and Arenas hung up a 3-1 victory. However, they lost Spooner with an eye injury and though Anthony Merrifield returned home the club failed to develop any consistency. Tario went back in goal and performed brilliantly during a 2-1 win in Arnprior but, generally, the goal keeping of Russell Whyte and scoring efforts of Ray Barnes gave the Woollen Town a decided edge. Arenas finished last, taking some solace in a final game 6-2 defeat of Renfrew. The Creamery Town swept Arnprior and Carleton Place aside enroute to UOVHL honours. Pembroke played two post-season exhibitions during which Lorne Wilson saw action.

*****

Nig Jones and the Andersons gave Calmax a third straight town league title and permanent possession of the Behan-Nighbor Trophy. Sparling and Campbell put up a cup for the new Jr division of Tuxis, SCBC, PCI and Scouts, the latter running away with it. This meant Calvin Church enjoyed winners in Both divisions. Calmax manager Sid Thomson received the Sr trophy from Dave Behan at a high-spirited banquet, while Scouts captain Bert Robinson accepted the new award from Elmer Sparling. It was a rare bright moment for Presbyterians; a vote favouring union with United worshippers caused die-hards to hold services in the Opera House.

*****

PHS had another poor GWVA Cup year, mainly because of an injury to Bert Anderson. He was rounding the net in practice and caught Larwell's goal-stick in the eye; there was a real danger of losing it for many days. A bright spot for the team was the spirited play of Vinnie McDonald.

*****

Arena girls, led by the scoring of Helen Kelly and Ella Kossatz, played often and lost but once. The rest of the team consisted of May Campbell, May Kenny, Lois Thompson, Julia Shields, Mary O'Donnell, Dorothy Murphy, Amanda Patzwald, Annie Bunke, Beatrice Ricket, Peggie Green, M. Ricket, Mary Lee, Keitha Fraser, Maxine Switzer, Margaret McCauley, Ann Behnke, Mona Thomas, Alma Boshart, Ida Smith, Grace Martin, Margaret Sullivan and Muriel Workman.

*****

At a specially arranged game between Ottawa Senators and members of the famous Boucher family, held March 25, 1925, in Ottawa, Lord and Lady Byng presented the first Lady Byng Trophy to Senators captain Frank Nighbor. With the inscription "To Encourage Clean Sport," it too spent the summer in Leacy's window. This was not a great year for Frank as he suffered a severe skate cut on the leg, putting him out for two weeks, a long time then. In fact, the whole team was shook up in a train crash near Perth. Lehman also had an injury-shortened campaign but Cameron enjoyed great success in Saskatoon

Participants

Popular town league player Frank Deloughery graduated from St. Augustine's Seminary and became a priest in Japan. Allan Wilson left Burma and moved to Vancouver. O'Driscoll Legge opened his dental practice in Timmins. Charles Devlin (1919 club) married a Detroit girl and took up residence in Cobalt.

Pembroke and New Westminster, B.C. shared grief

when Dr. Robert H. Scott died January 23, 1923 of a cerebral hemorrhage at forty-one. Robert had married a Victoria girl and they raised three children while he built a large practice in the suburban Vancouver community where he served as reeve for a decade. His excellent reputation was further enhanced by working twenty-four hours a day during the 1918 influenza epidemic, a dedication recognized at length by the *Coquitlam British Columbian*. Flags flew at half mast while the entire Board of Trade attended Dr. Scott's funeral.

Vic Ryan left Pembroke in the spring of 1923, taking a job at Winnipeg with CP airlines. He stayed there till 1949 then moved to Fort William, home of his wife Betty (Baird), and became a private mail contractor. They celebrated a fiftieth anniversary before Vic died in 1981.

Billy and Retta (Dickson) Williams had six children; Welland, the outstanding athlete killed overseas, Murray, a lawyer, Harry, the PHS star who became a surveyor, Dick, Margaret and Tom. William Welland Dickson "Dick" Williams enrolled in medicine at Toronto University and had locked up a defensive position with Conn Smythe's Varsity Grads but found noon hour and mid-afternoon practices interfered with studies. Upon graduating, Dick opened a general practice in Pembroke. The Doctor, who always felt he should have specialized in osteology but never did, lost a battle with cancer November 4, 1988.

Billy Williams, a semi-professional lacrosse player in Ottawa before becoming a member of Pembroke's first hockey team, opened a law office with Peter White in 1892. He became town solicitor and counsel for the railroad, eventually partnering with son Murray. William Henry "Billy" Williams, whose love affair with thoroughbreds earned him Royal Winter Fair judge status, died in 1947 at the age of seventy-nine.

Dr Michael Mulvihill, the last Pembroke player to wear "double-enders," quit playing after 23/24. He and Eileen raised five children, one being Terry, a hockeyist of note after WWII. Eileen died of a heart attack in 1953 and two years later Mike married Dr. Higginson's widow, Mary. Michael actually outlived his oldest son, Michael Jr, by two months, passing away at age ninety, December 22, 1985.

After five campaigns with Pembroke Srs, John Tennant "Jack" Anderson moved to Detroit, eventually becoming a foreman at Briggs Body Works. One of five children born to Mr and Mrs Jim Anderson, Jack married Hawkesbury's

Alma Jolly and they raised three youngsters. He died suddenly, April 22, 1953, at age fifty-four.

Louis Berlinquette, born in Papineauville, Que., lived most of his early life in Mattawa but made Pembroke a second home. The sixteen-year pro who played twelve seasons with the Montreal Canadiens, completed a then record career of 348 games with seventy-three goals in a checking role. Following a game at Ottawa January 18, 1922, Louis entrained to Pembroke, married Mary Culhane at 5:30am and, after a wedding breakfast, departed for a game in Montreal that evening. The couple moved to Gogama in 1940 where Louis became a Lands and Forests Chief Ranger, and then the Scaling Supervisor. He retired in 1957 and died June 2, 1959 at sixty-seven.

After the *Saskatoon Phoenix* did an article on Pembroke's contribution to pro hockey, including such players as Lehman, Cameron, Nighbor, Reise, Trapp, Fraser and Allan Wilson, Winnipeg's Lorne Ranson determined his old home town of 9000 souls ranked third in Canada, behind the city he lived in, and Ottawa. Ottawa remains the birthplace of more professional hockey players than any other community.

Adjuncts

When WWI veteran Christopher O'Kelly came home with his Victoria Cross, he settled in Winnipeg. Then, while prospecting in the Red Lake area, he and a friend were lost. The following spring, sourdough T.J. McManus found O'Kelly's body, washed ashore. One Pembroke native accidently found the remains of another, over a thousand miles from their original home.

A year after that, twenty-two-year-old Wally Stoqua, Anthony's brother, drowned while tending his traps where the Muskrat and Indian rivers meet. He surfaced twelve months later, right under the Pembroke St bridge.

Just above that bridge was the unused and deteriorating Pembroke Milling dam. During that weird spring we just described, the dam was partly destroyed by an ice flow unlike any seen before or since. Town council refused to help Milling Co. owner Alex Miller make repairs so residents had the pleasure of watching the dam gradually wash away over decades.

Even further upstream, the third Mary St bridge was opened under blazing lights and dancing feet. From budget to finish, costs tripled, just like today. Mary St is named after

Mary Moffat, granddaughter of Pembroke's first crown lands agent and village clerk, Alexander Moffat. Bridge number four came in the 1960s.

The summer and fall of 1923 produced some unusual accidents. An eight year old was badly injured when hit by a bicycle and a child half that age survived a kick from a horse. An Allumette Islander was killed by a bull. Two entire families were injured in separate accidents when their cars upset, and later a car loaded with eight people slammed into a pole, killing Reginald Chambers and causing Dr. James Mandeville to lose an eye. Also, *Ouiseau* steamship fireman Arthur Menard was shot from shoulder to hip when a passenger on the deck above accidently let his rifle off through the floorboards. After several days at death's door, Arthur miraculously recovered.

Buzz Armstrong's brother, William Bertram Armstrong, was a superb athlete, though he played little hockey. Bert turned his ankle while walking home from a baseball game and was therefore obliged next evening to watch his mates from the stands. Wouldn't you know it, he took a line drive smack between the eyes. Bert survived to pursue an interesting life: he gave up teaching to serve in WWII, then remained with the Far East repatriation forces, was a Department of Defence representative at the Geneva Convention and served a U.N. advisory group following the Korean War. Bert retired in 1956 and died a decade later at age sixty-three.

Three Royal Humane Society bravery medals were earned during this period. Bell employees Joe Carmody and Graham Thompson were working in Kingston when the former heard a cable snap and looked up to see his partner falling from thirty five feet. Carmody braced himself and Thompson bounced off his back. Joe apologized for Graham's minor injuries, saying he hadn't positioned himself properly. Number two winner was Constable Aime Jette who saved Mabel McDonald and Margaret Irving from drowning at Bell's Shore. Then young athlete Howard Riley picked up number three. When a group of Canadian Match employees dashed across the CPR tracks, Muriel Switzer got her heel stuck and, with a freight bearing down, fainted. Howard, who happened to be passing by, leapt across the tracks, pulling Muriel free; his foot actually glanced off the engine cow-catcher.

August Maves blasted Halloween pranksters with bird-shot, which cost him $57.75 . . . the town's second bus service was short-lived but a new one to Ottawa that only took

five hours proved a good alternative to the railroad . . . Phone service was extended to Mattawa, a town that almost totally burned December 2, 1925. Yearly municipal elections were finally moved from January to December . . . Two earthquakes shook things up and a storm nearly washed Murphy's ferry down the rapids. Librarian Alma Beatty opened the library building the year round . . . The fine for having no tail light went to $5 . . . Creation of Centenary Park began in 1925. Islanders went on another bridge tear . . . wanted notices came off post office walls, eliminating the only place some people ever saw their picture.

Having decided to build a new Cottage Hospital, governors considered the name Pembroke Protestant Hospital for a while. But "Cottage" remained until the wonderfully imaginative "Civic" handle was force-fed fifty odd years later.

October 1925 saw PCI replace the old PHS. The new school came within a whisker of being at O'Kelly Park but Mrs O'Kelly belatedly insisted on selling the whole eighteen acres at once. The Board then considered several locations before buying and demolishing the huge Mackie home at Pembroke and Christie Sts. But an educational facility would get the racetrack–fairground–circus site eventually; Champlain High School was built there in the early 1960s.

Parents paid stiff fines for not keeping youngsters under sixteen in school while Magistrate Stewart gave suspended sentences to eleven-and fourteen-year-olds for stealing guns and ammunition worth $600. Crown Attorney J.M. Burritt blasted him in open court for disparity. Stewart then gave a lad six months for stealing $20, perhaps inspired by another judge who imprisoned a postal employee three years for stealing "a posted letter," saying he'd gone easy on him as he was a wounded war veteran.

Fire Chief Blackler quit and Collingwood's Bob Dey took the job (Bob Deys in that family have reached eight in a row—and counting). Police Chief MacLaughlin also quit, his successor being William McKee, the most colourful and controversial chief Pembroke ever had. McKee arrived by way of Edinburgh, Winnipeg, Sudbury and Renfrew, beginning the $1800 a year job in bed with La Grippe. No sooner was he up and about, than he had a motorcycle accident, delaying orientation for a while.

April 1923: Tom Whalley sold the *Standard* to former *Wiarton Echo* publishers, A. Logan and Son. Just about then Dan Jones accepted his first beer ad. This was one month after the first of several immensely popular car shows. Of seventy-three available companies (already down to thirty-eight by 1925), only Ford, Studebaker and Chevrolet were not represented. McLaughlin Motor Co. distributed the first Ontario road maps and Grey Dort introduced cars in "Lake Louise Blue." Until then, you could have any colour you wanted as long as it was black.

Notable deaths were those of George Burns and Thomas Pink. In 1909, Burns and J.S. Wilson discovered what is now Dome Mines. George died in September, 1924 and Thomas the following February. Born in England, Pink came to Pembroke at age twenty-four from Perth, Ontario to begin a steel-working business which became one of the County Town's biggest enterprises.

Prominent Pembrokeites: D.P. Mulligan left the Windsor Hotel in Montreal to manage New York's Waldorf-Astoria in 1925. Paul Martin led his Toronto University debating team to Pittsburgh for the first ever Canada–U.S. competition, winning by seventy points. Senator Martin died in Windsor September 14, 1992 at age 89. Dr. Wilbert Fraser, whose practice was in Ottawa, married Alexandra Williamson Sterling, U.S. ladies golf champion three years running. Innes Bramley set a ladies world high jump record of 411", in Toronto . . .and Paul Quesnel, Ottawa's ski jumping champion and grandson of A.J. Fortier, succumbed to pleurisy at twenty.

We end with two runaways. When the PLC mill hoist blew off steam, a company team bolted with an empty wagon up Henry St and the full length of the main drag on a busy Saturday afternoon without hitting anything. The same cannot be said for what may be Pembroke's most spectacular example of unscheduled equine departure. Bill Hein's matched team took off westerly from Middleton's Feed up Pembroke St, connecting broadside with another outfit driven by Roy Tennant, who suffered the twin indignities of seeing his sleigh sliced in two plus being dragged forty feet on his nose. Hein's chargers never broke stride, disposing of the wagon when they broke a steel post off at ground level in front of the Opera House. Unencumbered, they eventually ground to a way up in the west end, purely from exhaustion. Neither steed suffered a scratch.

122

Chapter 10

HARVESTING

1925/26 to 1926/27

In lieu of rule changes, which were insignificant, here's Arenas 1925 statement:

INCOME:		
	Balance on hand	51.62
	Dance proceeds	132.50
	Gates	1827.02
	Gross receipts, special train	358.35
	TOTAL	2369.49
EXPENSES:		
	Guarantee to visitors	185.00
	Supplies and repairs	346.02
	Travel and hotel	342.00
	Special trains	435.08
	Rink rental	704.12
	Amusement tax	130.33
	League fees and donations	10.00
	Telephone and telegraph	12.92
	Advertising	99.35
	Referee fees	97.00
	Medical services	42.00
	Misc	14.49
	TOTAL	2418.31
	LOSS	(48.82)

Games

1925–26

Elmer Sparling ended his partnership with Jack Campbell, leaving Jack to run MacKay St Arena alone. Dave Behan turned over team presidency to Robert Coxford, then became UOVHL president the next day. Arenas treasurer Roy Kennedy took on the chore of league secretary as well.

Joe Freeman, a Belleville native who had been refereeing in Port Arthur, was hired to coach. Joe held clinics for everyone, including the very active girls Arenas.

The UOVHL rejected three applications: Hull, as they did not want to expand to Quebec; Almonte, on the basis of player quality; and Carleton Place, because the ODHA wouldn't let them leave the Rideau Group despite better train connections. So, there were three teams and eight games again. Bill O'Hara and Bill Smith did most of the officiating.

Coach Freeman was a spectator for the opening exhibition, a 9-0 clobbering of visiting Ottawa Royal Canadians during which Buzz lit the red light five times and Charlie Delahey made his annual appearance. Fans were tickled to see Roy Ludgate, Duff Groslouis and Wilf Cecile all back in proper uniform. Most pleasing was the solid blueline play of Dr. James Ritchie, Dr. I.D. Cotnam's new assistant.

Arenas began by thumping Renfrew 6-2, with Denny McMullen registering a hat trick and Tario tending goal. Then superb goaltending by Jim Mulvihill provided Arnprior with 3-1 and 3-2 victories over our heroes. Jim's cousins, Anthony and Ollie, helped form a solid Arnprior corp that included old pro Hank Stavenow and reliable Archie Dimmell.

Arenas continued the down slide by losing 7-3 in Renfrew, partly because Tario played most of the game with blurred vision thanks to a shot in the eye. At this point Nig Jones joined the team and helped halt the slide with a brilliant return match display, his club winning 3-1.

Next, Wilf Cecile almost singlehandedly defeated his former Arnprior teammates 4-2. Then McMullen did likewise when Pembroke upset Renfrew 5-2, and not all shots went in; one bounced off Harold Eady's eyebrow, putting the Renfrew goalie in hospital with a severe gash. RHS netminder Wally Easton, playing forward on the Creamery Town team because he couldn't bump the veteran, finished that contest in his preferred position.

The Arenas then lost 2-1 in Arnprior before clinching first place by virtue of an exciting 5-3 overtime victory in Renfrew. Buzz Armstrong registered four of the five goals. Dr Jim Cully, who generally gave way to Lorne Wilson for road games, suited up for this important schedule closer and tangled with Lip Anderson, a battle that cleared the benches and resulted in both men being ejected by referee Jim Evraire. Jim Kenny broke two ribs later in the contest.

The Pembroke Arnprior title series began with McMullen firing the first three goals and Armstrong the last four of a 7-1 victory. But Wilf Cecile took quite a pounding from his former teammates and couldn't answer the bell for Game Two, being replaced by Lorne Wilson. Buzz Armstrong and Archie Dimmell staged quite a show then, each registering hat tricks in the 5-5 tie that gave the Arenas another UOVHL title, 12-6 and Anderson-McKinnon Cup!

Rockland and Pembroke began the OVHL two-game championship at MacKay St Arena, a match that ended 2-2 after an erratically bouncing shot eluded Jones as time ran out. But Nig was perfect in game two, his counterpart only one goal less so when he deflected a rebound off the backboards into his own net. That 1-0 win gave Pembroke its first overall title since 1911.

Rockland officials provided a superb post-game spread then chauffeured their guests to the train at Bourget, Quebec. There, hospitality ceased, as they were refused entry to the CPR station and several players arrived home with frozen feet.

Arenas' next game was against Chesterville, a fast but individualistic team that succumbed easily, 7-1, 4-3 (11-4). However mixed the reports on coach Joe Freeman, he at least had his club playing as a team. Mind you, with Dub Murphy in Peterborough and Jim Kenny injured, only the humorously self-deprecating Armstrong was "singularly bent."

Alf Smith's hand-picked Ottawa Gunners met Pembroke in Beach Trophy play. Seventeen hundred fans packed MacKay St Arena for the opener, a contest that ended 3-3, thanks mostly to a fine effort by Wilf Cecile. Actually, Pembroke scored five goals but referee Alf Smith disallowed two of them. That's right, Gunners coach Alf Smith refereed despite long and loud protests by the home team. Only Pembroke's refusal to appear for game two resulted in the hiring of Toronto's Harold Mitchell. The Auditorium's largest crowd to date, over seven thousand, saw Mitchell call a sound game; Chuck O'Connor plus Tom and Harold O'Neill led the Gunners to a 5-1 (8-4) victory.

Joe Freeman missed his team's banquet, being called to referee the Allan Cup final, where Port Arthur defeated Toronto Varsity and Dave Trottier. But one hundred and fifty did attend, including Louis Berlinquette, Harry Cameron, Gordon Fraser and Frank Nighbor, who sported his second Lady Byng in a row. Players were given club bags and Mayor J. Parnell Duff used the occasion to present Howard Riley with his Humane Society medal. Arenas held the annual meeting shortly thereafter, electing Cecil Bailey president and declaring a 1925/26 profit of $13.

*****

Town league matches, with the Sunshine Orchestra regularly in attendance, featured such new blood as Jim Levoy, Emile Martin, Tom Ferneyhough, Joe Fournier, Reg Fraser and Jack Follis. Cecil Gallagher back-stopped his SCBC team to a narrow win over the Elks for the new Kittner Trophy. The Sparling-Campbell intermediate division, with the likes of Hugh Henderson, Charlie Knott, Joe Houlihan,

Tom Fitzgerald, Allan Ziegel and Aime Jette Jr, was taken by Allan Anderson's Scouts.

It was a poor season for Both Arena girls and PHS teams. Renfrew held the GWVA cup and declined all challenges until March, maintaining possession even then. Organized public school hockey was just becoming a fact of life.

1926/27

The annual ODHA meeting, in October, was a stormy affair. Increasingly bitter over favouritism toward city teams and officials, rural leagues unanimously sought to separate from the parent body. But pleas, even to CAHA secretary W.A. Hewitt, fell on deaf ears. However, the five "country cousins" were reclassified "intermediate," while city clubs remained Sr; Beach Trophy winners were still to come from a series between survivors of the two groups. Dr H.S. Hutt of Chesterville was elected ODHA president, while Leth Graham and George Powers were put in charge of officiating.

Meantime, Carleton Place was finally given permission to join the UOVHL.

Jack Campbell continued to manage MacKay St Arena. Pembroke Srs, still officially Arenas but often called Lumber Kings, had Louis Berlinquette lined up to coach when an offer arrived from Quebec City of the Canadian-American League that Louis couldn't refuse. So Dr Jim Cully took on the job, a potentially difficult task given that McMullen and Cecile turned pro with Windsor and Eddie Carmody, following a very promising 25/26 debut, moved to Toronto. Buzz also considered an outside offer but decided on Another year at home.

Charlie Delahey missed the Christmas exhibitions but town league graduates Harvey Schultz, John Workman, Gerry McLeod and goaltender Cecil Gallagher performed well during wins over Sudbury and Rockland. When Arenas opened the schedule in Renfrew, Cully had added Roy Ludgate's younger brother, Lloyd, to the line-up; all Lloyd did was get both goals in a 2-1 victory. This was the first time reserved seats were sold for a Renfrew hockey game.

Suddenly Carleton Place received a Rideau League schedule from secretary C.L. Comba of Almonte. Well, Carleton Place returned the document, so Comba took it up with the ODHA (still technically O&DAHA). Sure enough, that august body had reversed its previous decision by ordering the Junction Town back into Rideau League action and, when Carleton Place refused to comply, outlawed the entire

UOVHL!

Few could believe this manic manoeuvre by Ottawa Valley hockey's ivory tower. But when all UOVHL players were ordered to sign with "the nearest legitimate team" by January 20, 1927 or "hang em up," valley scribes got on the case: " . . . several Mussolini's in the hockey world down Ottawa way are ultimately due for a bump and by the time they recover someone else will be sitting in the seats of the high and mighty,"wrote one. Even the *Citizen* and *Journal* blasted their local hierarchy, the latter saying "it was not a just decision" and the O&DAHA should move "to the point of ridding the organization of the elements which are responsible for such reactionary situations."

The affair concluded with a demonstration of face-saving second to none. A CAHA committee, under the direction of secretary W.A. Hewitt, was sent to resolve the problem. First, it upheld the remarkable O&DAHA ruling, then asked all UOVHL clubs to apply for reinstatement! This was done. Then Carleton Place had to appoint an all new executive, which was also done. Additionally, Almonte was to join the UOVHL next year. Lastly, the 26/27 UOVHL champion, as punishment, could not compete beyond divisional playdowns. Noone agreed with that edict, of course, and the CAHA backed off.

When the season finally opened, Arenas took the home opener 6-2 over Renfrew, Buzz recording four goals. Nig Jones was happy because coach Cully proved able to prevent Jim Kenny's repeated circling in his own zone, a possessive habit that earned Jim the nickname "Corkscrew."

A home and home with Arnprior was memorable. In the Woollen Town, opposing goaltenders Cecil Gallagher and Leo Sargeant sparkled, Ollie Mulvihill scoring the only goal with 1:15 minutes left. But then Cecil took off for Temiskaming and Jones caught the flu, forcing Welly Tario into action for the second game. Allan McDonald gave Pembroke a 2-1 victory by firing the winning shot while Gordon Anderson skated through the Arnprior goaltender, sparking a full-scale donneybrook.

The Arenas then beat the Junction Town 5-4, despite a hat trick by one of Carleton Place's best ever, Carl "Buzz" Williams. Jones returned to action but he passed out at game's end. Actually, Pembroke played Carleton Place three in a row, winning the next two 4-1 and 7-1 with Gallagher returning for the latter contest. Once again, Kenny learned that reputations die hard, the newspaper reporting, "Yes— Jim Kenny actually passed the puck to Roy Ludgate for a goal!'' (Roy brought the house down one night by immediately making a souvenir of Jim's infrequent generosity.)

The press didn't let up either, though Armstrong and Kenny tallied two goals each in a 5-1 defeat of Arnprior at MacKay St Arena. The suggestion was made they could learn something from a McDonald–Anderson passing play that produced goal #5.

Arenas lost 5-0 in Arnprior, when Ollie scored four. They then secured first place with a 4-1 win in Carleton Place before finishing the schedule by losing twice to Renfrew.

With a pair of league games to be played and positions two to four undetermined, it was learned the UOVHL hadn't established a play-off format, creating protest potential in both matches. Neither Arnprior nor Renfrew gracefully accepted substitute referee Jesse Ketchum over the scheduled Leth Graham for one game, nor did Arnprior think it right that Carleton Place was short of player cards for the other.

This resulted in a meeting, of course. Ketchum was declared an acceptable replacement for Graham but Carleton Place indeed didn't have proper cards and thus were disqualified. This automatically pitted the Creamery and Woollen Towns against one another in the first round.

Final standing: Pembroke 7-5-14, Renfrew 6-6-12, Carleton Place 6-6-12, Arnprior 5-7-10. Buzz Williams had 16 goals, Ollie Mulvihill had 15, Buzz Armstrong and 13. Jones played seven games, Gallagher four and Tario one for Pembroke; Carleton Place's Ivan McIntosh and Leo Sargeant of Arnprior back-stopped all their team's matches, while in Renfrew Harold Eady faced the music ten times and Wally Easton twice. Carleton Place scored the most at forty seven.

Arnprior beat Renfrew 3-1 and 3-1 in two tense games. The winners even brought their own water into enemy territory for fear of being drugged.

Yet another protest. Renfrew didn't like Arnprior using Anthony Mulvihill. At first glance, that would seem ridiculous, as Tony was a native. However, close scrutiny showed the Arnprior star began 26/27 in Temiskaming and finished in Ottawa; this play-off being Tony's initial home town competition. That was in conflict with the residency rule, so Arnprior countered by claiming Anthony rated student exemption.

I relate this story because the resulting meeting is a classic example of how the O&DAHA fueled animosity over an issue that should have been a simple executive decision. The organization first disallowed Arnprior's flimsy defence, then put it to a vote anyway, while denying Carleton Place a ballot. Carleton Place officials were furious; they'd been booted from the play-offs but nobody said they were ejected from the league! Yet the ruling stood and Pembroke sided with Arnprior, enraging Renfrew representatives who claimed the County Town withdrew promised support in mid-stream. Surely the Pembroke delegation wouldn't have done a thing like that . . .

The Pembroke–Arnprior final began in MacKay St Arena February 21, 1927.

Fourteen hundred fans watched Lorne Wilson rush end to end for a first period goal and Jim Kenny set up Lloyd Ludgate for a late game marker—2-0 Arenas. Nig Jones was sharp and Leo Sargeant busy.

In Arnprior, goals by Lorne Wilson and Roy Ludgate were offset by a quick pair from Ollie Mulvihill. That score held until Ken Fraser gave the home team a 3-2 lead with twelve minutes left, setting up a half period of competition second to none. Arenas held on, winning the round 4-3 and securing another UOVHL title. But, angry with his club for nearly blowing a 4-0 advantage, coach Jim Cully dampened the celebration before it began.

Meantime, Almonte earned Rideau League honours by knocking off Perth. Coach E.F. McGregor enjoyed the services of Ray Edmonds, who scored twenty of the Factory Town's fifty goals. Also on the team were Eric Smith, Allan Leishman, Frank Honeyborne, George Houston, Rod Sullivan and goaltender Bert Horton; this club travelled to Pembroke and held the Arenas to an exciting 2-2 tie. But Horton had appendicitis when they dropped the puck in Almonte and it was 9-2 Pembroke before the determined goalie retired. His replacement fanned on every shot, making the final 14-3 (16-5).

Pembroke met Chesterville in what would have been the Shield round, had there been one. The village came to town and surprised Arenas, Jones coming up big to preserve a 3-2 victory. During game two at Chesterville, Pembroke's third contest in as many nights, Jim Kenny enjoyed the defensive game of his life in a scoreless tie that licenced his club to meet New Edinburgh for O&DAHA honours. Chesterville was led by left winger Johnny Sorrell, a native son destined for ten NHL seasons with Detroit and New York Americans. A decked-out town and banquet awaited Arenas return.

126

Encouraged by two thousand screaming fans, Pembroke held heavily favoured New Edinburgh to a 2-1 opening game victory, John Munroe scoring Burghs late winner. Seven thousand were in the Ottawa Auditorium when Burghs won 6-2, ending Arenas' impressive season. Territorially, the club held its own but couldn't beat Bill Beveridge, who tended goal for five NHL teams before retiring in 1943. Pembroke had alumni support too: telegrams arrived from Hugh Lehman; Varsity Grads Grant Gordon, Charlie Delahey and Dave Trottier; and Joe Freeman, who was coaching Port Arthur West-Ends to the Memorial Cup final. Nighbor, Gordon Fraser and Bob Trapp attended the final game, as did the entire town council, having postponed a meeting. For their efforts, each player received a ring.

In Allan Cup play, Toronto Varsity Grads hammered New Edinburgh 10-0 and 7-1; Both Trottier and Gordon were prominent. Major Smythe's team went on to take the Cup, upending Fort William in a best-of-five at Vancouver, 3-1-1. Trottier scored four of Grads 10 goals in that series and Delahey assisted Ross Taylor with the trophy winning tally.

*****

Scouts defeated SCBC and PHS enroute to the Sparling-Campbell Trophy. Calmax lost the Kittner round to HTC. Despite Mel Larwell having a fine final season, PHS couldn't hold the GWVA Cup, giving way to Renfrew.

*****

Northcote upset Eganville in Bonnechere League play for the George Cup; that famous Eganville family having long since ceased to be involved. Of those for whom it was named, William Basil George died at age forty-seven of appendicitis in 1933 and Greg was fifty-four when he passed away in 1942.

*****

Ted Behan, while setting up a practice in New Haven, coached Yale. Wilf Cecile warmed a Canadian Pro League bench in Windsor, was released, went to Moose Jaw, took influenza, and came home. Denny McMullen put in the full campaign with Windsor before he and his wife bought part interest in Pembroke's very first Arrow Visible Filling Station, where those new glass tanks let a person watch the gasoline come bubbling down.

The WHL having folded, Lord Stanley's Cup became exclusive NHL property. Hugh Lehman left Vancouver for Chicago Black Hawks. Gordon Fraser, whose Victoria team had won the Stanley Cup in 1925, recovered from a broken leg and arrived in the Windy City too, where Bob Trapp was already in harness. This was the only time I know of that three County Town boys played on the same NHL team. Fraser and Lionel "Big Train" Conacher, the Canadian Amateur Heavyweight Boxing Champion hockey player who split the season between Pittsburgh and New York Americans, fought to a vicious draw during a 26/27 contest, Gordon thus achieving a select level of notoriety.

Harry Cameron was named manager of the Saskatoon Shieks.

Frank Nighbor had a superb year with the Senators; so much so that Baz O'Meara, *Ottawa Journal* sports editor, felt compelled to write, "What Caruso is to singing, Beethoven is to music, what Hoppe is to billiards and Tilden to tennis, so is Frank Nighbor to hockey." Baz went on " . . .he will leave a monument that will keep his memory green in the game because every rookie that comes up from the leaky roof or kerosene circuit, every player who aspires to hockey greatness, will in the eyes of some enthusiastic manager be 'a second Nighbor.' The first one will have passed on, and the mold that cast him as a hockey great will be broken with his passing." Frank married Ottawa's Dorothy Slattery, June 16, 1926, and Dave Behan was best man. The couple drove around Lake Erie on their honeymoon.

Participants

Arenas, fast becoming known as the "Lumber Kings," peaked in 26/27. Lawrence Jones, though only twenty-four, eased out of the game, his natural skills subdued by nerves and criticism for wearing a mask. Jones married Helen Smith and opened a radio repair business which he operated until passing away in the early 1960s, a victim of eye cancer. Twenty-five-year-old Jim Kenny took an unsuccessful shot at the pros then virtually quit. Jack Armstrong spent the summer at his dad's Opeongo Lake mill, as usual, then turned pro. Lorne Wilson, twenty-two, went to Montreal with the Royal Bank and joined MAAA, winning an Allan Cup in 1930. Twenty-two-year-old Bert Anderson, Pembroke's best skater, also played two seasons in Montreal before enjoying several fine years at the

Lakehead. Frank Nighbor arranged a try-out for Roy Ludgate at the top of Lake Superior but he caught rheumatic fever and returned home. Lloyd Ludgate played one more season before embarking on a series of moves with Woolworth's. At least the club retained Albert Ellis, trainer and hi-jinks specialist. Cecil Gallagher didn't go anywhere either, except twice to hospital: he broke a leg playing baseball in 1925 and took a pitch on the head in 1926.

Delahey and Trottier had summer work in Jasper Park while Grant Gordon graduated from law school.

Dr J.E. Ritchie took over Dr Higginson's practice in Cobden, where he became prominent in both hockey and baseball.

Lindsay Joseph Fluker died suddenly, March 18, 1927, at age thirty-two. Fluker went from Pembroke Srs to the OHA club in Dunnville, where he worked for Monarch Knitting Mills before enlisting. After four years in France with the Canadian Engineers, Lindsay lived and played in Iroquois Falls. Brother Gordon was at Ottawa, where he passed away in 1956.

Last but not least, Jack "Buzz" Armstrong. The son of Mr and Mrs Fred Armstrong was born January 7, 1901, in the house beside 499 Pembroke St W which later became the Separate School Board office. Fred built 499 shortly after Jack was born and the family moved in. There was a frozen pond below the embankment at the back of the house where Jack and his buddies learned to play hockey. Frank Cone tagged him "Buzz," a comment on the centre's style.

During his decade in Pembroke colours, second longest to Bruce Giesebrecht (1950s), in terms of years, Jack had but three coaches: Gaul, whom he liked; Freeman, whom he did not; and Cully, from whom he finally learned it was a team game. Dr Cully also told him to shoot off a board all summer, Jack did and earned a chance at the pros. He, Kenny and McMullen attended the 27–28 Chicago camp; none stuck but Buzz was shipped to the Black Hawks farm team in Winnipeg. There, Buzz happened to be practicing with Babe Dye when the little Hall of Famer broke his leg so badly the bone protruded, virtually ending Babe's career.

However, Al Ritchie, the Cobden native coaching Regina Capitals, pursuaded Armstrong to join his team. It proved to be a professional error. Ritchie was replaced by Spunk Sparrow mid-season while Jack partied all year with roommates Andy Mulligan and Smokey Harris. In the end Jack came home with no money and little desire to try again.

He joined International Harvester in Ottawa and held several positions with that company before retiring in 1966. His wife, the former Janet Jones and sister of Lawrence, passed away in 1986. The couple had no children.

Of the many Buzz Armstrong stories, here are two: Dub Murphy generally kept a bottle in his gear at the rink. One night, expecting police to investigate, Murphy hid the flasked fortification among Jack's equipment. Sure enough, two officers routed the place, finding nothing. But Buzz discovered the merchandise before Dub could recover it, creating a "discussion" that left Murphy wondering which was the lesser of two evils—getting caught or tangling with Buzz.

Armstrong liked Conn Smythe and Harry Cameron equally as little. Jack was walking with Grant Gordon after a Grads game in Ottawa one evening when Conn appeared on the scene and gave Grant a prolonged blast for consorting with the enemy, any player not on his team was enemy to the militant Smythe. As for Cameron, he flattened Armstrong with a vicious check during one of those alumni games. Questioned by the recipient afterwards as to the need for such tenacity during a friendly exhibition, Harry snapped, "Either learn to protect yourself or quit."

Adjuncts

PCI opened at a cost of $220,000 . . . Hydro came to Westmeath on Dominion Day 1927 and electric signs began appearing, fouling radio transmission . . . The Temperance Act died June 1, 1927, sparking a furious growth of liquor and beer stores . . . and the minimum wage went to 25¢.

Ontario Hydro announced a dam would be built at Rapides Des Joachims; and it was, twenty years later. By the strangest coincidence, there was a renewed drive just at that time for a Georgian Bay canal. It was so pronounced that Hydro Chairman C.A. McGrath proclaimed, "The idea of handing over 200 miles of waterway to private interests is repugnant to all sane National views." . . . The bridge from Alumette Island remained a hot topic. In fact, the government did a study to determine the need. It found 3821 people lived between Sheenboro and Waltham and that Captain Murphy collected $10,000 a year in ferry fees! One private firm even offered to build a toll bridge but objections from Fort Coulonge and La Passe, who also wanted bridges, made the elected officials ponder, and ponder . . .

With the car show gaining popularity in leaps and bounds, everyone talked automobiles. People reminisced about Pembroke's first car, a 1903 #300 French D'Dion driven all the way from Ottawa by Bill Bromley at speeds approaching 15mph. Now they were moaning about paying $655 for a new Chevy. Headlights were deemed altogether too bright and those blasted horns would have to go. Naturally, the government recognized a new source of income; vehicle licences, costing $1, came into effect July 1, 1927. And any truck sporting four wheel brakes, enabling it to stop on a dime, required red warning triangles mounted on the back, like tractors today.

A Westmeath farmer, unaware that all one needed to fix a Ford was #9 wire, hitched the team to his balky machine and towed it to Blackwell's Garage. He sent the horses home alone and returned with the repaired vehicle shortly thereafter.

November 1927 saw Pembroke's first drunk driving charge. The accused was acquitted, then fined $100 for reckless driving.

Another fellow wanted to abandon a stolen car where it wouldn't be noticed immediately, so he left it in the middle of main street. Sure enough, police investigated three days later.

It was March 18, 1926 at 4am that W.S. Fraser left his team by the CNR station and went inside. The pair took off, down MacKay St and around the CPR station before charging head on into a locomotive. It may be the only time in history that a team was killed by a CPR train after having stopped at a CNR station.

Having been warned of vermin infestation, a mother forbid her offspring to enter MacKay St Arena, giving several "rink rats" a chuckle. About that time, local ladies took "The Little Scorpions" officially to task for swearing around their Indian River hockey shack, and peeping in windows to boot. Chief McKee surprised the lads by coming to their defence but his good humour ceased when someone spiked the west ward school tobaggan run, severely lacerating one youngster.

Everyone agreed that a Pembroke Hotel brawl in 1927 was the worst in history—five women settling an ancient feud.

Urban farmers found things getting tough. Pembroke passed legislation which made beekeeping well nigh impossible while Arnprior decreed a 100 foot buffer zone would be required between pigs and the nearest human abode.

On April 14, 1927, Renfrew's rink burned. Since the $52,000 building was insured for only $22,000 and $100,000 was required to replace it, the $2600 temporary outdoor substitute almost became permanent.

Nothing much burned in the County Town, unless you count six million board feet of Pembroke Lumber Company product, piled in the yard. There was another conflagration, a volunteer fireman lost his home, while he was at work. His cohorts responded to the call all right but the pumping station attendant responded to the call of nature, leaving them mere observers for want of a thrown switch.

Have I mentioned how J.M. Taylor came to be a Pembrokeite? Well, after a short career with the North-West Mounted Police, James returned to the militia in Ottawa, there becoming head of a gun crew that saluted visiting royalty. Unfortunately, he touched one off with the plunger still in place, firing it across Elgin St and through an ambassador's window. Taylor became a Pembroke resident within forty-eight hours.

Odd that J.M. should become mayor for 1928, given that the long-time voluntary fire chief and merchant had been a perennial thorn in council's side. Following one particularly protracted struggle, the chief was finally given a horse and buggy. James couldn't see this perfectly good transport stand idle most of the time so he kept the beast exercised by delivering goods from his paint and wallpaper store. But councils are vulnerable to voters and this one found personal use of publicly owned equipment unacceptable. They pulled the buggy out from under Taylor and sold the horse for $50, replacing both with a bicycle. James was not amused, so he rode the machine rather recklessly, eventually sliding off mud-covered planks on Peter St into an embankment. Taylor took the pieces to council, with specific suggestions as to what they should do with them. Pembroke's legislative body relented and bought back the horse, for $90.

And, at the end of 1926, Dan Jones sold his *Observer* to the *Standard*'s Logan family, creating the *Standard-Observer* and making Pembroke a one-newspaper town for the first time in sixty years.

Lastly, Canada's Great Elephant Hunt . . . In the summer of 1926, circus people had trouble with their pachyderms; several escaped in Edmonton and later again in

Calgary, though quickly recaptured each time. But in Cranbrook, helped by a barking dog, seven of the beasts panicked and trumpeted up main street, injuring five men and frightening locals no end. Three of the flat-footed creatures wandered into the Kootenay Indian Reserve, where little Mary Janet calmed them down with apples. The child later explained, "I suppose him just like one big horse . . .

so by and by I take off my shawl and tie his front feet together. You put old rotten rope on tame horse and he don't try to break it. Elephant just the same. He don't try break my shawl."

They should have hired her. While loading the runaways on freight cars later, one took off again, eluding capture for six hours.

1922/23 Pembroke Srs. This is a fine cross-section of the era's sporting fraternity. Edward "Ted" Rowan (coach), (Horace Gaul is missing) Frank Cohen, Roy Kennedy, Robert Coxford, Eugene Berry. J. Parnell Duff, Emmett Spooner, Lorne Wilson, Jack "Buzz" Armstrong, Gordon Anderson, J. McQueen. Victor Ryan, Jack Anderson, Omer Landriault, Wm. "Dub" Murphy, Jim Kenny. Wellington "Welly" Tario, Lawrence "Nig" Jones. The mascot is Ross Oshier, who later moved to Detroit where he made ice in the Olympia for ten years or more. Courtesy Hortense Lawn.

1922/23 Calmax team. Harry Williams, Jack Bowden, Sid Thomson, Jack Anderson, J. Sandwith, Dick Williams. Elymas Carmichael, Bert Armstrong, S.E. Smyth, Melvyn "Mac" McLeod (Gerry's brother), Bert Anderson. Charlie Delahey, Lawrence Jones, Lorne Wilson. Courtesy Pembroke Observer.

A pre-1900 Westmeath team. Note the hockey stick backdrop and that the photo was taken in the off season. Back row: James Bennie, Joseph Tucker, Charles Ryan, Wm. Carlson, W.F. Grylls. Front: Wm. Montgomery, Joseph Keyes, Irvin Dunn, Philip Montgomery (who was apparently timekeeper, if you look closely, you'll see a stop watch). Courtesy Ron and Gail Ethier.

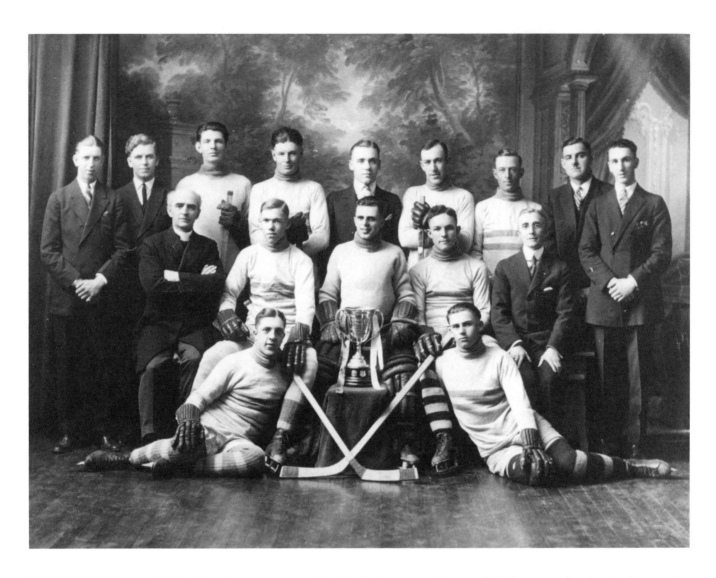

1923/24/25 Calmax. Ed Fitzjohn, Bert Armstrong, Jim Cook, Armstrong Fraser, Sid Thomson, Gordon Anderson, Jim Kenny, Mac McLeod, Ted Black. Rev. A.W. McIntosh, Bert Anderson, Lawrence Jones, Lorne Wilson, S.E. Smyth. Boyd Anderson, Harvey Schultz. Courtesy Norah Thomson.

1925/26 Pembroke Srs. The Anderson-McKinnon Cup. Courtesy Pembroke Observer.

An on-ice shot of the same team. Dr. Jim Cully, Gordon Anderson, Bert Anderson, Wilf Cecile, Denny McMullen, Nig Jones, Joe Freeman, (coach), Lorne Wilson, Buzz Armstrong, Jim Kenny, Ed Carmody. Courtesy Buzz Armstrong.

ABOVE: 1926/27 Pembroke Srs. This was the last Pembroke Sr team to be photographed until after WW2. Top row, left to right: Percy Doran, Jack Teevens, Wib Behan, Alvin Stroud, Bill Ellis. Louis Kahl, Robert Coxford, E. Allan Cone, Cecil Bailey, Cliff Godard, Roy Kennedy. Lawrence Jones, Armstrong Fraser, Gordon Anderson, Dr. Jim Cully, Bert Anderson, Lloyd Ludgate, Cecil Gallagher. Roy Ludgate, Lorne Wilson, Jack "Buzz" Armstrong, Harvey Schultz, Jim Kenny. Courtesy Roy and Lloyd Ludgate.

LEFT: 1926. Charlie Delahey. Courtesy Denise Casey, his daughter

1926/27 Scouts. Ken Oshier (manager), Len Remus, Bill Patterson, Ted Black (scoutmaster), Clarence Biesenthal, Harold Clauson, Burton Millar (assistant scoutmaster). Bob Dey, Clayton Eady, Dub Small, Allan Seigel, Allan Anderson. Courtesy Bob Dey.

1926/27 Arnprior Srs, including most stars of the era except Ollie Mulvihill. Tim Mulvihill, Sylvestre "Vesty" Sargeant, Bill Laderoute, C. Hyland (coach), Archie Dimmell, E. "Whitch" Close. Ken Fraser, Leo Sargeant, Harry Slaughter, Bill Anderson, Daulton "Dolly" Olivier. Tom "Bullet" Doyle, Harold McGregor. Courtesy Dolly Olivier.

1926/27 HTC. Len Kelly, Fred Fullerton, Harvey Fraser, Alec Brown, Connie Zeigel, Russell McDonald, Earl Hopper, Ted Brown, Percy Lewis. Lorne Lewis, Jack Follis, Tom Ferneyhough, Richie Lassman, Creighton Fraser, Gerald Lewis. Courtesy Joe Gauthier.

Chapter 11

UNIQUE

1927/28

There were very few rule changes, though the bells and whistles debate continued (the OHA still used bells). "Whistles simply cannot be heard," complained the local press, claiming bells made it more difficult for fans "with a misplaced sense of humour. True, referees have been known to use their bells as weapons to subdue recalcitrant players, a practice not to be encouraged, but league executives have frowned on that sort of thing and it has been largely abandoned."

Games

Under new president Conn Mulvihill, the O&DAHA finally came to grips with alignment. Carleton Place and Almonte joined Pembroke, Renfrew and Arnprior in the UOVHL; Smith's Falls, Perth, Chesterville and Finch became Central Division; Rideau disappeared and Russell moved to the Osgoode County League. With all groups outside Ottawa now classified Intermediate, the *Citizen* produced an appropriate Shield. When Valley leagues returned to Sr B in 32/33, they retained that same Shield (the *Citizen* did not produce an Intermediate replacement til 35/36.)

Arenas president Cecil Bailey became UOVHL vice-president behind president C.M. Logan of Renfrew. However, Logan quit within a few days and Bill Elliott took over. Eddie Rheaume and Happy Hooper aided referee-in-chief Ernie Evraire through the sixteen-game schedule.

Coach Cully began optimistic; Gallagher's goaltending matured, Eddie Carmody returned from the Toronto Merchantile League and Westmeath's Hector Ethier came on board, though he didn't finish the season. Enthusiasm cooled though, when Wilf Cecile was denied amateur reinstatement on a technicality and Denny McMullen, fed up with a Windsor to Duluth to Kansas City runaround, came home but didn't play.

Arenas opened with a 3-1 pre-season win over Queen's, a game in which Charlie Delahey played but not for the usual holiday reason. This time he was awaiting the arrival of his own club, Varsity Grads, enroute to Pembroke for an exhibition. Smythe couldn't avoid Pembroke on his pre-Olympic tour as he had three County Town boys on the roster.

Despite awful ice, they had great fun; Delahey, Trottier and Gordon played a half game for each club, the only time local fans ever saw the latter two in Pembroke colours. It was also the only time Ted Watt participated in a Sr contest. At the post-game banquet, J. Parnell Duff told of coaching young Dave in 1920 and Herb Mackie offered humorous advice to Grads on travel in Switzerland.

In fact, everyone skated on slush throughout January. Renfrew played more home games in Almonte and Pembroke than on its own unprotected surface.

Arenas maintained a 500 average until Renfrew beat them 2-1 in their own rink midway through the schedule. Even then, they might have recovered had Gallagher not been knocked off his game during the very next contest. Ollie Mulvihill skated right through him in Arnprior and since Pembroke had no back-up, the contest ended right there, in the home team's favour. Arenas won but once after that and missed the play-offs. Buzz Armstrong returned from Saskatchewan in time to lead his "old" mates to victory in the old-timers game.

Carleton Place finished first with 26 pts, Arnprior just a point back. Renfrew, in third with 13 pts and three games to go, could neither advance nor decline. So, in their third from last contest, Ed Anderson played goal and Harold Eady moved to defense. More or less a regular alignment faced Arnprior, who won 3-1, but the last match against Almonte was something else. A substitute goalie missed fourteen shots before Norman Budd was dragged out of the stands to finish up. Ray Edmonds scored eight times in the 17-4 slaughter; he later apologized to Carleton Place's Buzz Williams for slipping past him to the scoring title in such an undistinguished manner.

But Arnprior won the new Shield and, in fact, became initial UOVHL winners of the Beach Trophy by edging Ottawa Montagnards 4-3 over two games. The club lost it's first Allan Cup round to Montreal Victorias, 5-1 and 6-1 (11-2). Tim Mulvihill and Leo Sargeant shared Arnprior goaltending behind the likes of Archie Dimmell, Tim's brother Tony and cousin Ollie, Harry Slaughter and Daulton "Dolly" Olivier.

*****

After Calmax defeated HTC for town honours, the losers successfully protested Armstrong Fraser on grounds he had played with Arenas. That at least six others had done likewise was apparently irrelevant. However, Fraser was reinstated for the replay of game three! When HTC won the game, Calmax protested, claiming Holy Trinity dressed too many players. They were right. But HTC won game four also, finally securing its second straight Kittner.

Hockey fever ran high. Crowds flocked to Bonnechere and Laurentian League games and Pontiac towns fought for the Cahill Shield with great enthusiasm. Many militia teams sought the Sherwood Challenge Cup and girls clubs enjoyed excellent response.

*****

Frank Nighbor, strengthened by a summer of conditioning, enjoyed his thirteenth campaign with the Ottawa Senators. Lehman and Trapp stayed in Chicago but Fraser was traded to Detroit mid-season. Former Pembrokeite Fred Radke played with Toronto Sr Marlboroughs.

And Mickey McGuire's "Little Scorpions," rather than see their clubhouse burned again, tore it down, abandoning the Indian River location for the first time since Frank Nighbor and Leo Reise took their initial faltering strides on it.

Participants

Archie Dimmell, who had married Pembroke's Marguerite Cecile, became playing coach at Chapleau for 1928/29. He then worked and coached in several places before settling in Temagami. A father of four, he died in a North Bay hospital at the age of sixty-one, July 1956.

Charles F. Hout, one of Pembroke's earliest lacrosse and hockey players who held numerous cycling trophies, had been throwing light switches for PELC over twenty years when he made a mistake in January of 1928 and electrocuted himself. The husband and father of five was forty-seven.

Lloyd Ludgate transferred with Woolworth's to Sherbrooke, Quebec. during the summer of 1928. He played only a couple more seasons but stayed with the company forty-five years, retiring to Fergus in 1969. Born June 16, 1905, Lloyd married Ottawa nurse Vivian Barklay and they raised three children. It should be noted that this Ludgate family is not only related to the well-known Georgian Bay lumbering people but the famous Ludgate circus clan of London, England.

Adjuncts

A local lad died of blood poisoning after being punctured between the thumb and forefinger by a catfish horn ... John T. Mulcahy arrived from Orillia to be county court judge and his son John later became crown attorney . . . St. Louis Cardinals third baseman Frankie Frisch arrived on a fishing trip but spent most of the time in town talking anything but baseball . . . Tory E.A. Dunlop easily defeated Grit Paul Martin in a provincial by- election, as Mr Stewart had died in office.

In the spring of 1928, engineers were taking borings at the foot of Cecelia St with a view to running that bridge across from there. Two men rushed by, having escaped from the county jail. Turnkey Boland arrived moments later, completely out of puff. An engineer, assessing the situation much quicker than results were ever seen from his primary efforts, grabbed Boland's rifle and whistled a couple over the fleeing fugitives, fetching them to a grinding halt. As for the bridge, it was determined a span from that location would cost two million. Perhaps somewhere else . . .

That was the spring Councillor Demers got fed up. Halting winter traffic on main street was the only solution; $303 for snow removal could only be described as ridiculous. Council agreed, but then, there'd been a lot of snow and would such a move be legal? Besides, it would be a terrible inconvenience for doctors and taxi drivers.

One woman said there were far too many restrictions anyway. She'd lent her licence plate to a friend because her own vehicle was out of commission and got fined $10!

After two QPF officers and a guide nearly drowned, froze and starved while fetching a dead trapper out of the bush, the inquest determined he had wounded himself and, with no hope of discovery, took strychnine.

Pembroke's centennial, celebrated August 1928, was a humdinger. A popularity contest between Adele "Teddy" Kossatz, sponsored by industry, Catherine Murray, IODE, Olive Brunette, Kiwanis, and Margaret Bromley, PCI, generated tremendous interest. Teddy took the honours after a late charge. Steamer *Ouiseau* travelled the river continuously, fully loaded. Even Lennox Irving returned for the festivities, all the way from his home in Pasadena, California.

THE 1928 OLYMPICS, PEMBROKE'S CONTRIBUTION

The Olympic movement began in Athens, April 6-15, 1896 as strictly summer games, every four years. This remained so until 1908 when the London, England stretched version, April 27 and October 1, included six nations competing in figure skating. However, the Olympic Committee still viewed it as summer games and the 1912 meet in Stockholm reverted to form. Events planned for Berlin in 1916 were cancelled of course but the 1920 show in Antwerp ran five months again and featured both figure skating and hockey although they were still summer games. Canada sent the Winnipeg Falcons to Antwerp (hockey was actually played in Chaminox, France) and the team won easily. Falcons goaltender was Jack Cameron, an Ottawa lad who held the Pembroke golf course nine-hole record of 39 until J. McLaren Beatty pulled off a 37, many years later.

Paris, France decided to hold winter Olympic games in 1924, seeking official recognition when all was in readiness. The request fell on deaf ears. Undeterred, Paris went ahead anyway, holding a very successful tournament in which Toronto Granite Club won gold in hockey. When the Olympic Committee met in 1925 its most adamant winter games critic had passed on so, swayed by the Paris triumph, they reconsidered. It was not only decided to hold such games in 1928 but also to recognize 1924 after the fact!

So, contrary to records and popular opinion, Varsity Grads participated in the first pre-sanctioned winter Olympics.

However, to this day the Olympic Committee does not recognize winter games as "pure" Olympics. The term "Olympiad" cannot be used and consecutive numbering stops if interrupted. For instance, Calgary XV would have been XVll were it not for cancellations in 1940 and 1944. Count back the summer games and you'll find wartime pauses had no affect on the "spirit of continuity."

*****

Conn Smythe created the Varsity Grads in 1925, with 1928 firmly in mind. Grads had to win the Allan Cup in 1927 to qualify, and did so. Manager W.A. Hewitt actually coached in Switzerland because he and Smythe had a "wee tiff" and the club was disbanded at years end.

An outstanding team, lost only that one Allan Cup contest plus a 1-0 defeat by Boston University over the last two seasons of its existence. And the club didn't pick and choose either, playing all comers both at home and in Europe, winning eleven exhibitions abroad while outscoring the opposition 104-12.

Grads were given a bye to the final Olympic round which

consisted of three open-air contests that came within an ace of being cancelled due to weather. They went as follows:

- February 16, 1928: Grads 11, Sweden 0. Dave Trottier 5, Hugh Plaxton 2, Frank Sullivan 2, Dr Louis Hudson 2.
- February 18, 1928: Grads 14 Britain 0. Hugh Plaxton 6, Herb Plaxton 2, Dr. Louis Hudson 2, Dave Trottier 2, Red Porter 1, Frank Fisher 1.
- February 19, 1928: Grads 13, Switzerland 0. Dave Trottier 5, Hugh Plaxton 5, Ross Taylor 2, Red Porter 1.

Dr Joe Sullivan kept goal, backed up by Norbert Mueller. Only three assists were awarded: two to Dave and one to Hugh. Grant Gordon and Charlie Delahey were back-up in those days of few substitutions but did see action in the exhibition games. Yes that was the same Dr Hudson who died with Leafs Bill Barilko in a 1951 plane crash.

A story: the practicing Czechoslovakian club sought a referee among observers. The chap who volunteered immediately penalized two players for "intensive body checking." Realizing they didn't understand, the "official" offered to demonstrate, taking a stick and inviting anyone to knock him down. The guy went end to end six Times, scoring six goals, without being touched. The frustrated Czech goaltender asked who that was and, being told Dave Trottier from Canada, said "God help the States!" In fact, the U.S. wasn't represented.

*****

Grant Gordon was one of five children born to Mr and Mrs Robert W. Gordon. His father, who died in 1910, operated a large food and clothing supply store which became part of the new GTR station in 1914. Grant finished high school in Toronto, his mother moving back and forth between there and her Petawawa cottage until choosing the city permanently in 1925. The Osgoode Hall graduate joined Peter White's huge law firm and stayed with it until taken by cancer March 20, 1954 at the age of fifty-three. His wife of twenty-three years, the former Molly Bucknall, later married Jack Campbell and moved to Montreal; she passed away in 1987.

Grant and Molly raised Peter, Heather and Gerry; the latter owns an island off Petawawa Point and the original cottage, now a home, belongs to Jeanne Cringan, daughter of Grant's brother, Stanley.

Charlie "Duke" Delahey came into this world May 11, 1905. Dr Fred Delahey married his first wife's sister after Charlie's mother died and she took the boy to her bosom. An exceptionally gifted athlete, he gave sports priority over all else, frustrating his father no end. In fact, when Charlie married Toronto's Adele Phelan, a Roman Catholic, the strained relationship snapped, though the doctor, who suffered a stroke in 1932, was visiting his son in Toronto when he passed away two years later. Adele faced the music too, being forced by her grandfather to earn his approval by eating a dreaded bowl of porridge. But it was a good marriage; they raised Charlie Jr, Dwyne (Blick) and Denise (Casey) but the youngest, David, was only four when he drowned at the family cottage in 1950. Charlie taught aircraft identification during the war then operated Millgate Motors in Aurora for five years before moving on to Mother Parker's, Cara Foods and managing the Aero Motel. The last two were Phelan family enterprises. Charlie died of a heart attack at their Lake Joseph cottage March 17, 1973.

Delahey's sports record was impressive, as you'd expect for a fellow that one calm day booted a football the full length of a field on the fly! Between 1923 and 1930, Charlie ran and kicked one season for Trinity of the Little Big Four, two campaigns with Toronto U, then the rest with Balmy Beach. As for hockey, he followed the Grad years with a season at St. Mike's, then one with Sea Fleas of the Sr OHA before moving to Montreal where he joined Lorne Wilson on the MAAA and Royals roster. Charlie returned to Toronto in 1934, where he, naturally, became a scratch golfer.

Pembroke fans at least enjoyed the talents of Indian and Muskrat rivers graduate Dave Trottier to SCBC level before college called. Born June 25, 1906, he parlayed Grads stardom into a decade of success with Montreal Maroons, including a Stanley Cup in 1935. Maroons disbanded three years later so Trottier went to Detroit but the quick-tempered forward retired mid-campaign after suffering Another of his many injuries. Oddly enough, Dave was the only member of Smythe's famous team to become an NHL star. In fact, only Hugh Plaxton ever reached that level, playing seventeen games for the Maroons in 1933.

Also oddly enough, Dave's marvellous amateur scoring touch left him when he joined the new Maroons, until trainer Billy O'Brien, of Renfrew, told him to "cut 6 inches off that blamed stick." The response was immediate; Dave finished with 121 goals and 113 assists over 441 games plus seven play-off points. This was a far better record than many Hall of Famers. But he also recorded 517 penalty minutes— every one earned. Dave began his professional career taking a serious skate cut on the neck and finished it similarly injured. In between he suffered severe shoulder, heel and ankle damage plus one bad cut over the eye, administered during a stick-swinging duel with Dit Clapper. Dave also ran afoul of convention off ice but managed to survive.

Dave Trottier joined McCall-Frontenac Oil Co. in Halifax, there to marry Barbara Steele in 1941. His first wife, Kathleen Simpson of Westmount, had died shortly after the wedding. He and Barbara raised six daughters while becoming heavily involved in organizing local sports. He suffered a cerebral hemmorage at a football game and died November 14, 1956.

Chapter 12

THE SPORT EXPANDS

1928/29 to 1929/30

Everyone wanted to speed up the game and generate more scoring but no one knew quite how to go about it. Meanwhile, amateur hockey reached a level of defensive dominance unmatched before or since.

Game fixing occasionally reared its ugly head. Ottawa press, in particular, stayed on the topic, claiming those involved should be "subjected to a period of inactivity."

Sports reporting still left much to be desired. The *Renfrew Mercury* claimed reporters, "take a few longhand notes and depend upon their memory for the rest, with memory often making way for imagination tinctured with local prejudice."

Games

1928/29

All UOVHL clubs stayed in, even understaffed Carleton Place and buildingless Renfrew. Ernie Evraire and Eddie Rheaume carried the whistles.

Finally, Pembroke decided to use "Lumber Kings" officially. It was a good time for changes, since the old executive of Bailey, Duff, Behan and Cully all quit, leaving things in the hands of president J.B. Teevens, Dr J.C. Bradley, L.C. Tario and Jim Findlay. The first item of business was to ensure Cecile and McMullen had amateur cards as Cecile was a player while Denny McMullen was coach. Both Ludgates were gone but big Bob Warner returned from the north and Welly Tario decided to give Sr one more try.

Lorne Wilson and Bert Anderson brought MAAA to town for an exhibition, both tallied in their club's 2-0 victory. This immediately identified the Lumber Kings' season-long problem; they couldn't score.

Arnprior, with goalie Harold McGregor replacing Leo Sargeant, who went to northern Ontario, the east coast and Europe before returning in 1940, plus Jack Ferguson, Mort Kennedy, Dolly Olivier and that batch of Mulvihills, was expected to prevail. Coach Ed Anderson of Renfrew, in his fourteenth year, had added Ab "Snap" Rouselle, former Black Hawk Art Townsend, Fred Totten, Vince Utronki and Jack "Jiggs" McCormack to the regular line-up, and was therefore strong. Almonte, without a change, continued to improve, while Carleton Place depended on goaltender Jim "Taffy" Williams, a cousin of Buzz Williams, Watty McIlquham and Arnie McDaniels to carry the load.

Lumber Kings, when they did tally, usually found Harvey Schultz, Bob Warner and Wilf Cecile scoring. Scores were generally in the 2-0 or 2-1 range, thanks often as not to great work by Tario. Welly had two shut-outs: 5-0 over Carleton Place and a satisfying 1-0 defeat of Almonte. Plus one that should have been. Pembroke lead Renfrew 2-0 when the game ending buzzer sounded so Tario skated off, forgetting the referee must also blow his whistle. The official did, but not until Bob Perry's long shot slid into Welly's vacated goal.

Defenceman Jim Kenny played a few games, then quit. He and partner Boyd Anderson were booed unmercifully for hogging the puck. Resentment among their team-mates fueled friction and the team finished out of it. The Lumber Kings ended a pathetic season by hosting Westmeath, Laurentian League champions, then attended the return match in a collectively inebriated condition, drawing deserved criticism from all quarters.

Surprisingly, second-place Renfrew beat Almonte in the semi-final and narrowly upset pennant-winning Arnprior for the UOVHL title. Renfrew lost the first ODHA round to Cornwall, 5-3, 5-1 (10-4).

*****

Match-Splint prevented HTC from taking permanent possession of the Kittner Trophy by defeating them in a best-of-three final. Match-Splint leaders included goalkeeper Dub Small, Art Laronde, Jack Follis and league scoring champion Ivan Fraser. But games two and three of this town league play-off were a month apart due to an interruption by something new—Jr competition.

There had been talk of extending Jr hockey beyond the long-established Central Group for years but nothing came of it. Then, in late January 1929, Cecil Duncan got hold of Dave Behan, Sid Thomson and Dr Jim Cully, wanting to fulfill the dream. An organizational meeting was held in Pembroke's Legion Hall January 29 and, with young hopefuls lining the walls in eager anticipation, they decided on an immediate series of playdowns followed by formation of a league for 29/30. The *Citizen* had already produced a Shield. Each club would be allowed ten players, none of whom were to have played more than one Sr contest.

On-ice coach Behan and bench coach Cully (Dave refereed every game the team played) chose the following players from thirty who attended tryouts: Match-Splint goaltender David "Dub" Small, with PCI's Lloyd Reid his

back-up; defencemen Jim Timlin of PCI and SCBC's Aime Jette; centres Hugh Henderson from Jette's team and Joe Fraser of HTC; right wingers Tom Fitzgerald of PCI and Match-Splint's Ivan Fraser; left wingers D'Arcy Sammon and Bert Shepherd, SCBC teammates.

Jette and Henderson were in their last year of eligibility; Sammon and Fitzgerald had one more year; Small, Timlin and Joe Fraser had two; Shepherd and Reid, four; while Ivan Fraser (Gordon's nephew) had five, though the best of them were spent with Sudbury Wolf Cubs.

Aime Jette, Jr to his policeman father, had fallen from a building at age nine, puncturing his eardrum. He thus spoke very little and carried the "Dummy" handle. Aime's excellent peripheral vision and naturally refined awareness more than made up for his impaired hearing.

Each series was a two-game matchup. Pembroke Jrs opened in Chalk River February 18, winning 2-1 on Jette's deflection with four minutes to play. Bert Shepherd scored Pembroke's initial Jr goal, a long shot just as the first period ended. Gordon Tennant and Maurice McDonald shared net-minding duties for Chalk River; both were outstanding as was their lone goal scorer, Bill Tennant.

Three nights later in Pembroke, the visitors carried a 1-0 score into thirty-four minutes of overtime before D'Arcy Sammon shoved the puck under McDonald, giving his club a 1-1 (3-2) squeaker.

Meantime, the Arnprior–Almonte series made an immediate joke of the "one Sr game only" rule. Arnprior's Harold McGregor and Bob Houston had played three games each with their Sr club, while Bracewell and Brooks of Almonte had also exceeded the limit. Arnprior won the round 5-4 then dropped McGregor in favour of Austin Cram before facing Pembroke. However, they also added Vesty Sargeant, who had played every game with the Woollen Town Srs.

If the rule had been dropped, why didn't Behan and Cully use any of four Pembroke Srs who were under twenty years of age? Two possibilities: it was dropped and the Pembroke coaches figured they already had the best available, or, the two local teams weren't getting along that well. In support of the latter argument, Pembroke Jrs borrowed Lumber Kings sweaters to face Chalk River but were denied such generosity when Arnprior arrived, sending the club onto MacKay St Arena ice in an embarrassing sea of colour. Led by Ivan Fraser and aided by confusion, the rag-tag outfit won 4-2. But in Arnprior, sporting new uniforms, the Pembroke representatives never got out of their own end for forty minutes. Fortunately, Dub Small stood on his head during that time, allowing only Houston and Sargeant to score. That forced overtime that lasted twenty minutes before Henderson gave Pembroke a 1-2 (5-4) victory.

The Shield series opened in Chesterville against Morewood, the Central Group champions. Morewood players were huge in comparison to Pembroke, and bounced Pembroke around like kingpins enroute to winning 2-1. Then, at MacKay St Arena, Morewood secured the Shield by virtue of a 1-1 (2-1) tie. Or so it seemed . . .

Before that series began, Pembroke Jrs manager Sid Thomson had been advised to watch for "ringers." Indeed, Morewood played the second game with two new faces. So Sid called a Chesterville-area friend, who confirmed his suspicions. The jig was up; Cecil Duncan discovered players named Lynch and Gillespie had assumed the identity of two Morewood regulars. Duncan disqualified Morewood, banned the team executive for life, some players for several years, and then awarded Pembroke Jrs the first *Citizen* Shield.

That propelled the little team against Ottawa Shamrocks for ODHA honours. Led by George Rheaume, Shamrocks easily prevailed, defeating Pembroke Jrs 4-0, 8-0 (12-0). Still, they had enough success to inspire confidence yet keep visions of a John Ross Robertson Memorial Cup realistically distant.

*****

Harry Cameron played forward with both Minneapolis and St. Louis of the American Association, scoring well. Nighbor's last season in Ottawa was a poor one. Lehman quit goalkeeping to co-coach Chicago Black Hawks with the owner, Major Frederic McLaughlin.

1929/30

The same five UOVHL teams, under president James Muir of Almonte, made up the league. Mr. Teevens remained Lumber Kings head and Cecil Gallagher became manager, leaving goaltending exclusively to Welly Tario. South Porcupine's Fred Clark coached; he tended goal for the Ottawa Shamrocks the next season then headed back north.

Jim Kenny quit for keeps. Harvey Schultz left town and

Allan Anderson moved to Montreal, where he remained.

The Lumber Kings were supposed to open the season and Renfrew's new rink simultaneously, but, with the long-awaited building still unfinished, they played at MacKay St Arena instead, the visitors being the "home" team. Renfrew, missing Harold Eady, lost 3-1 to a Pembroke club with whom Gerry McLeod and Art Laronde had become regulars. Jr graduates Henderson and Jette also looked right at home.

Scoring was still a problem. The Kings were shut out in Almonte, then suffered a similar fate when they finally opened the Renfrew Arena, a structure that served the Creamery Town until 1989.

Following a narrow win over Carleton Place, Clark was obliged to suspend Boyd Anderson and Bob Warner. Though it was reported "a dove of peace flitted through the dressing room" following a meeting, the disciplinary measure sent the Lumber Kings into a six-game tailspin. New sweaters, white on red with a log crest superimposed over "P," provided no inspiration, and another team conference confirmed the club suffered considerable clubhouse animosity. They were broke to boot. Kings decided to play out the season and almost made it, defaulting only the last game.

One bright spot was young Allan Seigel. theexceptional player who moved from HTC to Jr to Sr during the season.

Arnprior had trouble too. After league officials discovered Tony Mulvihill had been playing without a card, all Woollen Town wins were declared ties, and the ties, losses. That mess was no sooner settled than the club earned total suspension after a disguised player was caught when his moustache fell off during play.

The Renfrew Maroons defeated Carleton Place in a two-game semi-final but fell to Almonte, who in turn lost the Shield round to Brockville.

*****

This season Joseph L. Murray donated the Murray Cup, a challenge trophy that survived two decades of post-season Upper Valley competition. There were few restrictions on team personnel. Dave Behan was an original trustee. All series were two-game, total goal.

Pembroke, Renfrew, Arnprior, Chalk River and Bonnechere All-Stars competed that first year. Using a mixture of Srs and Jrs, Pembroke shut out Chalk River twice but the Maroons had no trouble defeating Pembroke 5-1, 3-1 (8-2), becoming the first Murray Cup winners.

Sr town action began with a bang then folded mid-season, as did the first public school league. A Jr (juvenile) town league was hotly contested. Repeatedly protested finals ran well into April before the Lutherans, led by Arnie Junop and Joe Kruger, were finally awarded the Demers Trophy they had, in fact, won on the ice weeks earlier.

The Chalk River girls team shone, reaching provincial finals in Toronto before suffering defeat. Douglas broke Bromley's two-year hold on the George Cup, and Foresters Falls had the unmitigated gall to interrupt Westmeath's continuous hold on the Cotnam Shield.

The first full Jr season was organized a month after the stock market crash that took almost two years to ripple through rural Canada. Charter members of the new UOVJHL, under president J. Deacon Taylor, were Pembroke, Renfrew and Arnprior, with Almonte and Carleton Place both declining invitations. An eight-game schedule ran from January 3 to February 3, 1930.

The Deacon was also Pembroke Jrs head; his principal aids being team manager Sid Thomson, Percy Doran, Jim Findlay, Cecil Bailey, Jack Campbell and the Copeland Hotel's Ivan Roy. Official coach was Dr Jim Cully; on ice instructor Dave Behan not wishing to see his officiating frought with technical difficulties. Former goaltender now a barber, Roy Hamilton, was club trainer. Canadian Department Stores provided sweaters. Player additions were defencemen Joe Turcotte and Allan Mulligan plus forwards Gerald Lewis and Allan Seigel. John Stashick and Clayton Eady saw limited duty, as did back-up goalie Lloyd Reid.

This year, the annual Christmas exhibition game became a Jr–Sr affair which the Srs won 4-2.

Bert Lindsay coached Renfrew Jrs. Bert's son, Jim, tended goal and Andy Freemark backed him up. Other regulars were Alf and Lawrence Hickey, Bill Acton, Wilf Roach, Gus Brennan, Pat Villemaire and sharpshooter Ernie Troke. Prominent for Arnprior were goaltender George Tripp, Art St. Hilaire, Fred Cranston, Willis Close and Mel Slater.

Joe Turcotte's goal gave Pembroke a 1-0 victory over Renfrew to begin proceedings, then Ivan Fraser scored Both markers in a 2-0 win at Arnprior. Ivan then registered with an Ottawa business college, which meant he missed some games. Small finally gave up a goal in the return match but Pembroke still won, 3-1. Lindsay shut Pembroke out 1-0 in Renfrew before the County Town Jrs

blanked Arnprior twice, 5-0 and 1-0, then finished the regular campaign at 7-1 by beating Renfrew 4-1 and 3-2, outscoring the opposition 19-5 in the process.

Regular-season scoring, in what were generally clean, speedy matches, came mostly from Turcotte, Fraser, Allan Seigel and D'Arcy Sammon. But it was Tom Fitzgerald who led Pembroke to the title, his club defeating second-place Arnprior 3-2, 2-0 (5-2).

Cobden won a new rural Jr league, and met Pembroke in the first Shield round. After two-goal efforts by Mulligan and Seigel provided a 4-1 victory at MacKay St Arena, Pembroke skated onto the open-air ice at Cobden a tad overconfident losing 1-0, though still taking the series 4-2. Jim Parr was superb in the Cobden goal with Dub Small just as impressive, at least until Ollie Hart bounced one off his nose.

Despite success, Pembroke Jrs hadn't been drawing fans, until Rideau League champion Perth arrived for the Shield series. Dub Small didn't disappoint, shutting out the toughest team they had faced to date, 3-0. In fact, interest was so great the *Standard-Observer* revived its information service for game two; Pembroke lost 2-1 but earned its second successive Jr Shield by virtue of a 4-2 victory on the round, but an ODHA title was still beyond reach. Only Ivan Fraser could score as the club lost 3-1 at home to Ottawa Rideaus. Then Jim Timlin registered the team's only marker in a 5-1 loss at Ottawa. Dr I.D. Cotnam, MP, gave the boys a tour of Parliament Hill anyway. The club won two post-season exhibitions, then called it quits. Each player received a ring from town council, at the O'Brien Theatre one night between shows.

A.J. Frieman Stores donated a Jr trophy for "the most useful player to his club." Dr. Jim Cully, Bert Lindsay and T.P. O'Toole of Arnprior were named trustees. They awarded the first trophy to Tom Fitzgerald.

Participants

Melville "Fats" Larwell, son of Mr and Mrs George Larwell, turned up with Prince Albert Mintos in 1928, back-stopping that team to the provincial finals. The next year he was in Los Angeles, keeping goal for Richville Oilers and getting good press. An Oiler teammate was Tommy Westwick, son of Harry "Rats" Westwick, a rover with Ottawa Silver Seven, who scored eighty-seven goals in an eighty-seven game career.

Fats played with the Oakland Shieks of what was called

"The Mushroom League" in 1932, rating super-star status with some writers. The portly goaltender then drifted east, to Baltimore, where he played through 1936 before becoming a referee. Officiating appealed to Mel; in fact he wanted to referee at both the amateur and professional level but, as with players, certain restrictions applied.

In the famous Stanley Cup final between the Leafs and the Red Wings in the spring of 1942, Leafs were down 3-0. They came back to win four straight, the first team to pull off such a feat. Game four of the series, in Detroit, which Toronto won 4-3, was naturally tense. With just minutes remaining, referee Mel Harwood penalized Eddie Wares and Don Grosso, both Red Wings. Wares refused to enter the box and Harwood had a rough time regaining control. At game's end, Detroit manager Jack Adams took matters into his own hands, putting the run on Mr Harwood. Unfortunately for Detroit, NHL president Frank Calder was in attendance; he fined Harwood, Grosso, and Wares. Wares was charged an extra $100 for attempting to punch the referee, and Mr Adams, who did land one on the official, was suspended indefinitely. Mel Harwood, as you probably guessed, was our Mel Larwell, refereeing his one and only NHL game.

After a stint in the U.S. navy, Fats coached in Baltimore, then Oakland of the Pacific Coast League. During this time he attempted to recruit some of Pembroke's best players, without success. Returning to Baltimore, Mel Harwood suddenly died of a heart attack, March 6, 1948. He was only forty.

Eddie Carmody expected to play for the 29/30 Lumber Kings but was scouted by former Renfrew "Millionaire" Stan Burgoyne for Ted Oke's IHL Toronto Millionaires, where Hugh Lehman was manager. Gordon Fraser went from the Canadiens to Providence to Pittsburgh that season, and Bob Trapp stayed in Chicago, while Harry Cameron put in a campaign with St. Louis.

Cecil Daley, a graduate of SCBC who had been in the Nickel Belt League for some time, signed with Duluth, Minnesota. Arnprior's Leo Sargeant and George Aldrich "Ollie" Mulvihill went to South Porcupine. Leo stayed a couple of years then moved east and eventually went to England. Ollie went to Belleville the following season, then spent the remaining 1930s with AHL clubs in Kansas City, St. Louis, Wichita and Tulsa before returning home in 1940, where he occasionally coached Arnprior Srs. After a campaign in Hamilton, where he married prominent ath-

lete Eileen Welk, Renfrew's Harold Eady back-stopped the Sussex, New Brunswick team for several years, joined at one point by former teammate, Alton Dick.

Jim Coxford, working as a fire ranger near Chapeau, was hit by a train and killed in August of 1930. The forty-four-year-old former hockey player and WWI veteran was brought home for a full military funeral.

William J. "Dub" Murphy, born in 1900, retired from hockey in 1930. He left Atomic Energy in 1965 and passed away February 7,1971. One of twelve children born to Captain and Mrs W.L. Murphy over a period of twenty-five years, Dub married Pearl Kiely and their offspring totalled thirteen. There's a road in Petawawa named after the Murphy clan, a long one.

Burdened with poor eyesight but buoyed by determination, Lorne Wilson won an Allan Cup with MAAA Winged Wheelers in 1930, defeating Port Arthur Bearcats in Toronto. Foster Hewitt broadcast that series, frustrating fans of both teams; a Gordon Wilson played for Port Arthur and Foster tended to ignore first names. Lorne played till 1934, then began organizing minor leagues for Hampstead Recreation Association, an operation he managed for twenty years before easing from the scene. He had moved to Montreal with the Royal Bank but joined Shawinigan Water and Power in 1943. Lorne, born February 15, 1904,and Amy have one son, David.

William R. "Billy" Wallace succumbed to complications following an operation October 1, 1930, shortly after the fifty-year-year old Allumette Island native and Jean Behan were married. No one contributed more to local hockey than Billy Wallace. Except for time spent at his pharmacy course in Toronto, the man performed as either player, official or executive from 1898 till the day he died. Wallace was the fourth of that great 1906 club to pass away, behind Hugh Fraser, Tom Benson and, by two months, Jim Coxford.

Leo Reise ended his playing career splitting 1929/30 between New York Americans and Rangers. The son of Mr and Mrs William Reise was born in June of 1892 and learned to play on the river below his Moffat St home before going to live with his sister in Hamilton. He won an OHA Intermediate title with the Hamilton Tigers in 1914, played part of 1915 in New Liskeard, then returned to the Tigers, winning another Intermediate crown in 1917, before the club turned Sr and took an Allan Cup two years later. Hamilton Tigers then joined the NHL and Leo stayed with them until being traded in 1924 to the WHL Saskatoon Crescents, remaining with the Crescents until the league folded in 1926. Then Leo went to the New York Americans, which was actually his old Tigers, transplanted after a 1925 players strike ended professional hockey in the steel city.

Leo Reise went straight on to coaching, handling the London Tecumsehs, Brantford Jrs, Grimsby Beach Kings and Chatham Maroons before quitting to watch Leo Jr make his way to a pair of Stanley Cups through eight NHL seasons with the Red Wings and Rangers. Reise operated a fruit farm near Hamilton and worked for Brant County Historical Museum; he died July 7, 1975; his hockey career that much more remarkable for he was blind in one eye since the age of twenty.

Francis "Frank" Nighbor suffered a severe ankle injury in 1929 and was traded to Toronto. He finished 29/30 there and retired. His summary looks like this: Born January 28, 1893. Debaters 1910, Pembroke Srs 1911, Port Arthur 1912, Toronto 1913, Vancouver 1914-15, Ottawa 1916-29, Toronto 1930. Five Stanley Cups, three rings, two watches, first Hart Trophy, first two Lady Byng Trophies, 432 regular season games, 41 play-offs, 267 goals. If assists had been tabulated, 600? He spent 98 minutes in the penalty box while causing several members of the opposition to practically live there. Elected to the Hall of Fame in 1947.

To survive, the frail looking 160 lb. hockey player needed a trick or two. He prevailed upon friends to rush at him hour after hour to hone his skills. Still, it wasn't until switching from wing to centre while with Vancouver that Frank's uncanny ability to steal pucks off opposing sticks really surfaced. With stardom came nicknames and Nighbor had many: Pembroke Percolator, Old Master, The Black Prince, Gliding Ghost and Peerless Frank, but the two most popular were "Dutch" and "The Pembroke Peach."

Frank, who was Dave Behan's insurance partner, took a year off then, spent four seasons at the helm of the Buffalo Bisons, taking two titles while playing most of one campaign in Fort Erie for lack of home ice when the rink collapsed. Frank also coached the London Tecumsehs and New York Rovers before calling it quits.

Frank's first wife, Marion Dorothy Slattery, daughter of Mr and Mrs Bernard Slattery, an Ottawa family that owned part of what is now Byward Market, was only twenty-eight when she died of TB, May 3, 1931. Four-year-old Frank Jr

was their only child. On April 11, 1939, Frank married Ann Heney and the couple produced Pauline, Patrick and Cathy. Ann passed away in 1950. The Behan–Nighbor partnership had split and Frank Jr was in business with his father when Pembroke's most famous hockey player died of cancer, April 13, 1966.

Of many, here are three Frank Nighbor stories: During the 1923 Stanley Cup finals in Vancouver, Ottawa was a goal up with two minutes to play. Three Senators were penalized, leaving Frank and George Boucher protecting their goaltender to the game's end. Nighbor commenced stick-handling, working himself into such a frenzy that only jubilant teammates broke his momentum ten seconds after the game-ending whistle. Neither Boucher nor a competitor had touched the puck.

In the final 1927 Stanley Cup game, in Ottawa, against Boston, the Senators won thanks to an incredible third period by Frank Nighbor. Sports writers called Frank "the greatest player that ever lived—one whose prowess will never be equalled." Afterwards, Frank and his sister-in-law slipped away to eat, but searching fans eventually tracked them down. Surrounded by devotees, Nighbor rose to speak, but could not. You see, it was April 11 and Frank Jr had been born during the game, just blocks from the Auditorium. Some gambler got word to Frank, before the third period, that his wife had died and the child wasn't expected to live either. Frank had just learned the truth from Dorothy's sister.

Nighbor owned a one-man spaniel, which stayed with Frank Jr and his aunt Loretta while the widower was away coaching. Young Frank and the dog were playing outside one spring day when the pet suddenly took off down MacKay St, dashed around the corner, a half block up Pembroke St East, and jumped through its homecoming master's open car window.

Adjuncts

From it's new, and present, location on Alexander St, the *Standard-Observer* began publishing comics; rated the '29 crash a "market slump" till 1931; said the Pontiac MLA found any bridge to Allumette Island "not feasible'; and continued "old-fashioned" reporting with obituaries like "A familiar face will be missed on the street from now on for on wednesday evening the call came to Mr John

Morrison, and the silver cord was loosed and the golden bowl was broken, but he has passed the alloted span for on February 11 he had reached the age of 79 years."

A super little weekly called the *Pembroke Times* lasted but a year.

The O'Brien Theatre was converted for "talkies." Bakers, caught in a bread war that forced prices down to 6¢ a loaf, were also caught "short weighing." . . . Politicians reported an all-weather road would be built between Pembroke and Petawawa "come hell or high water."

Chief McKee asked for a police car again but council told him to spend as much time finding stolen autos as he did searching for bicycles and he'd likely get one for nothing. He could have gotten a new Essex at the car show for $840.

August 1930. A switch was left open at the foot of Arnold's Lane, causing a CPR wreck that killed two and injured many.

Dumb: How do you play truant from a correspondence school?
Smart: Send an empty envelope.
He: I'd die a thousand deaths for you.
She: Once is enough.

Bears were rare in the Ottawa Valley so when one was reported near Snake River it's easy to understand why fifty crack shots converged on the scene with every type of dog, including both those that hunt for you and those you're forever hunting. Amassed, they circled a piece of bush like a picket fence and commenced creating turmoil within. Sure enough, Mr Bruin burst forth, whereupon all manner of lead flew in his general direction. When the Great War replay ended, each marksman claimed a hit. Tracking proved otherwise. The undamaged bear left only a mauled dog as proof of its prowess.

Chapter 13

TOUGH TIMES BEGIN

1930/31to 1931/32

Games

1930/31

At the annual UOVSHL meeting, financially concerned Almonte officials were persuaded to hang in, for what proved to be the Factory Town's greatest campaign.

On the other hand, Lumber Kings players showed little enthusiasm despite merchant support, a dedicated executive, new blue and white striped uniforms and the best efforts of coach Cully. Throughout scheduled and Murray Cup play, many passed through the ranks, including Cobden's Aubrey Peever and Hector Robert, big Bill Tennant and Russell Field from Chalk River and defenceman Vince Chisnell of Shawville. Chisnell's protective equipment consisted of one elbow pad, a device he used to massage opponents. Cecil Gallagher played three games in goal, then Eganville school teacher Walter Zadow finished the regular season. Welly Tario back-stopped the Murray Cup crew.

Frustration reigned elsewhere too. Former NHLer Cy Denneny coached Renfrew to nine straight losses before quitting, and Carleton Place withdrew mid-campaign.

In an era of absolute defence when forward passing had not yet filtered down to the regional level, only shut outs ensured against defeat. Highest scoring contest was a 5-3 Kings loss to Almonte. This was the most goals Horton allowed in a game and Bill Tennant , Kings leading scorer with seven, registered all three goals in this game.

Arnprior finished a poor second, while Pembroke and Renfrew ended tied for third, necessitating a pre-play-off play-off. Wilson "Tat" Scott and his brother Bill combined on a Renfrew scoring play to offset Henderson's marker in game one, leaving it tied. Clarence Moore fired the only goal of game two, eliminating Pembroke and sending the Maroons against Arnprior for the hopeless privilege of facing Almonte. Renfrew managed a 2-2 tie before succumbing 2-0 (4-2).

Almonte enjoyed a 16-0 regular season with eleven shut outs and outscored the competition 49-8 while never being headed in a game! Waiting didn't hurt either; when Arnprior finally ended preliminaries, Horton rang up another pair of goose eggs 3-0, 4-0 (7-0).

Facing Brockville for the Shield, Bert Horton recorded his third straight blanking, 1-0, before getting generous and settling for a 1-1 tie enroute to securing the trophy round, 2-1.

Ottawa Montcalms met Almonte for the Beach Trophy in a fiesty mood. The city champions weren't accustomed to facing more than one hick town before proceeding on the Allan Cup trail but a systems glitch forced them to meet Shawville first and that Quebec team, featuring home town player Murph Chamberlain, didn't lie down and die, holding the Montcalms to 3-0 and 4-1 victories. Murph went on to twelve NHL seasons, most with Canadiens.

Gerald McCabe's late goal salvaged a 1-1 tie for Almonte in the first contest and game two, played on water, ended zip-zip, forcing a third encounter. That finished up 2-2, creating an unprecedented fourth meeting which took place before a large Auditorium crowd. The gallant little Almonte team bowed 2-1, concluding a twenty-four game campaign with nineteen wins, four ties, one loss and fifteen shut outs.

Almonte's record proves the worth of keeping a team together. Every regular player had at least three years with the club. Bert Horton was a rebellious but brilliant goaltender behind the defensive wall of George Houston and Frank Honeyborne. Eric Smith, 11-7-18 and points leader, was a perfect pivot to put between scorer Ray Edmonds (12-2-14) and checker Gerry McCabe. British-born Jack Bracewell, Claude Fraser, Danny Larocque and Ed McKenny saw regular duty while Bruce Morris, Art Horton, J. Brooks and the Gilmour boys played occasionally. Eddie Rheaume coached with Tom Blakeney the trainer. Lloyd Julian served as mascot. One of Ray and Jean Edmonds' four sons, Raymond McCrae "Mac" Edmonds, became a well-known insurance and real estate agent in Pembroke while another boy, Lawrence, is a splendid pen and ink artist; you'll find his work throughout the Almonte Legion.

Pembroke, Arnprior, Renfrew, Chalk River and Douglas entered Murray Cup competition, though the County Town representative wasn't exactly Lumber Kings. MacKay St Arena manager Arthur Allard put together a club he called Tigers, changing the name to Allard's Seconds after they won three warm-up matches. Allard's gang eliminated Chalk River and Douglas before falling 5-2 in game one of the final with Arnprior. Before they met again, as often happened with the late-season series, several wandering sons had returned, providing fans with upgraded hockey. Ollie Mulvihill dressed for his home town while the host team

featured Lorne Wilson and Charlie Delahey in addition to Jim Kenny and Timlin. The rugged battle ended 1-1, providing Arnprior a 6-3 margin.

*****

Pembroke Jrs fared even worse than their Sr brethren. The team tasted victory once, 2-1 over Arnprior, the Woollen Town's only loss. Renfrew finished 4-4. Part of Pembroke's problem was an opening game collision between Ivan Fraser and Bert Shepherd, putting Ivan out for the duration with a shoulder injury and leaving only Timlin with a scoring touch.

Arnprior was still strong with Harold McGregor in goal, George Tripp and Art St. Hiliare on defence and powerful forwards in Bob Houston, Wilf Dontigny, Willis Close and Mel Slater. But Renfrew caught them a tad overconfident, winning the league title 3-2, 1-1 (4-3), mostly thanks to the drive of Ernie Troke, Freiman Trophy winner #2. Troke was ably supported by Bill Acton, Joe Lora, Herb Handford, Pat Villemaire, Lawrence Hickey, Roy and Al McNab plus goalie Andy Freemark. Renfrew then defeated Chalk River and Cornwall before taking the Shield by hammering Chesterville. However, the Creamery Town lost to Ottawa Primrose, a club led by Bill Cowley and Stan Pratt that reached the Memorial Cup final, losing 2-1 to Winnipeg.

*****

Columbians defeated Match-Splint for another Kittner but Demers Trophy competition appeared to fade away. PCI, uniformed in pearl, crimson and indigo, lost 3-2 to Ottawa Glebe in the all-Ontario Interscholastic playdowns. Murray Doran scored both markers while Lloyd Reid tended goal. Frank Nighbor and Gerry McLeod officiated.

Arena girls enjoyed a glorious swan song. Leagued with Chalk River and Renfrew, Arenas defeated Conn Dover's crew 2-1, 1-0 (3-1) in one play-off then Renfrew 2-0, 0-0 (2-0) in the other. That gave them the Ogilvy Cup and a shot at Preston Rivulettes in Belleville for provincial honours, where they lost 4-2. This last Arenas team featured goaltender Eileen Fraser, her sister Lois and unrelated Dorothy Fraser; three Kossatz girls, Mary, Ella and Chris (who was by then a Biggs); Helen Kelly, Beatrice Tessier, Millie Dwyer, Genevieve Mullen, Audry Armstrong and top scorer May Campbell.

Westmeath, as was right and proper, won the Cotman.

1931/32

By this time, nobody could afford to photograph a team, let alone play hockey, so the ODHA granted approval of a more local league that would still qualify for Shield playdowns. While Renfrew, Arnprior, Almonte and Carleton Place maintained the UOVSHL label, Pembroke, Chalk River and Cobden organized an eight-game schedule under the North Renfrew Hockey League (NRHL) banner. Jim Bevans coached and Charlie Campbell was president of a Lumber Kings team consisting mostly of graduating Jrs; Bill Tennant went to Sudbury, Boyd Anderson and D'Arcy Sammon to South Porcupine and Vince Chisnell wasn't qualified, having played some late 30/31 minor pro games with Niagara Falls. Denny McMullen played a few early shifts and decided against it.

Only Pembroke played under cover, which increased the League's vulnerability to weather. But the clubs performed before exceptional crowds, particularly in Cobden where playing coach Dr Jim Ritchie had assembled Gerry Johnston, Stan McLaren, Carson Wilson, Ollie Hart and goalie Mac Angus to assist Lawrence (Lorne), Hector and team manager Ernie Robert, three brothers who frequently lost track of their emotional governors.

Chalk River began poorly but improved when Bill Tennant returned from Sudbury. He joined brothers Gordon and George plus an unrelated Tennant also named Bill. Others were siblings Russell and George Field, Percy Hallmer, Mervin McCarthy, Mansey Brown and goaltender Harry Dover.

Led by the scoring of Timlin, Jette and Harvey Schultz plus solid back-stopping by Walter Zadow, Lumber Kings finished 5-1-2 for first and Cobden took second. That season the largest score was 3-1.

Pembroke took a two-game series with Cobden 1-0, 2-1 (3-1) then met Carleton Place, who knocked them off 2-1, 2-0 (4-1). This ended the Kings season after only twelve games. In that second 2-1 defeat by Carleton Place, Bert Walker scored both Carleton Place goals, but in an unusual occurrence Pembroke's tally went off a Carleton Place defenceman and the referee declined to award anyone credit. Carleton Place defeated Chesterville for the Shield, then fell to the Ottawa Shamrocks.

Lumber Kings eliminated Chalk River and Bonnechere All-Stars but lost the final Murray Cup round to Arnprior. Anderson, Sammon and Tom Fitzgerald got home in time to participate.

With Dr Cully ailing, Dave Behan took over coaching the rookie-laden Jrs. Bert Lindsay, in his final season at Renfrew, required few replacements, only Walter Ireton and Graham Plaunt. Arnprior added Bernie Valin, Andy Bond, Felix Cranston and Godfrey Valliant.

The games were, again, tight, low-scoring affairs. Pembroke lost 1-0 to Renfrew on Troke's goal with three minutes left. Then the club played ninety minutes with Arnprior before Arnie Junop scored the game's only marker, then they went ninety minutes with Renfrew when nobody connected. Other than a 6-1 loss to Renfrew, the pattern remained consistent.

Ted Denault relieved Eddie Remus in goal halfway through the schedule. Ted's first action was another first, trailing 1-0, Arnprior coach Tim Mulvihill *pulled his goaltender*. Junop, who already had three overtime tallies to his credit, found the gaping twine too tempting to miss. Tim's club finished out of the play-offs but his all-purpose star, Garnet Anderson, earned the Freiman Trophy.

In the title round Renfrew won 3-1 in Pembroke and Pembroke won 3-2 in Renfrew, the Creamery Town thus prevailing 5-4. Mun Chaput was Pembroke's best player while Lora and Troke led the new champions, who lost the Shield series to Brockville.

*****

Scouts narrowly prevented Match-Splint from taking a third straight town title, keeping the Kittner in circulation. The Boy Scouts had actually won the Demers Trophy in 1931, which they did again in 1932, and in 1933, explaining why the Taylor-Doran Trophy came into existence for 1934.

The Trans-Canada Highway was a work-creating project between Pembroke and Mattawa at the time, and teams working on the road organized to play for the Findlayson Trophy. Emmett Spooner and Aime Jette were just two Pembroke lads who participated.

Participants

Cobden brothers Aubrey and Jim Peever helped win a league title for Kimberley, B.C. in 1924 and they remained out west until 1929. Jim, sixty-eight when he died in 1963 at a Sudbury sanitorium, was a fine one-armed goaltender and pitcher. When he was two years old his father ran over him with a hay mower as he lay sleeping in the field. Aubrey passed away in 1965, at fifty-seven.

David Dover immigrated from Lithuania with his Russian wife, Libby, to Eganville, then Cobden and finally Chalk River, where he gave up his horse and buggy business to become a storekeeper. Son Harry kept goal there for a number of years and his younger brother, Conn, despite losing a leg to blood poisoning at nineteen, organized hockey and ball teams all his life. Conn and Irene (Boucher) operated the Chalk River Hotel.

Gerald "Pin" Lewis extended an after-school job at Art Lemke's Shoe Store to a lifelong profession. Raymond, one of three children born to Gerald and Norine, followed suit. Gerald's brother Lorne (HTC) became a plumber in Red Rock but died there from TB at age thirty-six.

Like Gerald Lewis, Ivan Fraser never played Sr hockey. He was born April 1, 1913, and would have been a Black Hawk at seventeen, if Chicago manager Tommy Ivan had had his way, but Mrs Fraser couldn't see her son alone in a U.S. city. So Ivan joined Max Silverman's Sudbury Cub Wolves and won the 1932 Memorial Cup, though he missed the final series due to injury. Disenchanted with Silverman and told to decide one way or the other by his mining employer, Ivan quit playing. Fraser was married to Ada Nelles for twenty-five years, during which time he went from a grocery store in Coppercliff to real estate and insurance. After his first wife's death he married Naomi (Davidson) McNeil, sister of band leader Trump Davidson who played Casa Loma for years. They lived happily until he died of leukemia March 20, 1990.

Son of Norman and Margaret Tario, Joseph Wellington Tario hung 'em up after the 29/30 season. The Consolidated Paper Co. employee, WWI veteran and husband of Alexina Cecile passed away in September of 1956 at sixty-one. The couple had one daughter, Arden.

Lloyd Reid, youngest son of Westmeath's Norman and Phoebe Reid, became known as Pembroke's "baby doctor," delivering almost ten thousand babies before retiring. Lloyd and Dorothy raised seven of their own. He died January 26, 1985.

Cecil Gallagher quit playing after 30/31 in favour of officiating. He and Estelle had Edward, Arthur, Judy and David. Ed eventually took over his father's insurance business. Estelle died in 1959, Cecil in 1975, Edward and David in the mid-80s—all of cancer.

Roy Ludgate left the game after 31–32, at twenty-eight. Following four after-school years with druggist Billy Wallace and Bill Mulvihill, he intended to become a pharmacist but took up travelling for Gamble-Robinson after a bout of rheumatic fever. Roy married Captain Murphy's daugher Dorothy and was transferred all over northern Ontario before retiring in Kingston. The couple have one son, Rogers.

Just breaking into Sr hockey after two splendid Jr campaigns, Tom Fitzgerald took sick and spent the rest of his life on crutches. Undeterred, he worked as an ordinance clerk at Camp Petawawa and even received a Coronation Medal in 1953. Tom passed away a decade later.

A superb skater with a blistering wrist shot, Alexander Denzil "Denny" McMullen would have been NHL material had he been inclined to back-check. The son of a local builder, he spent several years with C.C. Parker Engineers before becoming a town employee. He became inspector on the 59/60 Lake–Nelson bridge construction. After that he formed a short-lived engineering partnership with Hugh Latimer, passing away August 8, 1964 at sixty-two.

In January 1932 Maple Leaf Dairy employee Daniel C. Vondette demolished his car but miraculously survived unhurt. The next morning, his delivery team bolted, crushing Dan between the sleigh and a retaining wall next to the post office. The thirty-year-old SCBC veteran died four days later.

Near midnight, October 12, 1932, returning from a hunt, twenty-one-year-old Jim Timlin rolled his car into a creek between Chichester and Sheenboro. Three passengers escaped but Jim died, leaving his mother and brother George in Pembroke, father John in Fort William and sister Mary in Montreal. Those teammates that weren't pall bearers formed an honour guard at the talented athlete's funeral.

Cobden's Dr James Evans Ritchie contributed greatly to sports, church, school board, village council and Lions Club before succumbing to heart trouble in February 1960 at sixty-two, leaving his second wife, Jessie (Leach). The Queen's graduate and Pakenham native had initially married Laura Steele, who died in 1951.

Almonte goaltender Albert Horton got married after his most remarkable hockey season ended but was almost immediately sentenced to eight months determinate and twelve months indeterminate for stealing $542 from his employer, Almonte Electric Power Co. Asked why he did such a thing, Bert said, "That's what I'd like to know." He missed most of 32/33 while figuring it out.

Tom Low, the sixty-year-old Quebec City native and former Minister of Trade and Commerce who rose from selling newspapers to owning a conglomerate under the umbrella of Renfrew Industries Ltd., passed away in February 1931. Mackenzie King attended his funeral. Until falling on harder times in later years, Low matched Renfrew's movers and shakers stride for stride.

Thirty-nine years after Pembroke's first hockey game, survivors of the team included: Lennox Irving (Victoria, B.C.), Albert Mackie and lawyer Peter White (Toronto), Bank of Nova Scotia manager J.R. Moffat (Ottawa), lawyers Billy Williams and Fred Supple (Pembroke). Of the Ottawa team: Weldy Young was a mining engineer out West; Albert Morrell, Chauncey Kirby and E.C. Grant were still in the capital while Halder Kirby, Bert Russell and Reg Bradley had "gone before the eternal scorer," as Lennox put it. By the way, Bert Russell was the father of Jeff Russell, for whom that famous CFL memorial trophy is named.

Lastly, a thumb-nail sketch of some of the distaffe Arenas: Beatrice Tessier, daughter of Captain Tessier who operated the *Ouiseau*, worked in a downtown store as did Miss Personality, Helen Kelly. May Campbell married Walter Zadow and the couple moved to Arnprior where Walter taught and coached for decades; a school there is named after him. Dorothy Fraser (sister to Russell and Harvey) married Stewart Hocking and moved to Pt. Alexander; their son Bryan is a prominent PC party member. Mary, Ella and Chris Kossatz were daughters of a riverboat engineer who came from Prussia in 1853.

Eileen and Lois Fraser were excellant skaters, Eileen ending up in goal only because "no one else was stupid enough to do it." The young lady even played without gloves, until Conn Mulvihill gave her a pair. This was a mixed blessing because her mother found blood on them and hit the roof. But Eileen survived to marry Ross Harris and, after Ross died in 1950, become the wife of insurance adjuster Chris Tytler. Eileen outlived Chris too. Lois married Gordon Gunter after WWII, in Vancouver, returning to Pembroke in the early 1950s.

Adjuncts

1931 was the driest summer on record. July and August days often surpassed 100 degrees while June and September frequently reached 90. Even the horses went crazy; one bolted from a downtown stable and plunged headfirst into a moving car, killing itself . . . Just as the Canadian government slapped a $1 licence fee on radios, the U.S. Federal Radio Commission announced technology was available to put television in homes . . . The treasurer of Renfrew County was sentenced to three and a half years in prison for embezzling several hundred thousand dollars.

An eight foot high fence was installed around 360 acres at Petawawa to house Wapiti Elk. Before disease forced its closure after WWII, the game park supplied animals to many areas of North America. Partridge season opened early, closed, then re-opened during deer season, when you had to have a deer licence to take one. In those pre-freezer days, the law required that partridge be "either eaten or stuffed" within ten days of season's close and all venison had to be devoured by March 31, the year following.

Forty-four names were submitted for the 1933 municipal elections, including eleven for mayor, but not a single mayoralty candidate qualified and George Biggs was returned by acclamation, as did the longest-reigning reeve in Pembroke's history, J.D.L. Leitch. The town's worst political period followed; conflict-of-interest charges forced many resignations, creating a near-rookie 1934 council and more early departures.

Auctioneer: You're bidding against yourself, sir.
Bidder: No I ain't. Me father an' me brother asked me to bid on this ere grammyphone an' I'm kinda anxious to see which one o' them gits it.

161

Canadian Olympic Hockey Team
at St. Moritz, Switzerland, 1928
The University of Toronto Alumni Team "The Grads" Amateur Champions of the World

FRANK FISHER	GRANT GORDON	ROGER PLAXTON	CHARLIE DELAHEY	BERT PLAXTON	FRANK SULLIVAN	NOBERT (Stuffy) MUELLER
DEFENCE	FORWARD	FORWARD	FORWARD	FORWARD	FORWARD	GOALER
ROSS TAYLOR	Dr. LOUIS HUDSON	JOHN C. PORTER	W. A. HEWITT	HUGH PLAXTON	DAVE TROTTIER	Dr. JOE SULLIVAN
DEFENCE	RIGHT WING	DEFENCE AND CAPTAIN	MANAGER	CENTRE	LEFT WING	GOALER

1927/28 Varsity Grads, Canada's Olympic team. Charlie Delahey, Grant Gordon and Dave Trottier are the only Pembrokeites to date who have played on an Olympic hockey club. Courtesy Ted White.

Grant Gordon, in Olympic uniform. Courtesy Gerry Gordon.

That great Carleton Place performer, Carol "Buzz" Williams, taken in 1928. Courtesy Buzz Williams.

August 1928. Centennial parade, looking west from the post office, now city hall. Courtesy Margaret Sheraton.

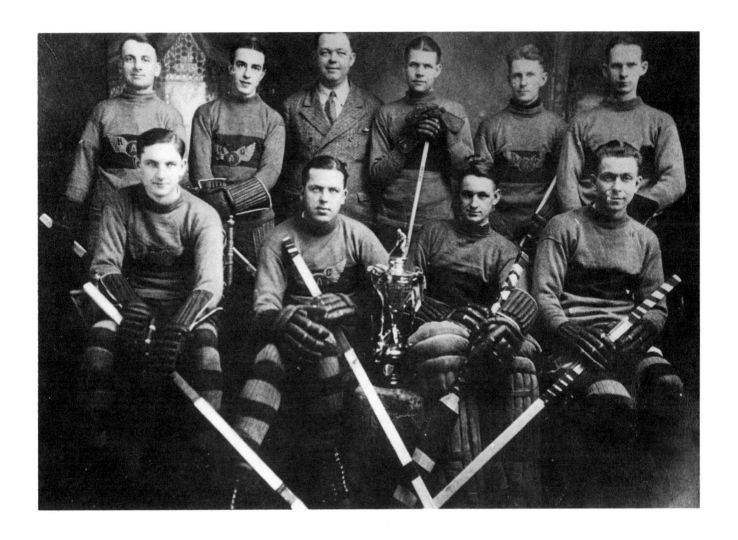

1927/28 Almonte Srs with the Stewart Cup. Wilbert Monterville, Eric Smith, Jack McCabe, (manager), Allan Leishman, George Houston, Dr. Ross MacDowall. Gerry McCabe, Morris McCabe, Bert Horton, Ray Edmonds. Courtesy Mac Edmonds.

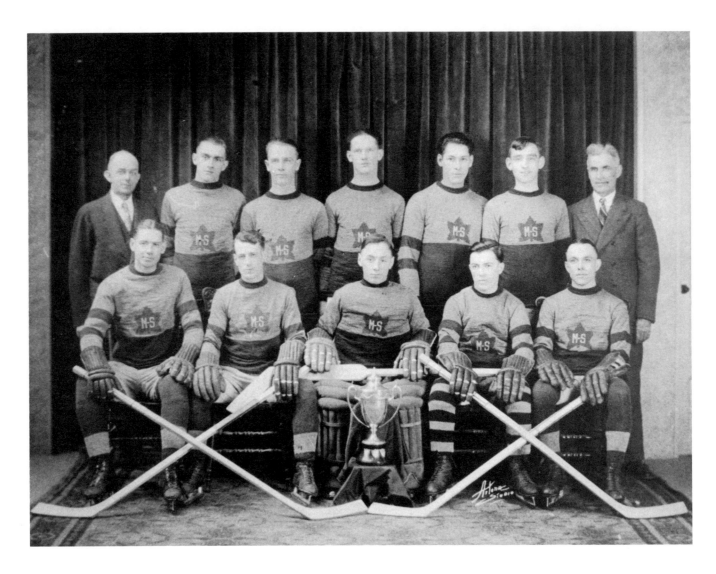

Match-Splint club of 1928/29. Alvin Y. Stroud, Ernie Deloughery, Lorne Biggs, Ivan Fraser, Art Laronde, Connie Zeigel, Robert Knott. Jack Follis, Wilf Jones, Dub Small, Creighton Fraser, Lorne Gardner. Courtesy Crystal Biggs and Adele Cameron.

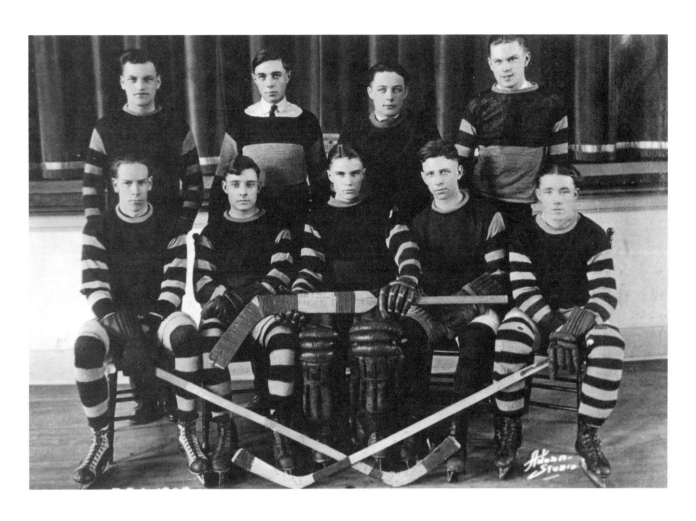

1928/29 PCI. Wib McLaughlin, Art Wallace, a rare picture of Jim Timlin, Bert Shepherd. Harold Clauson, Tom Fitzgerald, Lloyd Reid, Gordon Maves, Allan Mulligan. Courtesy Bob Dey.

Pembroke's first Jr hockey club, 1929. Sid Thomson (manager), Aime Jette, Bert Shepherd, D'Arcy Sammon, David "Dub" Small, Dave Behan (coach). Tom Fitzgerald, Joe Fraser, J. Deacon Taylor (president), Hugh Henderson, Ivan Fraser. Mascot is Emmett Fraser. Courtesy Stuart Taylor, son of J. Deacon Taylor.

LEFT Aime Jette's Citizen Shield. Courtesy Lawrence Jette, a nephew.

BELOW: 1929/30 Pembroke Jrs and the Shield. Percy Doran, J. Deacon Taylor, Jim Findlay, Dr. Jim Cully, Jack Campbell. Roy Hamilton, Allan Seigel, Lloyd Reid, Bert Shepherd, D'Arcy Sammon, Sid Thomson. Allan Mulligan, Joe Turcotte, Dub Small, Tom Fitzgerald, Gerald Lewis. Courtesy Ted White.

169

Sunshine Orchestra. Taken during the later 1920s. Lorne Wilson, Cecil Hughes who continued his music in the Ottawa area, Owen Levans, who became vice-president of Canadian Splint, Charlie Neapole, who went on to become a high-ranking officer of the Royal Bank, and our own Sid Thomson. Courtesy Norah Thomson.

Ed Reaume, Coach

T. Blakeney, Trainer

F. Honeyborne, R.D.

A. Horton, Sub.

L. Julian, Mascot

R. Edmonds, R.W.

Claude Fraser, Sub

J. Bracewell, Center, R.W.

B. Horton, Goal

E. Smith, Center

E. McKenney, Sub.

G. McCabe, L.W.

Geo. Houston, L.D.

D. LaRoque, Sub.

1930/31 PCI Jrs. Joe Houlihan, Jim Scully, Clarence Biesenthal, Bob Dey, Tom Fitzgerald. Wib McLaughlin, Austin Malloy, Lloyd Reid, Duncan McLean, Harold Clauson. Courtesy Bob Dey.

The 1932 launching of the W.L. Murphy ferry. The replaced boiler is lying in front. Courtesy Jack Murphy, the captain's son.

Chapter 14

TOUGH TIMES CONTINUE

1932/33 to 1934/35

Forward passing finally filtered down from the pros. Most rule changes encompassed all hockey quickly but this one met considerable resistance at the amateur level, although the measure was but a stride toward what we know today. Players could only pass ahead within a zone, until the centre red line was adopted in 1943/44. Regionally, we visit the first of two eras that employed "creative scheduling." The phenomenon on this occasion was a money-saving technique brought on by hard times. It occurred again after WWII, even more dramatically, when artificial ice slithered up the Valley, one rink at a time.

Games

1932/33

The NRHL died. Pembroke returned to UOVSHL play and Cobden was also accepted. With the Depression at its worst, everyone paid their own way 100 percent and admission prices fell to pennies. The cost-saving schedule looked like this: Pembroke played Cobden six times, Renfrew four times and the others just twice. Cobden the same. That left Renfrew playing four more games than everyone else, a situation corrected by giving the Creamery

Town only one point for a win over either Pembroke or Cobden.

Francis George Follis was named Lumber Kings president and Eddie Carmody, back home with two seasons of forward passing under his belt, became coach.

Dr MacKercher presided over the Cobden team that Ernie Robert handled. Ernie added Bromley's Gerry Johnston and Jack Stitt of Douglas from the Bonnechere League to several carry-overs that included his brothers. Wilber Neville took over in goal.

Neither town fared well. Cobden finished last with six points, defeating Pembroke twice and Renfrew once. Pembroke was fifth with 13 points. Ritchie Lassman played a few games in goal, then moved to forward when Dub Small took over. But goaltending wasn't the problem. The Lumber Kings only tallied once in the first four encounters! Pembroke's only hat trick belonged to Bob Warner and it came during a 5-4 loss to Renfrew. Bob also scored twice during the club's most decisive showing, 6-0 over Cobden.

Almonte and Carleton Place tied for first place with 20 points but Almonte had the better for and against ratio. Renfrew finished with 19 and Arnprior 18. Arnprior defeated Carleton Place in one semi-final while Almonte, with a well-rested Bert Horton, eliminated the Creamery Town. But Bert's boys lost a best-of-three to Arnprior 2-1. The Woollen Town then went on to beat Maxville before losing the Shield round 10-3 to Brockville Magedonas.

Pembroke did not contest the Murray Cup, which was won by Renfrew. In fact, the only real notice a Lumber King drew all year was when Pat Villemaire spent much of the summer sitting on a flag pole.

*****

Conversely, Pembroke Jrs enjoyed a very successful 32/33 season. However it didn't generate fan interest when Arnprior dropped out and a Carleton Place application was rejected, leaving Pembroke and Renfrew to go it alone through a four-game schedule and automatic play-off.

Coach Fred Totten added Roy McNabb, Buster Scott, Stan Freemark, Felix Dobec and Alex Thur plus Bert and Jim Reeves to his Renfrew club while Dave Behan promoted Peter O'Brien, Vince Marion, Harvey Coumbs and Chapeau's Clarence Keon. NOTE: This Harvey Coumbs is not the man who became a well-known carpenter–builder–supplier in Pembroke; it's his cousin who moved to Kirkland Lake before WWII.

Sporting new red, white and blue jerseys, the County Town Jrs took all four games; 3-1, 2-1 in overtime, 3-0 and 3-2. Murray Doran and Bud Levoy recorded most of the goals. Interwoven among that quartet were decisive exhibition wins over three Ottawa clubs.

However, the title round wasn't nearly as tight, as Joe Kruger and Arnie Junop joined Doran and Levoy to lead scoring in the 8-1 and 6-2 Pembroke victories.

Kruger remained hot during the first Shield series, in which Pembroke defeated Carleton Place 6-1 and 3-2. While waiting for another opponent, Pembroke Jrs defeated Ottawa Primrose 4-2, which was only that team's second loss of the season. Levoy's hat trick and great goaltending by Denault, who edged Remus in games played, led Pembroke to a 4-0 victory in the first game of series two at Iroquois. Fans suddenly began noticing Behan's little gang and a good crowd was on hand when the clubs arrived at MacKay St Arena for game two. That exciting contest ended 3-3, the first lost point for Pembroke in fourteen games. A 7-3 win on the round qualified Behan and Company to meet Cornwall in final Shield action.

A terrific struggle in Cornwall ended 1-1, Keon scored for the visitors—generating eighteen hundred fans for the return match. Gord Levoy's goal wasn't enough as the home side lost 2-1, leaving Pembroke Jrs with little to show for a season in which they lost but once while outscoring the opposition more than three to one.

Still, Valley hockey needed those two games. The clubs praised one another for fine sportsmanship and the losers offered no excuse, even though Ted Denault unwisely left hospital just long enough to play game two after having suffered a serious eye injury in Cornwall. The biggest disappointment was seeing Bert Shepherd come that close to a third Shield in his last of five Jr seasons. After one Sr year, Bert transferred to Toronto with the Steel Equipment Company.

Pembroke Jrs won three more games after that, including a 4-1 defeat of Cecil Duncan's Jr Senators in the Auditorium, following an NHL contest.

Had Behan's boys avoided that 2-1 loss, hindsight suggests the club stood a better than even chance of facing Newmarket in the Memorial Cup finals. The 1932/33 Pembroke Jrs team was lined up as follows:

NAME	AGE	HT	WT	POS	SHOT
Ted "Rhumba" Denault	18	5'6"	128	G	
Eddie Remus	18	5'6"	145	G	
Bert Shepherd	19	6'1"	172	D	L
Murray Doran	18	5'8"	168	D	L
Arnie "Ace" Junop	19	5'10"	169	C	L
"Bullet" Joe Kruger	19	5'7"	150	LW	L
Gordon "Bud" Levoy	19	5'7"	130	RW	R
Clarence "Cooney" Keon	17	5'7"	139	C	R
Jack "Tiny" Latimer	17	5'5"	142	RW–C	R

Peter "Speedy" O'Brien	17	5'7"	146	LW	L
Frank "Clip" Fitzgerald	17	5'6"	148	LW–D	R
Frank Quinn	17	5'7"	139	LW	L
Harvey Coumbs	18	5'8"	142	RW	R

Statistics on Vince Marion and Billy Howe are unavailable.

The modern trend of listing players a head higher and 30 lbs heavier than actual had not yet become fashionable. But age cheating had, an area in which Pembroke officials held their own. On this occasion, we have Joe Kruger, who led team scoring by a wide margin. Joe was born January 21, 1912 but he carried his brother Clifford's birth certificate which was dated April 12, 1914. This not only kept Joe on the team, but his quite talented brother off. Joe Kruger was awarded the Freiman Trophy.

*****

Having added Chapeau and Petawawa, the town league became Pembroke and District Hockey League. Led by Carmen and Earl Keon, Mike and Guy Dempsey and Louie Lacourse, Chapeau upset Rover Scouts for the title. Meantime, Young Scouts defeated SCBC for their third straight Demers Trophy. Managed by Percy Doran and coached by Tom Fitzgerald, this exceptional outfit consisted of goalies Herb and Harvey Kaden plus Frank Zadow, Everett Doran—son of Percy and Murray's younger brother, Allan Levoy—Bud's brother, Jack Duff and Jim Stewart, father's of whom we crossed paths with earlier, Ramsay Garrow, Art Dixon, Elliot Cohen and Doug Thrasher. Some SCBC stalwarts were goaltender Willard Gray, Toots Tremblay, Jim Slattery and Jack Murphy plus Jim and Ken Fortin.

1933/34

Under president W.E. Scott, the UOVSHL became seven teams strong by adding Petawawa. The entire division upgraded to Sr B but still contested the old Shield as the *Citizen* did not create a new intermediate version until 1936.

The schedule was arranged so that Pembroke, Petawawa and Cobden were to play 4-pointers and meet all teams twice; Renfrew, Arnprior, Almonte and Carleton Place playing only 2-pointers, but played each other four times. Add the fact Petawawa and Cobden played outdoors and

it's no wonder only one team, Lumber Kings, finished up playing the intended number of games.

Under president J. Deacon Taylor, a Pembroke Hockey Association was formed for the first time, taking all clubs under its wing. There were internal problems; Eddie Carmody retired and it looked as though Jim Bevans would handle the Kings until Dave Behan took over, having lost his beloved Jrs to Dean Rogers.

Actually, Dave saw few new faces as his team was virtually all former Jrs. He counted on having Dub Small but the little goalie joined a club in Lake Placid, N.Y., making him rarely available. Renfrew and Arnprior were in the same boat except several former Jrs had been in the Sr boat longer. Buzz Williams coached a veteran club in Carleton Place while Almonte still retained most of that 1931 unit. Cobden changed little, while Petawawa relied on goalie Tom Ferneyhough and Art Laronde plus buddies Bert Hall and Jerry Kyle, two lads from Arnprior who were working at the Relief Camp. Petawawa native Oscar Clouthier also dressed with his home club that season. Clouthier later played in Sudbury and with Niagara Falls of the OHA, where he lost an eye. He died of a bee sting in 1972.

The Lumber Kings struggled, finishing fifth with 18 points. Their top scorer was Arnie Junop. Cobden had eight and Petawawa never earned a point. Almonte finished with 39, Renfrew 35, Arnprior 27 and Carleton Place 21. Almonte also won the play-off, 6-4, over Tim Mulvihill's Arnprior team.

The feature 33/34 UOVSHL story came out of Cobden, one night when Carleton Place visited. Poor lighting and similar sweaters revived the fading practice of calling for a pass from one's opponent. This had often been a successful manoeuvre under such conditions, bringing ordinary tempers to the boiling point let, alone the shorter fuses of Mssrs Robert, Robert and Robert.

The referee was Tommy Westwick. Carleton Place was leading 2-0 when Tom chose to penalize Lawrence Robert. Ernie began screaming immediately from the bench but Hector contained himself for all of three seconds before coming at Westwick. He bruised the official's jaw, bloodied his nose, blackened his eye, cut his forehead and knocked him cold. The game ended right there. Hector played no more hockey that year and Ernie, though allowed to continue, was severely censored.

Buzz Williams, who took Westwick to Dr MacKercher for repairs that night, knew Ernie well. Buzz was refereeing a year or two earlier when the Cobden mentor took exception to a call and blind-sided him; Buzz's headache didn't last nearly as long as Ernie's suspension. Among Hector's past transgressions was a 1932 attack on Conn Dover, for which he paid a stiff fine.

*****

At the last minute, Arnprior joined Pembroke and Renfrew in UOVJHL play for an eight-game schedule. Coach Rogers opened camp with forty hopefuls and only four carry-overs began the season. Everett Doran and Allan Levoy replaced their overage brothers and George Timlin put that surname back on the Jr roster. Carmen Keon was expected to fill Clarence's shoes but he elected to play in Ottawa.

Actually, Ted Denault was the only non-rookie when they opened in Renfrew, tying 2-2, Greg Haggarty's first game in the Creamery Town goal. The initial match in Arnprior was also a tie, 1-1, where coach Wilf Dontigny displayed a new goalie, Ed Gram. Other Arnprior additions were Stan Smith, Bernie Valin, Jerome Mulvihill—Bill's son, and Jack Carthy, who fashioned a splendid hockey career including a stint with the 1950s Lumber Kings.

The home opener, Mun Chaput's first Jr game, was painful. Leading Renfrew 2-1 with five minutes left, referee Dave Behan gave Harvey Coumbs a five-minute penalty, allowing Elmer Manion to score twice and win it for the visitors.

There were few goals scored again that season, which ended Renfrew 10, Pembroke 8, Arnprior 6. This time, Pembroke was never in it, losing 2-0, 5-1 (7-1) to a Renfrew club led by Bert Reeves and Ken Briscoe. Ellis Hout fired Pembroke's lone goal.

*****

The town league folded. Scouts, in what was finally being called a juvenile division, outscored the competition 53-10 enroute to its fourth straight title and new Doran-Taylor Trophy. This remarkable club lost but one game in those four years! The Scouts even gave the Jrs a run, losing an exhibition 6-4, with George Timlin scoring all six Jr goals.

Douglas won the George Cup and there's no need to say who took Laurentian League honours.

Frank Nighbor had a rough year. He led Buffalo to first place but lost the play-offs. His mother and sister Inez died five days apart. Then, just before leaving for the 1934/35 training camp, he got a call saying Mickey Roach would be taking his place. However, London coach Toots Holway came down sick and Frank took over that club.

1934/35

Costs and controversy nearly killed the UOVSHL, Dr Box of Arnprior became the third new president even before play began. Almonte and Carleton Place joined the Lanark Group with Smith's Falls and Perth, while Cobden and Petawawa never gave a thought to doing it again, leaving Pembroke, Renfrew and Arnprior to struggle through an eight-game schedule.

Internal strife and strain alone caused the fledgling Pembroke Hockey Association to fold, as did the Lumber Kings. Boyd Anderson joined forces with Lloyd Lewis and Jim Kenny to create the Pembroke Falcons, thus maintaining UOVSHL membership. J.B. Teevens accepted team presidency and, while Charlie Campbell was initially named coach, Wilf Cecile was behind the bench when play began.

The three clubs played it tight, each finishing with eight points. Falcons would have taken first place had they not dropped the final game 9-3 to Renfrew, leaving them third. Pennant-winning Arnprior allowed the least goals and second-place Renfrew scored the most. Pembroke's leading marksman was Bud Levoy with 10 points. Bill Guest and goaltender Joe Zyvitski led the Creamery Town to a 3-2, 4-2 (7-4) victory over the Falcons but superior efforts by Harold McGregor and Vesty Sargeant gave Arnprior the title, 0-0, 7-2 (7-2). In turn, the Woollen Town lost to Smith's Falls in Shield play.

Falcons, sporting a youngster from Petawawa named Roy Giesebrecht, defeated Bonnechere All-Stars in the first round of Murray Cup play but were then disqualified for dressing too many men. All-Stars rode that second wind to their first post-season trophy.

*****

Dave Behan returned to his beloved Jrs, then fought all season with ODHA secretary Cecil Duncan over playing rights to young Giesebrecht, the first of Charlie's sons to make the Giesebrecht name and Ottawa Valley hockey synonymous. Roy, who turned sixteen on September 14, 1933, had been playing with Connie Brown and Hec Kilrea at St. Malachy's in Ottawa the previous season and intended to join the Jr Senators (a club close to Duncan's heart) for 34/35 but a promised job never materialized so he returned home at Christmas, hopefully to play for Behan and Company.

Giesebrecht managed one exhibition game, a 5-3 defeat of St. Malachy's in which he scored twice, before the ODHA secretary advised Dave Behan in writing that Roy must return to the Senators. Dave wrote back, pointing out a rule that said players were to register with their nearest team. Cecil replied that rules were rules indeed and if he allowed one player to skip then any number would do likewise. Behan then claimed the big centre would increase local fan support. This was a mistake as the Senators required similar assistance. Duncan coolly reminded Behan of the "no exceptions" rule again, then used the 1929 Pembroke-Morewood incident as an analogy which, in fact, bore no resemblance whatsoever to the current issue. By late January, letters were dated just two days apart (an impossibility today) and increasingly hostile, the sequence ending with a note from Duncan saying Giesebrecht would play nowhere, period. Within days, Behan learned Roy was again playing for the Senators. He blew his gasket but Duncan merely blasted the Pembroke coach in turn for allowing Roy to participate in a pre-season contest without his permission. Communications abruptly ceased and Roy Giesebrecht, whose personal written plea to Cecil Duncan also fell on deaf ears, was out of competitive hockey for the season.

Meantime, Behan had a team to coach. With just three carry-overs—Billy Howe, Jack Duff and Allan Levoy and Everett Doran who only played one 33/34 game—he recruited several juveniles including goalie Herb Kaden, while brothers Clarence and Carmen Keon returned from a season with Ottawa St. Pats. The club opened with a H&H aginst Renfrew, where 33/34 Freiman Trophy winner Greg Haggarty was still tending goal. Levoy teamed with the Keons for all six markers in a pair of 3-2 wins and it wasn't until game four that Doran broke their scoring monopoly.

Coach Tom Fishenden blended several rookies into his Renfrew club, including Jerry and Elmer Manion, Ed Hickey and Corrie Legris. Legris was with McIntyre Mines when they opened the new Schumacker arena in 1938 before playing in the U.S. Arnprior coach Wilf Dontigny added Norm McNaughton, Ken Moorehouse and Bill Featherstone plus a hot goaltender named Mac Beattie.

Pembroke cruised in first place until Tom Godin returned to Eganville and a flu bug hit Garrow, Howe, Dixon and Kaden. That forced Bob McQuirter from the back-up role and increased ice time for Herb Correll and Chalk River's Delmar McDonald. Losing the last three games left Pembroke tied with Arnprior at 9 points, Renfrew was out of it with 4.

The two-game title round began in Arnprior, where Carmen Keon and Allan Levoy offset markers by Eric Burton and Freiman Trophy winner Stan Smith, sending Pembroke Jrs home on even terms. But they could do nothing right, ending the disappointing season with a 3-1 loss, even though coach Behan kept Arnprior stalwart Jim McDermott out of the game by successfully protesting his lack of a baptismal or birth certificate. Arnprior then lost the Shield series to Brockville.

Since anyone so inclined had traditionally participated in post-season activity, it was considered hilarious that Cecil Duncan suddenly sent written permission for Roy Giesebrecht to do so. Roy played with a clear conscience.

*****

SCBC finally ended the Scouts Taylor-Doran reign, partly by catching them with an overage goalie.

And Frank Nighbor, after leading London to the finals, came home with a broken leg. Frank hadn't been playing; he vacationed at Grand Bend and fell down the river bank.

Participants

Hugh and Ellen (Ryan) Cameron brought Harold Hugh "Harry" Cameron into this world February 2, 1890. After her husband was killed by lightning while working on a log boom, Ellen married Andrew Grace. She died in 1915, at age fifty-seven.

The "free spirit," as we'd call Harry today, never learned to skate until reaching age seventeen but within days of first strapping on the blades he was flying through friend and foe alike.

Toronto Blueshirts playing–manager Jack Marshall,

moved the 154 pounder from forward to blueline in 1912/13 creating hockey's first "rushing defenceman." During the fourteen NHA–NHL years of his twenty-year pro career, Cameron scored an amazing 171 goals in 312 games, plus ten more in 28 play-off contests. How much time he lost to penalty and suspension is anyone's guess. Many of those goals can be attributed to another first for which Harry is credited, a curved shot. Few players developed that knack until bent blades blasting blistering bullets made indirect flight common '50s fare.

Harry holds another claim to fame which will probably never be matched. He's the only player to have won Stanley Cups with three different teams based in the same city: 1913/14 Toronto Blueshirts, 1917/18 Arenas; 1921/22 St. Pats.

Cameron continued playing professionally in the USHL with Minneapolis and St. Louis after leaving Saskatoon Shieks. He returned to coach the 32/33 Saskatoon Sr Quakers. When that club folded he took up WHL officiating, even responding when Frank Patrick called him to referee a Bruins–Maroons game, after which both men agreed it wasn't Harry's cup of tea.

Harry and Ellen (an Ethier from Westmeath) married in 1909 and raised Grace, Marie, Estelle and Andrew; Grace liked her maiden name so well she married a Cameron. Of many grand-and great-grandchildren there were no hockey players but several swimmers, one of whom won a 1958 British Empire Games bronze medal. The couple retired to Vancouver in 1942 and enjoyed six relatively stationary years before the little guy was hit by a stroke. Harry Cameron battled but never fully recovered, being taken by a heart attack October 10, 1953. In 1962, he was the third, and last, Pembroke native elected to the Hockey Hall of Fame.

Eddie Carmody gave up coaching after one frustrating year. Born on Halloween 1906, Eddie spent one season, between his two with Pembroke Srs, in Toronto Merchantile League hockey. After a good 28/29 campaign in Haileybury, he passed up an assaying course at Queen's in favour of joining Ted Oke's IHL Toronto Millionaires. Oke assigned him to the Kitchener Dutchmen of the Canadian Pro League, all of which Ted owned. Eddie played two months in Kitchener before being transferred to Guelph Maple Leafs, where he remained until the Depression forced Oke, a broker, to fold his hockey operations.

Eddie then surveyed out of Amos, Quebec until enlisting in 1942. After the war he worked in a radar parts factory before joining DND at Toronto. He never married, and retired to Ottawa in 1960, and was there when he died on August 24, 1992. His brothers, twins Tom and John, were town league players for some time.

July 19, 1933 was a sad day, for Pembroke's Dr James H. Cully died. Born May 3, 1895 to Mr and Mrs John Cully, Jim moved with dispatch through Ottawa U and McGill to a doctorate. Despite learning of a heart defect early on, the powerfully built young man played all sports and played them well, even enjoying a friendly wrestle. He and Muriel Small were married only a year when a bout of pneumonia in 1931 really set him back. However, the doctor practised until ten days before his death.

A 1906 Thanksgiving day baby, Gerry McLeod was fifteen when he moved from Alice to town and began thirteen years of steady attachment to baseball and hockey. Gerry preferred baseball, though memories of the game included losing his father at a 1925 tournament in Temiskaming. John McLeod had accompanied his son to the weekend affair and was helping a farm friend while Gerry played; a team bolted, John grabbed the bridles and was crushed. Had it not been for the accident, John probably would have lived beyond eighty. His wife and four children sailed past that roadblock with ease. Gerry, a lifetime Canada Bread employee, who married Eleanor Fraser in 1939 they raised a millionares family, passed away June 19, 1992.

Notoriety once lightly touched Gerry McLeod. For four seasons in the early thirties he operated a skating rink at what is now Rotary Park, charging the youngsters 10¢ a day to cover costs. MacKay St Arena president Billy Bogart pressured town council about the "unfair competition" and Gerry finally decided he didn't need the hassle.

Born May 3, 1914 to Mr and Mrs Peter Chaput, Edmond "Nun" Chaput skated better than most youngsters, causing the local Jrs and Srs to anticipate his maturing with enthusiasm. Sure enough, his first Jr year showed great promise, so much so that he spent 32/33 with St. Mikes, only returning home for his last season of eligibility. Then Mun joined International Paper in Temiskaming for $20 a week with lots of his preferred sport, baseball, thrown in. Nun, Eva (Cayen) and their three children moved to the capital when war broke out. There he worked for Ottawa Car and Aircraft, sold insurance, then spent his last decade before retirement in the Psychology Department of Ottawa University.

Allan Seigel, son of Mr and Mrs Dan Seigel, showed all kinds of hockey promise as a Jr. But Allan took sick in 1932 and never recovered, passing away July 5, 1934 at the age of twenty-three.

Another original team member, John R. Moffat, died in 1935, at seventy-two. The retired Bank of Nova Scotia (Ottawa) manager whose brother, Roy, was lost in the Klondike gold rush, left his wife and four children.

Charles Roach passed away in June of 1935. An outstanding local athlete in his day, Charles had been living in Timmins where he served on the NOHA executive for many years.

1935 was the summer Pembroke's Jim Slattery pitched for Brantford Alerts of the OBAA Jr circuit. You could say Jim had a decent season, going 14-0 while his team won the league title.

Arnie Junop, son of Christie and Minnie, turned twenty-one on May 18, 1934 and immediately took off for Kirkland Lake, where a job and sports beckoned. Arnie worked that area until hostilities broke out, then set up military laundries from Gander to Prince Rupert throughout WWII, playing baseball and hockey, once with Doug Bentley, all the while. He came home in 1946, married Leona Waito, and operated the laundry at Atomic Energy till retirement.

Arnie and his Jr teammates were paid $13.50 a week, except Joe Kruger, who got $20 weekly, and Jim Timlin, who was paid $20 a game. Jim's not in the team pictures because his $10 posing fee was refused.

Dub Small went to work in Noranda after 33/34, intending to play goal for the mine team. Unfortunately, he crushed his foot on the job and couldn't suit up till the playoffs. No sooner was he able to play, on March 7, 1935 to be exact, than a sliding ore pile fractured his pelvis and put him in hospital for ages. We don't know where Dub got to after that, but we do know he spent his depression-era summers at Riverside Park, for a newspaper ad read:

Instructor is on duty at beach
Dubby Small is in charge again
Bathing suits needed

Wilf Cecile withdrew from hockey after 1934, following a long and varied career. Though born August 29, 1901 in Westmeath, he was a Pembroke resident by 1907. His family moved to town after his father died and their hotel burned down. Aside from hockey excursions, Wilf never left the County Town, selling Daly Tea before becoming

court reporter in 1939. He married Gertrude Goltz in 1945 and they had sons Michael and David. He became purchasing agent at Consolidated Paper Co. until retirement in 1966. He was working as a night clerk at a local motel when he died of lung cancer August 19, 1969.

Wilf Cecile swore a lot, until 1927. Rushed home from Moose Jaw with pneumonia, it was nip and tuck for several days whether he would survive . One of the nursing sisters, disenchanted with his vocabulary, said she'd pray for him if he'd clean up his tongue. He did, and she did.

John Workman's life as a firefighter was only interrupted by service to his country. After the war he was fire chief at Petawawa before becoming deputy fire marshall in Spryfield, N.S. John died of a heart attack March 22, 1959, leaving his Eganville-born wife, Annie Green, and two children.

Dave Behan's protest of McDermott was a pretty bold move, given that he had another twenty-two-year-old on his roster. Born in 1913 at Sutherland, Saskatchewan, Clarence Keon returned while an infant with his family to the Chapeau, Quebec homestead. One of seven children, he attended PCI and, following the 34/35 Jr season, took employment in Timmins. Clarence came back to operate the family hotel in the spring of 1939, married Laura May Carroll on July 1, 1939. The following September 15 he entered hospital for an appendix operation. He did not survive the anaesthetic. Laura never remarried and passed away October 13, 1992.

Aside from an odd local game and brief stint with the 37/38 Renfrew club, Murray Doran left hockey to join his father's business, Doran's Ladies Wear. He enlisted when the war began and came home after it ended. He married Rose Daniel, and they had two children, Jeffrey and Deborah. His brother, Everett, who local hockey legend Art Bogart says was the smoothest skater he ever saw, entered dentistry at Ann Arbor, Michigan after the 35/36 campaign and served as a dental technician in Halifax during WWII. Everett married Jessie Rattray, Charles's daughter, in 1942 and they had one child, Carol. He too moved into the family business and, after Percy died in 1951, became partners with Murray. Born June 10, 1917, Everett married Erna Lowe after Jessie died in 1980, himself being taken by Lou Gehrig's disease, October 2, 1987. Murray died October 20, 1975, at the age of sixty-two.

While a teenager, Everett Doran caught a stick in the spokes of his bicycle and went face first down a side hill.

In hospital, his temperature soared, breaking just hours before a scheduled arm amputation. Meantime, his brown hair turned snow white.

A significant contributor to Valley hockey was Carl "Buzz" Williams, born in 1906, at Carleton Place. Coincidentally, Buzz Williams and Buzz Armstrong were both born near Christmas, both were named Carol and both arbitrarily shortened it. Williams, also like Armstrong, was playing Sr hockey at fifteen and remained a team leader until attending Clarkson College in 1928. He then saw service with the IHL Detroit Olympics and Can-Am League Boston Cubs before the Depression dropped salaries to pennies and Buzz returned home, joining brother George in his drugstore, before hooking up with another brother, Howard, in the grocery business. A third brother, Jim, was one of Carleton Place's earliest hockey players.

Brockville Madgedomas are an interesting story. MLA George Pulford lifted a town league team he had been sponsoring to Sr B company, renaming the club after four family members: Madge, George, Dorothy and Mary. Prominent for nearly a decade, Madgedomas travelled by specially equipped bus or private plane and the players either worked on Pulford's thirty-five acre estate or his private yacht.

Who first wore #99 in the NHL? Joe Lamb of the 34/35 Canadiens. And #88? Roger Jenkins of the same team. In fact, almost every player on the club wore high double digit numbers.

Adjuncts

During the Depression, people had no money to buy anything. Nowadays, people have money that won't buy anything.

For those in Pembroke and area, the *Standard-Observer* was not only their one connection to the outside world but also with neighbouring communities. The Chartrand family in Sheenboro, Quebec, twenty miles away by road but only a few as the crow flies, eagerly awaited that newspaper. But their subscription ran past due a year, so Mrs Chartrand, fearful of having delivery stopped, dropped into the office and enquired if they could pay up with a load of wood. The editor, realizing the distance and carrying most people anyway, told her to relax and pay when they could. But Mrs Chartrand said they paid for flour with wood and

there was no reason they couldn't do the same for newspapers. Sure enough, a week later family members pulled up with a load of the best, worth $4.50 a cord.

By the way, Dan Jones couldn't live without ink stains; he bought the *Rouyn-Noranda Press* and hung onto it until retiring in 1948 after fifty-two years in the business. Dan and his wife then retired in Pembroke.

Martin Ringrose, of Claredon Township, Quebec was eighty-one when he died July 5, 1934 in Windsor. From the time he came to Pembroke as a young man and began publishing the *Ottawa Valley Advocate*, which he later merged with the *Observer*, till mellowing late in life, Martin wrote editorials that would keep a bevy of lawyers in spending money today. Personally, I suspect he enjoyed himself and would have been fun to know.

Edward A. Dunlop died New Year's Day 1934. His father, Arunah, had died New Year's Day 1892. Plagued by heart trouble, E.A. passed away in a Toronto hospital at fifty-seven. The prominent business and industrial leader who served on almost every area board, including sports, was just twenty-seven when he won that famous political battle with Lorne Hale in 1903 and first became MPP. Following the 1928 landslide victory over Paul Martin, he stayed in office and was provincial treasurer at the time of his death. Premier George Henry and several cabinet ministers attended Dunlop's County Town funeral and we still have his big MacKay St home to remember him by; it is known yet as the "Dunlop estate."

Ed Meilleur, who for three decades was the first person every year to walk across Ottawa River ice, made his earliest trek in 1933—November 22 . . . There was still much talk about that bridge but no one listened . . . The first quintuplets to survive, the Dionne girls were born May 28, 1934 at Corbiel (not Callander!) . . . McLaughlin-Buick introduced "knee action." Officials decided to build an Alaska Highway north from Hazelton, B.C in 1934 but it fell through at the last minute . . . Mae West visited Lord Byng and called him "Dearie." . . . King George celebrated his silver jubilee May 6, 1935 and one of the jubilee medals went to J. Parnell Duff for his VON work.

Someone described the new "autogiro" as "the clumsiest, craziest, flimsiest-looking flying machine ever devised" to which the inventor replied, "The sky has become a place to laze in, to browse in. A vantage point from which to make calm, ordered, well-reasoned study of mortal problems beneath." Not much study went into this contraption; it whirled counter to the rotor blades!

Raymond Hamilton was born between Pembroke and Mattawa at Deux Rivieres. He began stealing as a child, next came major robberies and murder, even killing a prison guard. That earned him U.S. Public Enemy #1 status, as had been John Dillinger, Charles "Pretty Boy" Floyd and George "Baby Face" Nelson. Hamilton escaped from various prisons, including a 1934 dash from the death house in Huntsville. He was recaptured in Texas, all before his twenty-second birthday.

In March 1935, Leslie Scheuneman and Herb Berger had been logging together in Alice township and were discussing disposal of the timber at Herb's Woito Station residence. An argument ensued and Leslie chopped Herb's head off, with the man's own axe. Leslie then set fire to the place and walked away, having pulled Herb halfway out. Naturally, the departed partner wasn't fully consumed by the fire and when Leslie explained, "He was nothing but a damn dog anyway," the court took little time committing him.

Pembroke nearly hosted its third hanging in the fall of 1935 following execution of a Mr Auger in 1873 and a Mr Gogelin fourteen years later. Both those men were woman killers and so was twenty-seven-year-old Albert Cowan of Barry's Bay. Convinced his wife had been cozy with his younger brother, Albert shot her, but a February 26, 1936 date with the noose was changed to life imprisonment after a last minute appeal for clemency.

Again, Chief McKee begged council to replace his motorcycle with a four-wheeled vehicle. How much, they asked. Seven hundred, said Bill. Ridiculous, get a used one, came the reply. How much, asked Bill. Two-fifty, tops. He found one, but they changed their mind.

Later, Bill was given $100 to get the cells cleaned. Rather than hire help he did it himself. Council charged him with misappropriation of funds. Seventeen citizens testified against him and McKee ended up facing seven charges, including improper handling of fines. But Judge John T. Mulcahy exonerated Bill, so four councillors quit.

Next spring, the Chief asked for an $85 raise, to round off his salary at $1700. The town fathers dithered, too long, and McKee quit. When council reconsidered, so did McKee.

With a population of 10,000, Pembroke had a three-man police force. Now at 13,500, twenty-five officers aren't enough.

*****

July 1933. Joe Bradley operated a two-hundred-acre farm near Demers Centre on Allumette Island, which he bought from Pembroke's Napolean Lafrance. Joe's son, Michael, worked with him and lived just down the road with his wife, Emma, and several children. Father and son didn't get along; Joe was a demanding man and Michael, feeling he wasn't getting a fair financial break, grew increasingly frustrated. Finally, during the winter of 1933, Michael crossed the river to visit Mr Lafrance, asking him to split the property so he could go it alone. Napolean explained, though payments were long overdue, he had no authority to do that. Try to work it out with your dad, he advised.

Mike took that suggestion to his father, making Joe more adamant than ever and the relationship further deteriorated. So, on the evening of July 20, while his family slept, Michael Bradley set out across the fields to his father's barn, armed with a 32 Special and plenty of ammunition. He intended to await Joe's appearance at dawn, shoot him, and return home.

Michael did exactly that, but, before he could leave, his father's retarded brother appeared and he was obliged to shoot him too.

The angry young man had just finished stuffing his second victim under a haystack when his sister arrived on the scene. She dashed for the house, her brother in hot pursuit with a bag over his head, firing as he ran. Wounded, she managed to reach the kitchen before Mike got close enough to finish her off. Mrs Bradley turned from the stove, she lived only seconds longer than her daughter. Upstairs, Michael caught his brother before he could escape from the bedroom.

He backtracked home, hid the smoking rifle under the kitchen floorboards and rested a while.

Meantime, neighbors had heard the shots and the girl had been seen being chased from barn to house. Someone got up enough nerve to peek through a kitchen window, and called the police in Campbell's Bay. Pembroke police were also notified and they advised Mr Lafrance who immediately, with his son Leo, boated across, arriving as a mystified Michael appeared. They offered him condolences.

189

Quebec police had no trouble finding four bodies thus suspected Joe's brother, until they searched the haystack. That left only Michael as a suspect. A search warrant was obtained, the gun found and soon confirmed as the murder weapon.

Michael's trial was first booked for the fall in Campbell's Bay but with the usual string of delays it didn't take place until July 16, 1934. Amazingly, the jury returned hung, generating another trial, this time in Hull the following January. Found guilty and sentenced to hang April 5, Michael Bradley fainted and had to be carried from the courtroom.

Though a commutation petition was circulated, Michael died as prescribed, the first ever hanging in Pontiac County.

By that time, Emma Bradley was working at the Mackay House for Tom and Josephine Landriault; she stayed with them until Josephine died in 1935. Eventually, Emma remarried and moved to Toronto.

Island residents were regular sellers at the Pembroke market. For years after the tragedy they identified themselves as "being from where the murders happened," presumably to aid sales. Some say it worked.

The 1931/32/33 Scouts. Bob McQuirter, Herb Harvey, Clarence Wright, Art Dixon, Percy Doran, Herb Kaden, Doug Thrasher. Lloyd Bailey, Everett Doran, Don Stewart, Frank Zadow, Ramsay Garrow, Jack Duff, Allan Levoy. Courtesy Don Stewart.

The 1933/34 Scouts made it four titles in a row. Nate Cohen, Clarence Wright (scoutmaster), Art Dixon, Andrew Mackie, Lloyd Bailey, Walter Zadow (coach), Percy Doran. Reg Smith, Ramsay Garrow, Everett Doran, Herb Kaden, Jack Duff, Don Stewart, Bud Cohen. Goaltender Bob McQuirter is missing. Courtesy Don Stewart.

McKay St Arena, shortly after WWII, by the look of the vehicles. Courtesy Ted White.

1935/36 Match-Splint. Murray Doran, D'Arcy Sammon, Len Kathen, E.L. Smith, James Parr, Connie Ziegel, Charlie Knott. Hugh Hart (president), Herb Harvey, John Workman, Walter Zadow, E. Jones, Jack Duff, Owen Levans (manager–coach). Don Stewart, Wilf Jones. Courtesy Don Stewart.

1935/36 Little Lumber Kings. Courtesy Ted White.

1935/36 Little Lumber Kings in Toronto, before the final game. Courtesy Allan Levoy.

1935/36 West Toronto Nationals. Courtesy Brownie Andrews.

1948/49 Fort Frances Canadians. Coach Gordon Fraser is back right. Joe Balzan, rear left, took this club to the Allan Cup in 1952. The captain was Walter "Sambo" Fedoruk, standing second from right. Courtesy N–W Ontario Sports Hall of Fame.

ABOVE: 1936 shot of Captain William Murphy (wearing sweater) and his engineer, Peter Rouleau. Courtesy Jack Murphy.

RIGHT: Ted Lindsay. Courtesy Ted Lindsay.

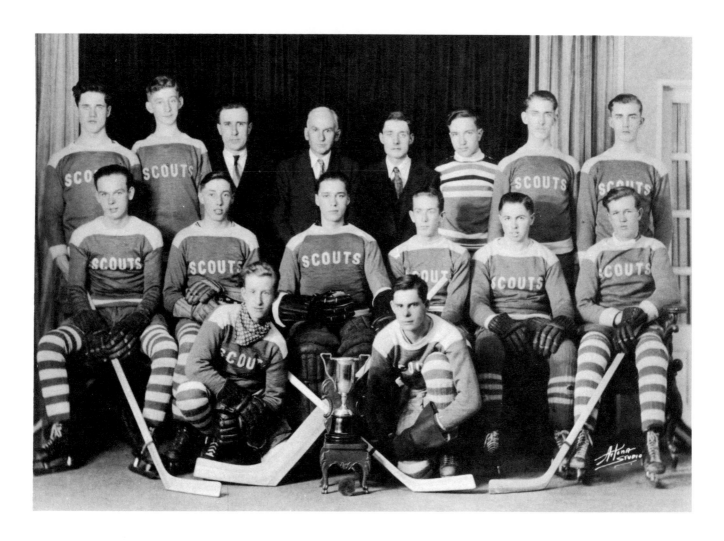

1935/36 Scouts. Back: Frank Remus (captain), Fred Romhild, Clarence W. Wright (scoutmaster), Percy C. Doran (manager), Tom Fitzgerald (coach), Earl Sweeney (spare goaltender), Basil O'Dacre, Gerald Buder. Front: Gillan Johnston, Tom O'Brien, Frank Gauthier (goaltender), Harold Choppin, Martin Sullivan, Chris Corrigan. Kneeling: Bert Gagnon, Boyd Briscoe. Courtesy Tom O'Brien.

LEFT: Frank Nighbor and Dave Behan, 1935. Courtesy Pat Nighbor.

BELOW: 1935/36. Everett Doran, whose hair turned white after an accident. Here, thanks to the miracles of modern science, it is brown. Courtesy daughter Carol Doran.

Chapter 15

JUST WHAT THE TOWN NEEDED

1935/36

Let's do this one backwards; more or less. First; town and Sr hockey, then participants, closing with Pembroke Little Lumber Kings outstanding campaign. There were no significant rule changes and we'll dispense with further adjuncts.

All games but Jr

1935/36

The Pembroke Hockey Association surfaced again, sputtering through the war before taking a firm hold.

Under president Ken Currie, the town league had a fine year. Chalk River, Tuxis, Match-Splint, SCBC, Milling Co. and PCI battled for the Board of Trade Cup. Conn Dover's Chalk River gang lost the final to Match-Splint, managed by Hugh Hart. The Scouts secured a fifth juvenile title in six years, beating SCBC. Westmeath won another Cotnam Shield of course, and Northcote took the George Cup.

Little changed in UOVHL Sr hockey except Arnprior opened a new rink. Falcons president Jim Teevens and coach Emmett Spooner welcomed Arnprior's Bert Hall and Jerry Kyle from Petawawa, and Lawrence Robert came up

from Cobden once again. Wearing black-crested yellow sweaters, the club came back from a 2-0 deficit to win its opener 3-2 over Renfrew. The highest score of the season was 4-3, a Pembroke loss in Arnprior that gave Hall and Kyle reason to wish they'd never visited home. Not only did the Falcons lose, with Arnprior's Mac Mooney firing the season's only hat trick, but the pair followed a snowplow for miles and, when it got stuck, spent nearly three hours shoveling themselves around it, arriving at the game with frozen feet.

In the final standing Renfrew had 9 points, Pembroke 8, and Arnprior. Renfrew's Felix Dobec won the scoring title with five goals and one assist! Bud Levoy had as many points but only two goals. Arnprior scored nine goals in the eight games and Pembroke tallied fifteen.

Another first that season was the *best-of-five* series between the Creamery and County towns. Renfrew took it three straight: 6-3, 7-1 and 4-3. Alton Dick, Dobec and Bill Scott did most of the damage while Boyd Anderson and Bert Hall had the honour of scoring the last goals for a Pembroke Sr hockey team till 41/42. Renfrew then lost to Smith's Falls Mic-Macs, with whom Bill Tennant played. That club won the Shield by defeating Prescott.

Participants

Gordon "Bud" Levoy, one of nine children born to Mr and Mrs Peter Levoy, came into this world October 18, 1912, which means he was another of Behan's Jrs that slipped in an extra season. Levoy had been learning the shoemaking business from Joe Tessier of Fraser and Grieve, a company that produced wooden-pegged river driver boots, but after the Srs folded he went to Sault Ste Marie, remaining there until enlisting in 1943. Bud married Marg Lovelace of Deloro, Ontario after the War and became a Crown Life agent in Pembroke. The couple raised three children.

A gifted sax and banjo player, Boyd Anderson also played hockey well. But he bucked the system, hitting bottom in 1932 by being the wheel man for Alvin Donahue and Lawrence Gareau when they robbed Alice postmaster Charles Moss at gunpoint. They went up for two and a half years plus ten lashes while Boyd got two and five. Upon his release, Anderson helped organize the Falcons and, meeting anyone with waywardly intentions, he'd merely take off his shirt.

Boyd and Eva moved to Kingston before the war and remained there till he died in the mid 1970s. Of their four children, Jim became well-known in the hockey world, coming up through the Kingston minor system to the Windsor Spitfires, Glace Bay and Edmonton before spending twelve years with the incomparable Eddie Shore and his Springfield Indians. Jim stayed in Springfield, working for Miller Breweries and scouting for the Los Angeles Kings.

Though Aime Jette continued to play with the road building crew, his last Pembroke team was the 34/35 Falcons. Aime, who never married, took a job building the new hydro dam at Rolphton in 1948. A temporary suspension bridge that had been in place only four hours, gave way, sending Aime and five fellow workmen into the torrent below. His drowned peers were recovered within hours but Aime battled the current considerable distance before succumbing. The thirty-eight-year-old was found several days later, one arm torn from its socket and a leg completely missing. A coroners jury determined the 170-foot span was "just too long."

Lawrence Robert returned home and managed Cobden's Bonnechere League team. Suddenly, March 2, 1939, while building a new rink, Lawrence died of a heart attack, he was only thirty. Ernie died of TB during WWII. Hector was born

January 10, 1910. He earned his living painting and paper hanging, until he passed away October 14, 1978.

Bert Hall and Jerry Kyle made 20¢ a day when they started at the Petawawa relief camp cookery. Naturally, the pair jumped at Gordon Fraser's invitation to join his Baltimore club. Jerry quit after one season but Bert carried on longer. While playing for his RCAF team in 1940, Hall broke a leg, getting himself kicked back into civvies. He married Helen Slater. and they had four children. Bert eventually returned to hockey, taking a hit from Pembroke's Cully Simon in 1947 that ended his playing and gave him knee trouble for life. Bert Hall put in three decades as Arnprior's recreation director before retiring.

Daulton "Dolly" Olivier, usually mispronounced Oliver, played over twenty years, all of them for his home town except one campaign in Chesterville. Always a top performer, Dolly's hockey career almost ended before it began. Woollen Town players stepped onto the ice under an overhead door; it fell on Dolly one night, putting the little playmaker out of commission for some time. But he survived to father two children and live a long life in his favourite community.

1935/36 Pembroke Little Lumber Kings

Success

- or -

How a few local lads provided desperately needed distraction from desperate times

The Pembroke Jrs became the Little Lumber Kings officially, and the Baby Kings unofficially. J. Deacon Taylor and Sid Thomson remained president and secretary respectively, while Archie O'Connor became treasurer. The management committee consisted of Cecil Bailey, J. Parnell Duff, Bill Radke, N.B. "Chick" Giroux, Cecil Gallagher, Joe Sikorski, Albert Marcotte, Jim Findlay and Percy Doran. Mailman Jack Sarsfield remained trainer, father figure and curfew enforcer, with the help of Jim Hill. Dave Behan coached once again. The club played a six-week, eight-game schedule with Arnprior and Renfrew beginning December 30, 1935.

The goaltenders were the small but quick Bob McQuirter, backed up by reliable John Poirier.

The defencemen were Ottawans Don Grant (Jr Senators)

and Cliff McBain (Gladstone), the only two from beyond spitting distance. A clever player but poor skater, Grant was worked to exhaustion by the fundamentalist coach, emerging on a par with most teammates by season's end. McBain, his reliable partner, proved unflinching on ice and off; Taylor spun his car into a snowback one night and the dozing defenceman never woke up. Supporting this pair were Lloyd Bailey, who seldom ventured up ice, and Len Turcotte, he of the wicked but unpredicable shot.

The forwards included Roy Giesebrecht at centre. Big for his day at six foot and 165 lbs, the first of five brothers, he was destined to reach hockey prominence. He joined the Detroit Red Wings, before several sparkling post-War years with the Pembroke Sr Lumber Kings. Carmen Keon, a diminutive sharp shooter from Chapeau, patrolled the right wing and Allan Levoy, who employed an after-goal dance like Tiger Williams and an evasive action like Serge Savard, held down the left side. Often compared to Frank Nighbor, centre Everett Doran checked ferociously and scored timely goals. The most well-rounded athlete was Ramsay Garrow, one of those disgusting guys who did everything well the first time he tried it. Art Dixon, who weighed 140 lbs if he was carrying a tool box, stirred the pot as required. Jim Slattery, Herb Currell and Don Stewart filled in admirably as and where necessary.

The Little Kings played four preseason exhibitions, defeating Ottawa Quakers 6-1 and Ottawa U 2-1 before Poirier got his first start and lost a tough 2-1 decision to St. Pats. John would have played the next game too only he widened his nose in a car accident, allowing McQuirter back between the pipes to defeat New Edinburgh 4-2.

Pembroke opened in Renfrew and fell behind 2-0 before scoring the game's last five goals. A return match ended 4-3 for the home side. Then Arnprior Greenshirts lost 6-1 and 5-3 to Behan's boys, Roy Giesebrecht establishing a steady pattern of two goals a game. Doran and Levoy led their club to a 5-3 win in Renfrew, then Keon's hat trick was enough for a 5-2 victory back home. Roy might have scored his second of that contest if he hadn't catapulted head first into the goal post, putting himself in hospital. Fortunately, the big fellow recovered quickly.

Len Turcotte joined the Little Kings at that point. He, Giesebrecht and McQuirter immediately turned up in Arnprior sans skates; they played due to local generosity. The Kings prevailed 6-1, then took the return match 5-1.

So Pembroke took all eight games while Renfrew and

Arnprior finished tied. At 12-12-24, Giesebrecht topped league scoring and a string of teammates followed before we find Renfrew's Elmer Manion and Herb Clarke of Arnprior Greenshirts with five points each.

The Renfrew–Arnprior two-game series had its moments. Each team won 2-0, forcing a third contest, in Renfrew. Ken Moorehouse and Ludger Diotte gave Arnprior a 2-0 lead in that match before Elmer Manion made it close. With two minutes left, Billy Lockwood lifted a shot that Gerry Manion deflected past Mac Beattie to tie the score. Referee Alex Barnet, of Renfrew, was about to drop the puck at centre ice when judge of play Tim Mulvihill, of Arnprior, called no goal, claiming Manion was in the crease (a no-no for even the goal scorer then). They argued, while the clock was allowed to run out. That fueled the fire. Eventually, Barnet ordered overtime but Arnprior coach Jim Mulvihill, Tim's cousin, packed up his team and went home. So Barnet conducted a face-off and Lockwood put it in the empty net. Renfrew won.

Cecil Duncan did not agree, and ordered game four, in Arnprior. Ottawa's George Seed refereed, without a judge of play, and Bernie Valin led the Greenshirts to a 4-3 victory.

Mulvihill's team fought hard in game one of the two-game final, earning a home ice 3-3 tie. But at MacKay St Arena on February 20, 1936, the Little Kings took league honours by way of a 10-1 landslide, six players sharing the ten goals, including Roy's usual two.

Next, came a trip to Perth, where Roy broke the routine with a hat trick, his club winning 11-0. That humiliated coach Rusty White and his proud Blue Wings; they came into Pembroke breathing fire and, though they lost, it was just 3-2 and only a late pair by Keon made the difference.

The Little Kings then faced Fyre Fyters of Westboro, a community now swallowed in the Capital. Again, Pembroke romped to an easy win in the first game, 11-1, before coasting through a 2-2 tie. Though Roy recorded eight points in the two games, every Pembroke player except McQuirter got at least one point, prompting a Westboro fan to ask, "They told us Pembroke was a one man team, which one?"

Coach Behan's line-up required an adjustment to meet the Shield holding Brockville Cubs because Everett Doran came down with measles. With Don Grant playing forward in game one at the Island City, Cubs surged to a 3-1 lead, forcing Don's return to the blueline and Jack Poirier to take over in goal. Jack played brilliantly, though the Cubs won 4-3 after Roy scored twice to make it close. Goaltender Dave McFaulds and the line of Jack and Bill Imerson plus Doug Frye dominated Brockville's statistics.

The *Standard-Observer* resurrected its information hotline for that match, March 3, and interest was such that Pembroke's first riot went almost unnoticed. (Unhappy with relief distribution, a large crowd damaged the town hall and five people were arrested.)

The second game was played in a packed MacKay St Arena. Poirier was brilliant again, especially early, allowing only Russ Rourke and Steve Foldeak markers while his mates got untracked. Hat tricks by Giesebrecht and Grant eventually secured the Shield, 9-3 (12-7). The Cubs leading defenceman was Cully Simon, a Brockville native who dressed with the 37/38 Little Kings, then returned after WWII by way of Detroit Red Wings to marry Roy Giesebrecht's sister and become a big part of post-war hockey in the County Town.

Now, the big stumbling block, ODHA honours. Beat Ottawa University and it's the Memorial Cup express.

First, PCI coach Allan Levoy took his team to Beachburg for a fun game. Giesebrecht went along though neither lad was supposed to play. However, they couldn't resist the temptation and dressed for the third period. Making a rush, Levoy jumped to avoid being sandwiched at the blue-line. His skate caught Henry Metcalfe on the neck, severing an artery. Henry dashed to the club house while Roy drove for a doctor with his skates on and Allan employed what he'd learned in Boy Scouts, clamping the blood vessel off with his fingers. Henry was unconscious when Roy returned with medical assistance to find Allan still locked on the artery. Metcalfe fully recovered and was even able to attend Little Kings games before they finished the season.

With MacKay St Arena pure slush, the Ottawa U–Little Kings two-game series was played in the Auditorium, March 13 and 14, 1936. Cecil Gallagher and Jack Duggan officiated. Poirier hung tough in the first contest till four straight third-period goals gave the students a convincing 5-2 victory. Roy Giesebrecht played only because the train waited twenty minutes in Pembroke for the Petawawa lad to dig himself out of a snowdrift.

Coach Ally Garland's garnet and grey team, led by Ken Kilrea, Gord Pantalone and goaltender Jacques Garceau, had thrown a blanket over big Roy and figured to do it one more time, then proceed in search of a Memorial Cup. But forty-five hundred fans, half of them from Pembroke, witnessed little Art Dixon grasp his moment of fame, sandwiching goals by Doran, Garrow and Giesebrecht between two of his own for a 5-1 (7-6) upset of the century. Bob McQuirter had back-stopped his club to the first ODHA Jr crown not taken by a city team, in comeback fashion, against a club that had not lost all year. It was little wonder the County Town went nuts!

The disappointed losers were good sports, visiting the jubilant winners' dressing room almost to a man, as did several Perth and Westboro players.

The Little Kings next opponent was the Amherst Canucks, necessitating a trip to Moncton, N.B. The train left town at 3am but Pembroke's hockey players, complete with bowler hats and scarves, were bundled into sleeper cars long before then by parading townspeople. In addition to the executive, Ellseworth Smythe went along as did cheerleader Oscar Landriau. The *Citizen* sent Jack Koffman, and Cecil Gallagher made regular reports to the *Standard-Observer*.

What was promoted as a best-of-three began March 19. Only twelve hundred fans trudged through pouring rain to watch a game frequently halted by fog. Tied 3-3 after fifteen minutes of play, Pembroke pulled away to a 9-4 victory. Amherst had not lost a game to that point but found Grant and McBain impenetrable and Giesebrecht's line too fast. Roy had a four and two night, giving goalie Norbert White nightmares. Keon scored two, McBain one, Levoy one and the season's prettiest goal came off Garrow's stick after a three-way, end-to-end rush. The Amherst line of brothers Frank and Carl Ripley plus Creighton Lowther registered a goal each while Elmer Fraser also scored once.

Before the second game began, officials declared Pembroke would take the series if it ended tied. Since that resembled neither a two-game nor a best-of-three, the match was played under a cloak of mystery. Sure enough, it was a 2-2 tie after sixty minutes. A lengthy discussion followed and they decided on overtime. Lowther made it a three point night by notching the winner, forcing game three.

The crowds were poor, but after Dave Behan, aided by Everett Doran on the piano, fired off a sales pitch on local radio, three thousand fans crammed the rink, March 23. Meantime, telegrams arrived from hundreds, including Nighbor, Lorne Wilson, Lennox Irving and young MacKay St Arena manager Art Bogart. Peter White sent Dave $25 to help with expenses, while the Windigokan Sturgeon Mining Syndicate provided 200 shares to the club for "promoting clean and up-to-the-minute hockey in Pembroke."

The Ripley brothers gave Amherst a third-game 2-0 lead, then Giesebrecht cut the margin in half. But the Canucks made it 3-1 on a goal everyone, except the referee, said came nowhere near going in. The umpire was therefore replaced as a matter of form. Roy scored a second-period marker and at 6:10 of the third, McBain, Garrow and Doran combined to tie it up. The frantic pace continued unabated until Giesebrecht went end-to-end for the hat trick winner with 1:40 left in regulation time. Naturally, the Little Lumber Kings returned home to cheering masses.

The CAHA had scheduled the Eastern Ontario–Maritimes winner to play Quebec, and Quebec Aces were ready to go. The survivor of that series was to meet the Ontario champions in the Eastern Canada Memorial Cup finals. Suddenly, the CAHA reversed the procedure.

The Toronto West Nationals won the Jr OHA title one night before Pembroke eliminated Amherst. The Nationals then played South Porcupine two games, four nights apart, winning 13-5 on the round. Next, Nationals played Quebec, two games, three nights apart, Nats winning the round 16-4.

Dave Behan's team could have been playing the Aces while the Nationals and South Porcupine met, delaying no-one, under the original plan. The mysterious switch forced Little Kings to wait twelve days, losing momentum in a town with no ice!

Within twenty-four hours of learning about the reversal, Pembroke Citizens had donated $1000 toward practice at the Auditorium, during which time Frank Boucher lent Dave a hand and the Ottawa press wrote encouragement.

A CNR bid to deliver three thousand fans for the best-of-three opener in Ottawa, April 4, 1936, edged a CPR price by 20¢ a head. The Aud's largest crowd to date, over nine thousand, watched Harold Ballard's club take a 3-0 lead, slip to 4-3, then recover for an 8-3 romp. The Nationals used

a method abandoned in the Ottawa Valley since lighting improved; that of hoisting bouncers at the goaltender. McQuirter had trouble with them.

The teams next met in Maple Leaf Gardens, April 7. Coupling the mysterious scheduling change with an established local coolness toward Ballard's hand-picked team, only a thousand fans showed up. This was too bad, because Pembroke Little Lumber Kings gave it their all. McQuirter was brilliant, back-stopping his mates to a 3-1 lead after forty minutes. But they wilted under terrific forechecking, and more long shots, falling 4-3. Doran scored a goal and Giesebrecht maintained his two goals a game pattern to the very end.

The Nationals then defeated Saskatoon Wesley's, 5-1 and 4-2, for the Memorial Cup. Six Nats went on to the NHL: Johnny Crawford, Roy Conacher, Bill Jennings, Red Heron, Jack Shill and Johnny "Peanuts" O'Flaherty.

Since winning the Shield, the Little Kings had scored twenty-eight goals in seven games, allowing the same number. Roy Giesebrecht led with a 12-4-16 record and Carmen Keon followed at 4-6-10. Jock Walton, a local butcher, promised Allan Levoy a pound of sausage per goal all season; Allan recorded twenty-one markers and ate well. Roy Giesebrecht took the Freiman Trophy and still has it; for some reason the award was never presented again.

Five hundred people jammed PCI auditorium later in April for a memorable banquet. With Mayor Albert Cockburn officiating, D'Arcy Finn presented the *Citizen* Shield, and newly elected CAHA president, Cecil Duncan, delivered the ODHA Ahearne Trophy. Oscar Landriau also presented a "Cup," one he had made for the boys while down east. Tom Fishenden represented Renfrew, and Frank Boucher came up from Ottawa. Pembroke town council gave each member of the Little Lumber Kings a gold watch. The Anderson Orchestra—Greg George, Charlie Hale, Bill Anderson and Boyd Anderson—provided music. So did Everett Doran. It was a heck of a night.

Epilogue

The story doesn't end here, of course. Some may think it's only the beginning, which is quite understandable as many have passed on, even from the great 1936 Jr club.

There is certainly an intriguing tale within the confines of 1937 and 1961, after which Sr hockey died throughout the land. It begins with a Jr club every bit as polished as its immediate predecessor, only the season's conclusion being significantly different.

Next, another war; a time when Petawawa Camp housed hockey talent of the highest calibre—if frequently packaged in shotgun casings.

The 1940s spawned a string of remarkably proficient Pembroke Juvenile teams, clubs that didn't always receive a fair shake from the ODHA hierarchy.

When the war ended, Pembroke slammed back into Sr hockey with a gusto, beginning a string of 'golden years' talked about to this day. Jr competition was hit and miss then, a stigma thrown off with flair as the 1950s drew to a close. A new arena and, of course, new names came into play.

On the adjunct side: politics, dams, murder, mystery, horses on a military payroll— and that blessed bridge. Indeed, something for everyone.

I'm working on it.

Harold Garton

References

A Canadian Millionaire by Michael Bliss; MacMillan of Canada.

Hockeys' Captains, Colonels and Kings by J.W. Fitsell; Boston Mills Press.

The Trail of the Stanley Cup by Charles L. Coleman: Volume one published by Kendall–Hunt Publishing Co., Debuque, Iowa; volumes two and three published by Progressive Publishing Inc., Sherbrooke, Que.

Photo List

*****

CTM, Champlain Trail Museum
N–W Ont, North Western Ontario Sports Hall of Fame
MLG, Maple Leaf Gardens

Contributors

The following people gave in-depth interviews:

John Carroll "Buzz" Armstrong, Ottawa;
Dave Behan, Pembroke;
Crystal Biggs, Pembroke;
Art Bogart, Pembroke;
Gertrude Cecile, Aylmer,
Que; Roy Giesebrecht, Petawawa;
Lois Gunter, Pembroke;
Bert Hall, Arnprior;
Arnie Junop, Pembroke;
Allan Levoy, Pembroke;

Gordon "Bud" Levoy, Pembroke;
Gerald Lewis, Pembroke;
Lloyd Ludgate, Fergus;
Roy Ludgate, Kingston;
Gerry McLeod, Pembroke;
Daulton "Dolly" Olivier, Arnprior;
Don Stewart, Pembroke;
Eileen Tytler, Pembroke;
Dr. W.W.D. "Dick" Williams, Pembroke;
Margaret Willison, Pembroke.

The following people also contributed.
They are all Pembroke and area residents, unless otherwise specified.

Sharon Adams;
Jim Anderson, Springfield, Mass;
Don "Brownie" Andrews;
Eileen Andrews;
Kathleen Barry;
Bill Beal;
Dick Billsborrow;
Dwyne Blick, Toronto;
Ken Briscoe, Northcote;
Hazel Bromley;
Grace Cameron, Victoria, B.C;
Angus Campbell
Eddie Carmody, Ottawa;
Mrs Tom Carmody;
Denise Casey, Toronto;
Bob Chouinard, Beaconsfield, Que;
Sister Clotilde Chusroskie;
Lillian Corner;
Dorothy Cotnam;
Jeanne Cringan, Petawawa;
Norma Daley, Petawawa;
Mac Davis, Almonte;
Charlie Delahey, Toronto;
Bill Deloughery;
Noreen Desjardins, Westmeath;

Marjorie Devine;
Bob Dey;
Helen Dey;
Moodie Doering;
Irene Dover, Deep River;
Benny Duke;
Lawrence Edmonds, Ottawa;
Raymond McCrea "Mac" Edmonds;
Ed. Eldridge, Ft. Frances;
Emmett Ethier, Westmeath;
Lawrence Ethier, Westmeath;
Ron Ethier, Westmeath;
Sambo Fedoruk, Ft. Frances;
George Fishenden, Renfrew;
Kay Fishenden, Renfrew;
John Flavelle;
Des Fleurie, Ft. Frances;
Emmett Fraser, Morrisburg;
Helen Fraser, Morrisburg;
Orin Frood Jr., Ottawa;
Leo Gagne;
Joe Gauthier;
Vic Gauthier;
Vince Gervais, Westmeath;
Gerry Gordon, Toronto;

Martha Graham;
Wilbert Hamilton;
Francis Henessey, Westmeath;
Evelyn Higgins;
Mary Hill;
Harry Hinchley, Renfrew;
Joe Houlihan;
Allan Huckabone;
Lawrence Jette;
Keith Jordan;
Ed Kelly;
Angus Kennedy;
Laura May Keon, Chapeau, Que;
Gary Knott;
Kay Knott;
Reg Knott;
Alec Kohls;
Elsie Kohls;
Oscar Kohls;
Felix Kutchaw;
Ed Landriault;
Marguerite Landriault;
Hortense Lawn;
Fred Larose, Almonte;
Mary Lee, Renfrew;

Corrie Legris, Calabogie;
Edith Leishman, Almonte;
Ed Lehman;
Cassie Lemke;
Mrs Geo. Lemke;
Gerald Lett;
Norene Lewis;
Tom Liberty, Almonte;
Blake Lindsay, Birmingham, Mich;
Margaret Lindsay, Renfrew;
Ted Lindsay, Metamora, Mich;
Myrtle Lucas, Toronto;
Dorothy Ludgate, Kingston;
Vivian Ludgate, Fergus;
Dr. Andrew Mackie, Kitchener;
Dave Markus;
Elizabeth Martin;
Lucille Martin;
Subhash Mehta;
Hazel Moore, Beachburg;
Murray Moore;
Reg Morton, Almonte;
Terry Mulvihill, Petawawa;
Audry Mulvihill, Petawawa;
Jack Murphy;
James Murphy;

Michael J. Murray, Ottawa;
Aubrey Nesbitt, Carleton Place;
Frank Nighbor;
Pat Nighbor;
Mrs Lloyd Oates, Cobden;
Mrs Daulton Olivier, Arnprior;
Cecil Palmer;
Olive Palmer;
Bill Patterson;
Janice Peterson, Almonte;
Linda Ready;
Terry Reid;
Leo Reise Jr., Ancaster;
Eddie Remus;
Helen Risto;
Larry Ritza, Renfrew;
Margaret Ritza, Renfrew;
Elmer Robinson;
William Robinson, Westmeath;
Ann Rogers, Vancouver B.C;
Father R.J. Roney;
Jim Ross, Barrie;
Jim Rutherford, Perth;
Garry Ryan;
Earl St. James;
Gus Schroeder;

Don Shaw;
Marie Shaw;
Jack Sheraton;
Margaret Sheraton;
Ken Smith, Perth;
Jack Smithson, Almonte;
Aurelia Spotswood, Westmeath;
Margaret Stanley, Toronto;
Cyril "Red" Strike, Arnprior;
Helen Stutgarth, Beaverton, Oregon;
John Summers;
Francis Sylvestre;
Stuart Taylor;
Ed Thomas;
Norah Thomson;
Stan Trapp;
Mel Turner;
Sheila Turner;
Mrs Art Wallace;
Emily Weedmark, Beachburg;
Mrs Forbes Weedmark, Beachburg;
Carl "Buzz" Williams, Carleton Place;
Lorne Wilson, Rosemere, Que;
Ron "Rusty" White, Perth;
Ted White.

A sincere thank you to all contibutors.

Team Rosters

1893/94 to 1935/39

Pembroke Hockey Team 1893/94

Wallace Pink (g)
Lennox Irving
Peter White
William Henry "Billy" Williams
Robert E. Gibson

Albert Mackie (g)
Edward Irving
John Robert Moffat
Fred Supple

Pembroke Hockey Team 1894/95

Frank Pink (g)
W. Hawkins (g)
Edward Irving (g and fwd)
J. Robert Moffat
H. Dickson
T. White
C. Kennedy
H. Short
Herb Mackie
Wallace Pink
John Lorne Hale
William Halpenny

Wallace Pink (g)
Cliff McPhee (g)
Robert E. Gibson
Billy Williams
E. Dickson
F. Porter
David P. Kennedy
H. Beatty
Edward MacKenzie Jones
Fred Supple
W. Herbert Supple

Pembroke Hockey Team 1895/96

Wallace Pink (g)
David P. Kennedy
Ed. Jones
Edward Irving
Fred Cockburn
Andy Thomson
A.J. Foster (manager)

J. Robert Moffat
Robert E. Gibson
Billy Williams
Herb Supple
James Ward Stewart
H. McCurdy

Pembroke Hockey Team 1897/98

Wallace Pink (g)
Tom Dunbar (fwd)
Frank J. McDonnell
Billy Wallace
Jack Poff

Cliff McPhee (g and fwd)
Bert McPhee
Dr. A.V. "Bert" Summers
Jim Stewart
David P. Kennedy

Pembroke Srs 1898/99

OVHL, Pembroke, Renfrew, Arnprior, Carleton Place
Buchanan (g)
Ed Jones
Bert Summers
Billy Wallace
Cliff McPhee
Edward A. Dunlop (president)
Peter White Jr (commissioner)

G. Peden (g and pt)
Frank McDonnell
Jim Stewart
J. Lorne Hale
Ed. Irving (captain)
Fred W. Cockburn (vice president)
R. Ranson (commissioner)

Pembroke Srs 1899/1900

OVHL, Pembroke, Renfrew, Arnprior, Carleton Place

Tom Dunbar (g)	Frank McDonnell
Jack Wallace	Bert Summers
Sam "Shinny" Shaughnessy	Jim Stewart
Billy Wallace	Eugene "Paddy" Howe

Pembroke Srs 1900/01

OVHL, Pembroke, Renfrew, Arnprior, Carleton Place

Tom Dunbar (g)	Jack Douglas (g)
David P. Kennedy	John Albert "Jack" Poff
Jack Wallace	Eugene "Paddy" Howe
Jim Stewart	Billy Wallace
Allan Hale	B. Howarth
Shinny Shaughnessy	

Pembroke Srs 1901/02

OVHL, Pembroke, Renfrew, Arnprior

Tom Dunbar (g)	Jack Poff (g and fwd)
Paddy Howe	Lorne Kennedy
B. Howarth	Billy Wallace
Bert McPhee	Cliff McPhee
Shinny Shaughnessy	Lorne Ranson
Tom Jones	

Pembroke Srs 1902/03

UOVHL, Pembroke, Renfrew, Arnprior, Almonte

Jack Poff (g)	Frederick Hugh Lehman (g)
Roy McVean	Paddy Howe
Lorne Kennedy	Lorne Ranson
Bob Scott	Tom Jones

Pembroke Srs 1903/04

UOVHL, Pembroke, Renfrew, Arnprior, Almonte

Hugh Lehman (g)	Jack Poff (g)
Paddy Howe	Frank Sargeant
Lorne Kennedy	Tom Jones
Tom Dunbar (fwd)	T.J. "Jim" Dunbar (fwd)
Lorne Ranson	Bert McPhee
Emile Hout	Roy McVean
Billy Wallace	Hugh Matheson "Rusty" Fraser

Pembroke Srs 1904/05

UOVHL, Pembroke, Renfrew, Arnprior, Almonte

Hugh Lehman (g)	Jack Poff (pt and cover pt)
Paddy Howe	Tom Jones
Billy Wallace	Tom Benson, capt.
Gordon "Curley" Campbell	Tom Dunbar (fwd)
Lorne Ranson	J.A. Merkley
Roy Anderson	

Pembroke Srs 1905/06

UOVHL, Pembroke, Renfrew, Amprior,

Hugh Lehman (g)	J.A. Merkley
Tom Benson	Tom Jones
Billy Wallace	Hugh Fraser
Orin Frood	Roy McVean
Jim Coxford	

Pembroke Srs 1906/07

UOVHL, Pembroke, Renfrew, Amprior

Jack Poff (g)	Hugh Lehman (g)
Roy McVean	Tom Benson
Orin Frood	Tom Jones
Roy Anderson	Billy Wallace
Hugh Fraser	Curley Campbell
Eddie Roberts	H. Scott
George Valin	Anthony Kutchaw
Ernie Taylor	Erskine "Skene" Ronan
Charles Douglas "Baldy" Spittal	Samuel Hamilton "Hamby" Shore

Pembroke Srs 1907/08

UOVHL, Pembroke, Renfrew, Amprior

Hugh Lehman (g)	Roy McVean
Hugh Fraser	Dr Bob Scott
Orin Frood	Tom Jones
Eddie J. "Dutch" "Germany" Schaeffer	
Billy Wallace	Roy Anderson
George "Mick" Beamish	Albert Leonard Beamish
Alex Thrasher	Allan "Rus" Wilson
Art Ross	Tom Hooper
Jack Chipchase	

Pembroke Srs 1908/09

UOVHL, Pembroke, Renfrew, Almonte, Carleton Place

Jack Poff (g)	Calvin Rowan Stewart
Fred Thrasher	Alex Thrasher
James P. McAlindon	Billy Wallace
Hugh Fraser	Harold Hugh "Harry" Cameron
Milt "Bluebell" Horn	Roy McVean
Allan Wilson	Emmett Duff

Pembroke Srs 1909/10

UOVHL, Pembroke, Amprior, Almonte, Carleton Place

Jim Dunbar (g)	J. Brown
Ralph Lett	Rowan Stewart
J. Parnell Duff	Emmett Duff (captain)
Fred Thrasher	Harry Cameron
Gordon "Brick" Fraser	Ernest Cunnyworth

Pembroke Srs 1910/11
UOVHL, Pembroke, Arnprior, Almonte, Carleton Place

Jim Dunbar (g)	Rowan Stewart
Harry Cameron	Francis "Frank" Nighbor
Brick Fraser	J. Parnell Duff
Percy Wilson	J. Reginald "Bedu" Morand Jr.
Lindsay Fiuker	Graham Fenton
Joe Murray (coach and president)	

Pembroke Srs 1911/12
UOVHL, Pembroke, Arnprior, Almonte, Smiths Falls

Sylvestre "Vessie" Cadden (g)	Solomon L. "Hum" Lance (g)
Jim Coxford	Allan Wilson
Sarsfield J. Brennan	Bedu Morand
Edward "Teddy" Behan	David Edward Behan
Fred Thrasher	Percy Wilson
P.J. O'Brien	Howard Box
Smilin" Billy O'Brien, (trainer)	

Pembroke Srs 1912/13
Interprovincial Union, U.O.V. Section, Pembroke, Renfrew, Almonte, Carleton Place

Hum Lance (g)	Charles Thorpe (g)
Ted Behan	Daniel D. Durack
Bedu Morand	Sarsfield Brennan
Gordon Fluker	Horace Ross
Harold Duff	Dave Behan
Oliver "Dooney" Landriault	Milton Horn
Jim Cully	Billy O'Brien, (trainer)

Pembroke Srs 1913/14
Interprovincial Union, U.O.V. Section, Pembroke, Renfrew, Almonte, Carleton Place

Hum Lance (g)	Bedu Morand
Jim McAlindon	Dave Behan
Omer "Schauf" Landriault	Dan Durack
Archie Dimmell	Joe Tierney
Gordon Beal	Harold Duff
Jim Cully	Charlie Ramsay
Ted Behan	Hugh Fraser
G. Trottier	

Pembroke Srs 1914/15
UOVHL, Pembroke, Renfrew, Arnprior, Almonte, Carleton Place

Hum Lance (g)	Bedu Morand
Omer Landriault	Dooney Landriault
Harold Duff	Dan Durack
Arthur O. Bourdon	Jim McAlindon
A.B. Box	Luke Imbleau
Ian McKinnon	Emile Zadow
Horace Ross	Eric Ross
Sarsfield Brennan	Dave Behan
Harold Bresnahan	

Pembroke Royals Hockey Club 1915/16

Exhibitions only

Hum Lance (g)	Wellington "Welly" Tario (g)
Art Bourdon	Dave Behan
Fred Thrasher	George Dimmell
Bedu Morand	Hugh Fraser
Ted Behan	Sarsfield Brennan
Dan Durack	Jack Anderson
Omer Landriault	William J. "Dub" Murphy

Pembroke Srs 1916/17

OVHL, Pembroke, Renfrew, Arnprior, Almonte, Carleton Place, 240th.

Welly Tario (g)	Hum Lance (g)
Bedu Morand	Sarsfield Brennan
Dub Murphy	Jack Anderson
Dooney Landriault	Omer Landriault
Eugene "Ching" Landriault	Gordon Fraser
Archie Dimmell	George Dimmell
Art Bourdon	

Pembroke Munitions 1917/18

No league, exhibitions only.

Bert McAndrews (g)	Welly Tario (g)
Jack McKell	Whitey Mullen
Bill Mooney	Bill Mills
Dewhurst	Johnston
Eddie Gorman	Jack Anderson
Archie Dimmell	George Dimmell
Ching Landriault	Omer Landriault
Dooney Landriault	Gordon Fraser
Dub Murphy	Neil Campbell
Emmett "Ducky" Spooner	Roy McVean (trainer)
Mr De La Ronde (manager)	

Pembroke Arenas Hockey Club 1918/19

No league, exhibitions only

Lawrence S. "Nig" Jones (g)	Hec Fraser (g)
Hum Lance (g)	O. Sabourin
Ken Dunfield	Ching Landriault
Omer Landriault	Bolan
Archie Dimmell	John Carroll "Buzz" Armstrong
Wilfred Edward Cecile	Dub Murphy
Luke Imbleau	Charles H. Devlin
B.E. "Barney" McFarlane	Dave Behan
Sarsfield Brennan	Michael J. Lee
Alexander Denzil "Denny" McMullen	

Pembroke Arenas 1919/20
UOVHL, Pembroke, Arnprior, Almonte, Carleton Place

Nig Jones (g)	Welly Tario (g)
Dr Michael J. Mulvihill	Omer Landriault
Dub Murphy	Jack Anderson
Wilf Cecile	Buzz Armstrong
Richard Gournalle "Betsy" Bethel	Emmett Spooner
Dave Behan	Rowan Stewart
Denny McMullen	Michael Lee
O'Driscoll Legge	

Pembroke Arenas 1920/21
UOVHL, Pembroke, Renfrew, Arnprior, Almonte, Carleton Place

Nig Jones (g)	Welly Tario (g)
Dr Mike Mulvihill	Dave Behan
Buzz Armstrong	Denny McMullen
Betsy Bethel	Emmett Spooner
Randolph Spooner	Wilf Cecile
Dub Murphy	Omar Landriault

Pembroke Arenas (Lumber Kings) 1921/22
UOVHL, Pembroke, Renfrew, Arnprior, Almonte, Carleton Place

Welly Tario (g)	Buzz Armstrong
Omer Landriault	Betsy Bethel
Wilf Cecile	Dub Murphy
Jack Anderson	Emmett Spooner
James W. Kenny	Victor Ryan
Adolphe "Duff" Groslouis	

Pembroke Arenas 1922/23
UOVHL, Pembroke, Renfrew, Arnprior, Carleton Place

Welly Tario (g)	Nig Jones (g)
Wallace McKay	Jack Anderson
Betsy Bethel	Jim Cully
Ted Behan	Jim Kenny
Dub Murphy	Buzz Armstrong
Vic Ryan	Duff Groslouis
Dave Behan	Wilf Cecile
Omer Landriault (captain)	Emmett Spooner
Gordon Anderson	Lorne Wilson
Edward A. Rowan (coach)	Horace Gaul (coach)

Pembroke Arenas 1923/24
UOVHL, Pembroke, Renfrew, Arnprior, Almonte

Welly Tario (g)	Nig Jones (g)
Melville "Fats" Larwell (g)	Emmett Spooner
Buzz Armstrong	Jack Anderson
William Welland Dickson Williams	Jim Kenny
Bill Mulvihill	Gordon Anderson
Omer Landriault	Charles "Duke" Delahey
Desmond Irwin	Denny McMullen
Lorne Wilson	Dub Murphy
Dr Michael J. Mulvihill	Lloyd Ludgate
Dave Behan (playing coach)	J. Parnell Duff (manager)

Pembroke Arenas 1924/25
UOVHL, Pembroke, Renfrew, Arnprior,

Peter Donlevy (g)	Welly Tario (g)
Dr. Jim Cully	Gordon Anderson
Buzz Armstrong	Denny McMullen
Jim Kenny	Emmett Spooner
Roy Ludgate	W. Anthony "Betsy" Merryfield
Charlie Delahey	Bill Mulvihill
Allan McDonald	Lorne Wilson

Pembroke Arenas 1925/26
UOVHL, Pembroke, Renfrew, Arnprior

Welly Tario (g)	Nig Jones (g)
Dr James E. Ritchie	Robert Watson "Bert" Anderson
Wilf Cecile	Denny McMullen (captain)
Buzz Armstrong	Jim Kenny
Duff Groslouis	Roy Ludgate
Dr Jim Cully	Lorne Wilson
Bill Mulvihill	Gordon Anderson
Clayton Eady	Eddie Carmody
Charlie Delahey	Joe Freeman (coach)

Pembroke Arenas 1926/27
UOVHL, Pembroke, Renfrew, Arnprior, Carleton Place

Nig Jones (g)	Cecil Gallagher (g)
Welly Tario (g)	Mel Larwell (g)
Bert Anderson	Buzz Armstrong
Lorne Wilson	Roy Ludgate
Lloyd Ludgate	Harvey Schultz
Gordon Anderson	Bill Fraser
Armstrong Fraser	Allan McDonald
Boyd Anderson	John Workman
Jim Kenny	Gerry McLeod
Dr Jim Cully (coach)	Albert Ellis (trainer)

Pembroke Arenas (Lumber Kings) 1927/28;

UOVIHL, Pembroke, Renfrew, Arnprior, Almonte, Carleton Place

Cecil Gallagher (g)	Ivan McDonnell
Hector Ethier	Harvey Schultz
Roy Ludgate	Lloyd Ludgate
Eddie Carmody	Armstrong Fraser
Gerry McLeod	Ted Watt
Allan Anderson	Gordon Anderson
Vinnie McDonald	Charlie Knott
Boyd Anderson	Bill Fraser
Bert Anderson	Charlie Delahey
Dave Trottier (Grads game)	Dr Jim Cully (coach)
Grant Gordon (Grads game)	

Pembroke Lumber Kings 1928/29

UOVIHL, Pembroke, Renfrew, Arnprior, Almonte, Carleton Place

Welly Tario (g)	Cecil Gallagher (g)
Jim Kenny	Boyd Anderson
Harvey Schultz	Allan Siegel
Bob Warner	Des Irwin
Michael J. Neville	Allan Campbell
Wilf Cecile	Charlie Knott
Armstrong Fraser	Allan Anderson
Denny McMullen (coach)	

Pembroke Jrs 1929

David "Dub" Small (g)	Lloyd Reid (g)
Jim Timlin	Aime Jette
Hugh Henderson	Joe Fraser
Tommy Fitzgerald	Ivan Fraser
Bert Shepherd	D'Arcy Sammon
Dave Behan (coach)	Dr Cully (coach))
Sid Thomson (manager)	

Pembroke Lumber Kings 1929/30

UOVIHL, Pembroke, Renfrew, Arnprior, Almonte, Carleton Place; plus Murray Cup

Welly Tario (g)	Boyd Anderson
Aime Jette	Hugh Henderson
Roy Ludgate	John Workman
Bob Warner	Mike Neville
Charlie Knott	Gerry McLeod
Art Laronde	Allan Seigel
Ivan Fraser	Wilf Cecile
Dub Murphy	Guy Larwell
Bill Patterson	Armstrong Fraser
Jim Timlin	Joe Turcotte
Allan Mulligan	Fred Clarke (coach)

Pembroke Jrs 1929/30

UOVJHL, Pembroke, Renfrew, Arnprior

Dub Small (g)
Jim Timlin
Allan Mulligan
D'Arcy Sammon
Ivan Fraser
Clayton Eady
John Stashick
Sid Thomson (manager)

Lloyd Reid (g)
Joe Turcotte
Tom Fitzgerald
Bert Shepherd
Gerald Lewis
Allan Seigel
Dr Jim Cully (coach)
Roy Hamilton (trainer)

Pembroke Lumber Kings 1930/31

UOVIHL, Pembroke, Renfrew, Arnprior, Almonte, Carleton Place

Cecil Gallagher (g)
Vince Chisnell
Boyd Anderson
Hugh Henderson
Bill Tennant
Mike Neville
Hector Robert
Gerry McLeod
Russell Field
Added for Murray Cup:
Welly Tario (g)
Allan Mulligan
D'Arcy Sammon
Charlie Delahey

Walter Zadow (g)
Wilf Cecile
Bob Warner
John Workman
Aime Jette
Roy Ludgate
Richie Lassman
Aubrey Peever
Dr Jim Cully (coach)

Jim Timlin
Ivan Fraser
Lorne Wilson
Jim Bevens (coach)

Pembroke Jrs 1930/31

UOVJHL, Pembroke, Renfrew, Arnprior

Leonard Whelan (g)
Jim Timlin
Allan Mulligan
Allan Seigel
Arnie Junop
Gerald "Pin" Lewis
Ivan Fraser

Ab. Gravelle (g)
Joe Turcotte
Gordon "Bud" Levoy
Bert Shepherd
Bill Patterson
D'Arcy Sammon
Dr Jim Cully (coach)

Arena Girls 1930/31

Provincial finalists

Eileen Fraser (g)
Dorothy Fraser
Ella Kossatz
Beatrice Tessier
May Campbell
Genevieve Mullen

Lois Fraser
Mary Kossatz
Chris (Kossatz) Biggs
Helen Kelly
Mildred Dwyer
Audry Armstrong

Pembroke Lumber Kings 1931/32

NRHL, Pembroke, Cobden, Chalk River

Walter Zadow (g)

Joe Turcotte

Jim Timlin

Allan Seigel

Narcisse "Cec" Thomas

Art Laronde

Denny McMullen

Arnie Junop

Boyd Anderson

D'Arcy Sammon

Roy Ludgate

Charlie Knott

John Workman

Aime Jette

Lionel "Nel" Thomas

Ivan Fraser

Harvey Schultz

Tom Fitzgerald

Joe Kruger

Jim Bevens (coach)

Pembroke Jrs 1931/32

UOVJHL, Pembroke, Renfrew, Arnprior

Eddie Remus (g)

Bill Patterson

Arnie Junop

Frank Fitzgerald

Edmund "Mun" Chaput

Bud Levoy

Borden Lyttle

Dave Behan (coach)

Ted Denault (g)

Art Patterson

Joe Kruger

Murray Doran

Frank Quinn

Bert Shepherd

Jack Latimer

J. Deacon Taylor, pres.

Pembroke Lumber Kings 1932/33

UOVSHL, Pembroke, Cobden, Renfrew, Arnprior, Carleton Place, Almonte

Richie Lassman (g) #1

Vinnie McDonald #4

Harvey Schultz

D'Arcy Sammon #8

Charlie Knott #10

Nel Thomas #7

Art Laronde #12

Eddy Carmody (coach).

Dub Small (g)

Joe Turcotte #6

Bob Warner #2

Allan Mulligan

Harold Selkirk #9

John Workman #3

Patrick J. Villemaire

Pembroke Jrs 1932/33

UOVJHL, Pembroke, Renfrew

Ted "Rhumba" Denault (g)

Dub Small (g-exh)

Bert Shepherd

Joe "Bullet" Kruger

Jack "Tiny" Latimer

Frank "Clip" Fitzgerald

Peter "Speedy" O'Brien

Vince Marion

Carmen Keon

Eddie Remus (g)

Murray Doran

Clarence "Cooney" Keon

Gordon "Bud" Levoy

Frank Quinn

Harvey Coumbs

Arnie "Ace" Junop

Billy Howe

Dave Behan (coach)

Pembroke Lumber Kings 1933/34
UOVSHL, Petawawa, Pembroke, Cobden, Renfrew, Arnprior, Carleton Place, Almonte

Ted Denault (g)
Richie Lassman (g)
Joe Turcotte
Joe Kruger
Bert Shepherd
Tom St. Amand
Gerry McLeod
Murray Doran
Harvey Schultz
Dave Behan (coach)

Dub Small (g)
Wilfred Hein
Arnie Junop
Andy Fitzgerald
Aime Jette
Bob Warner
Bud Levoy
D'Arcy Sammon
Harvey Coumbs

Pembroke Jrs 1933/34
UOVJHL, Pembroke, Renfrew, Arnprior

Ted Denault (g)
Vinnie Marion
Billy Howe
Gordon Johnston
Jack Duff
Allan Levoy
Jim Slattery
Harvey Coumbs
Frank Quinn

Herb Kaden (g)
Ellis Hout
Frank Fitzgerald
Mun Chaput
Peter Vondette
Everett Doran
George Timlin
Jack Murphy
Dean Rogers (coach).

Pembroke Falcons 1934/35
UOVSHL, Pembroke, Renfrew, Arnprior

Richie Lassman (g)
Joe Kruger
Hector Robert
D'Arcy Sammon
Joe Turcotte
Andy Fitzgerald
John Workman
Aime Jette
Jake Scully
Everett Maxwell Doran
Clarence Keon
Wilf Cecile (playing coach)

Len Whelan (g)
Murray Doran
Lawrence "Lorne" Robert
Vinnie Marion
Boyd Anderson
Bud Levoy
Harvey Schultz
George Timlin
Roy Giesebrecht
Carmen Keon
Allan Levoy
Charlie Campbell (coach)

Pembroke Jrs 1934/35

UOVJHL, Pembroke, Renfrew, Arnprior

Bob McQuirter (g)
Billy Howe
Jim McDermott
Clarence Keon
Tom Godin
Ramsay Garrow
Everett Doran
Herb Currell
Don Stewart
Roy Giesebrecht
Dave Behan (coach).

Herb Kaden (g)
Jim Slattery
Allan Levoy
Carmen Keon
Delmar McDonald
George Wilson
Art Dixon
Jack Duff
Ken Fortin
Murray Doran (exh.)

Pembroke Falcons 1935/36

UOVSHL, Pembroke, Renfrew, Arnprior

Ted Denault (g)
Boyd Anderson
Harvey Schultz
Joe Kruger
Bud Levoy
Richie Lassman
Vinnie Marion
Emmett Spooner (coach)

Len Whelan (g)
Jerry Kyle
Andy Fitzgerald
Bert Hall
Lawrence Robert
Arnie Junop
Jim Slattery

Pembroke Little Lumber Kings 1935/36

UOVJHL, Pembroke, Renfrew, Arnprior

Bob McQuirter (g)
Don Grant #2
Roy Giesebrecht #6
Allan Levoy #8
Ramsay Garrow #10
Cliff McBain #4
Jim Slattery
Don Stewart
Jack Sarsfield (trainer)

Jack Poirier (g)
Lloyd Bailey #9
Carmen Keon #7
Everett Doran #5
Art Dixon #12
Herb Currell
Len Turcotte
Dave Behan (coach)
Jim Hill (assistant trainer)

PEMBROKE MAYORS,
SINCE BECOMING A TOWN JANUARY 1, 1877

1877,78	William Moffat
1879-81	Dr. W.W. Dickson
1882	J.H. Metcalf
1883,84	Walter Beatty
1885-,87	Archibald Foster
1888,89	William Murray
1890	Thomas Deacon
1891-93	W.R. White
1894-96	F.E. Fortin
1897-1900	Thomas Murray
1901	J.P. Millar
1902	Peter White Jr.
1903,04	Gideon Delahey
1905,06	W.H. Bromley
1907	Isidore Martin
1908,09	J.S. Fraser
1910,11	W.L. Hunter
1912,13	William Lacey
1914,15	J.L. Morris
1916,17	Edward Behan
1918,19	W.R. Beatty
1920,21	Daniel A. Jones
1922,23	Walter L. Smyth
1924,25	L.S. Barrand
1926,27	J. Parnell Duff
1928-30	James M. Taylor
1931-33	George D. Biggs
1934	Dr. J.C. Bradley
1935	Dr. Matthew McKay
1936	Albert E. Cockburn